COMPLETE CONDITIONING FOR HOCKEY

Peter Twist
Twist Conditioning, Inc.

Human Kinetics

Library of Congress Cataloging-in-Publication Data

Twist, Peter, 1963-
  Complete conditioning for hockey / Peter Twist.
    p. cm.
  Includes index.
  ISBN-13: 978-0-7360-6034-9 (soft cover)
  ISBN-10: 0-7360-6034-0 (soft cover)
  1. Hockey--Training. 2. Physical fitness. I. Title.
  GV848.3.T85 2007
  796.962--dc22

                            2006025106

ISBN-10: 0-7360-6034-0
ISBN-13: 978-0-7360-6034-9

Developmental Editor: Cynthia McEntire; **Assistant Editor:** Scott Hawkins; **Copyeditor:** Bob Replinger; **Proofreader:** Sarah Wiseman; **Indexer:** Dan Connolly; **Graphic Designer and Graphic Artist:** Andrew Tietz; **Photo Manager:** Joe Jovanovich; **Cover Designer:** Keith Blomberg; **Photographer (cover):** © Jamie Squire/Getty Images; **Photographer (interior):** Neilpix unless otherwise noted; **Art Manager:** Kelly Hendren; **Illustrator:** Tammy Page; **Printer:** United Graphics

We thank Twist Conditioning, Inc., in Vancouver, British Columbia, for assistance in providing the location for the photo shoot for this book.

Human Kinetics books are available at special discounts for bulk purchase. Special editions or book excerpts can also be created to specification. For details, contact the Special Sales Manager at Human Kinetics.

Printed in the United States of America   10 9 8 7 6 5 4 3 2

Human Kinetics
Web site: www.HumanKinetics.com

United States: Human Kinetics
P.O. Box 5076
Champaign, IL 61825-5076
800-747-4457
e-mail: humank@hkusa.com

Canada: Human Kinetics
475 Devonshire Road, Unit 100
Windsor, ON N8Y 2L5
800-465-7301 (in Canada only)
e-mail: orders@hkcanada.com

Europe: Human Kinetics
107 Bradford Road
Stanningley
Leeds LS28 6AT, United Kingdom
+44 (0)113 255 5665
e-mail: hk@hkeurope.com

Australia: Human Kinetics
57A Price Avenue
Lower Mitcham, South Australia 5062
08 8372 0999
e-mail: info@hkaustralia.com

New Zealand: Human Kinetics
Division of Sports Distributors NZ Ltd.
P.O. Box 300 226 Albany
North Shore City, Auckland
0064 9 448 1207
e-mail: info@humankinetics.co.nz

This book is dedicated to my father, William (Bill) Twist, the person who introduced me to this great game and who role-modeled passion for hockey and sports. Bill Twist taught me the skills, supported my participation, and demonstrated competitive fire as well as enjoyment and ethics. He made sure I learned to try harder, to give more. Bill Twist loved to battle on the ice and compete hard while coaching behind the bench. He gave so much to the game.

Coaching Peterborough to the Ontario championships and then to the gold medal at the 1971 Canadian Winter Games, Bill Twist was much more than a hockey player, coach, volunteer, and enthusiast of the game. He was a tireless volunteer in sports, church, and community. In hockey and in life, he worked so hard, he gave so much, he was so strong—of body, mind, and spirit.

Bill Twist was a gracious, humble, and proud Canadian; respectful of people; a dedicated family man; a good friend to many; a man of integrity. I asked my six-year-old Zoe what I should say in the dedication. She succinctly noted, "he was a great dad. And he was very kind." Smart kid. It is pretty awesome to have a father you can be proud of, respect, and call a friend.

Although he lost a brief and vicious battle with cancer, Bill Twist continues to profoundly impact me every day.

Contents

DVD Contents

Foreword

After being drafted by the Vancouver Canucks, we were surprised at the physical improvement still needed to succeed at the next level. We thought we were ready for the NHL, but learned we had more to improve and more upside.

It was very helpful to be exposed to Peter Twist's leading edge program right in our draft year. The workout program was much different than those in fitness clubs and was also much different than what other athletes were doing. The program we followed was more hockey-specific. The training style transfers very well to on-ice demands.

We all know that exercising itself can sometimes be boring, but with Twist's exercises and drills you do not get bored. The exercises are more interesting than the standard ones and make you feel more athletic as a hockey player. Because of that, we've stayed motivated throughout the hockey-specific dryland workouts, on-ice drills, and off-season programs. And most important, we've both experienced significant improvements in strength, speed, power, balance, quickness and agility, and overall conditioning.

The type of exercises and intensity needed to succeed in the training program added that dimension of physicality to compete successfully, night in night out in the NHL. Twist's regimen helped us realize more of our full potential as players so that we could match up with the more dominant players today.

Peter Twist made us realize what it takes to excel at the highest level. You can be a good player in the NHL by working out hard, but to be among the best you have to put time into working out with the right focus and intensity. Twist's exercises are very challenging and require hard work, which are good features for athletes.

Fortunately, you can access the same training program and get similar results through this *Complete Conditioning for Hockey* book and DVD. And if you follow the program, you'll find out how great it feels to be strong on your skates and fast on the ice. It sure makes the game more fun to play!

Daniel and Henrik Sedin

Acknowledgments

After writing the original *Complete Conditioning for Hockey* in 1995, some things have stayed the same while a few things changed. I still got to listen to great music during all-night writing shifts, and my dog Rico is still with me and can still run through the mountains with great enthusiasm. But the music changed from 1960s bands to Audio Slave and Pearl Jam, and Rico slept through it all. Most everything else has changed. The exercise content has changed dramatically, along with a few other changes—marriage, houses, kids, another dog, retirement from the NHL, development of a sport-fitness business, and much more time in the mountains. What remains consistent is my love for the game, for helping athletes achieve their goals, and a sincere appreciation for many people who directly and indirectly influenced this project.

Lorne Goldenberg, Dr. Greg Anderson, Peter Freisen, Dr. Mark Kling, Scott Livingston, and Sean Skinner are six hockey conditioning coaches who helped redefine what a pro player's program looks like but more importantly stand out for the volume of education they share with minor hockey coaches, parents, and personal trainers to help improve the game. J.J. McQueen and Randy Lee are two long-time pro coaches who have tested drills in the NHL trenches. Ron Bulloch of Powering Athletics contributed to our hockey programs through his passion for hockey and design know-how as well as assumption of risk to introduce innovative training equipment solutions to the specificity needed in a hockey dryland environment.

I met many talented people in and around the NHL; Barry Smith, Tom Renney, Pat Quinn, Mike Johnson, Glen Hanlon, and Brian Burke are noteworthy coaches and executives because they are outstanding people, generously shared their knowledge of the game with the hockey community, and influenced the way I coach athletes and lead and treat staff and clients. Many of my hockey-specific presentations were tied to Hockey Canada's Paul Carson and Johnny Misley, and BCAHA's Bill Ennos, who all have profoundly impacted the game through the educational opportunities they afford coaches. Stan Smyl, Terry Bangen, Rick Ley, Curt Fraser, Mike Babcock, Jack Mcilhargey, Tim Hunter, David Nonis, and Steve Tambellini influenced my coaching and training with conversations on the art of coaching and developing hockey players, as well as seeing them in action as hockey leaders and quality people.

My current teammates at Twist Conditioning are all awesome people who keep our training center, camps, franchises, product distribution, and business infrastructure clicking while I tackle education projects. Specific to the fulfillment of this book, Jeff Roux, Dean Shiels, Gerard Recio, and Andrew Clark helped review and edit full chapters; Lisa Northrup, Ashley Schenstead, and Mason Gratto helped with exercise descriptions.

Thank you to the athletes who demonstrated exercises in the book and DVD: Dean Shiels, Ian Lampshire, Jeff Lynch, and Stephane Gervais on-ice; Dean Shiels, Andrew Clark, Nicole Lark, Haleigh Callison, and Karl Alzner off-ice. Their energy and precise execution is well appreciated. And much gratitude to Ted Miller, Cynthia McEntire, and Doug Fink of Human Kinetics for producing and editing the content into a finished package at the level Human Kinetics is well known for.

To my family—Julie Rogers, daughters Zoe and Mackenzie, dogs Rico and Loosy—and many tremendous like-minded friends on the west coast, thanks for making life so full and fulfilling.

Introduction

The hockey community has awakened to the dramatic effect that training can have on performance. Even the most traditional coach now recognizes the basic role of fitness. Forward-thinking coaches have adopted new training principles, significantly upgrading their player development processes.

The information in this book is the culmination of a fortunate journey that included delivering hundreds of lectures and workshops around the globe, writing hundreds of articles, and working daily with National Hockey League (NHL), minor professional, college, junior and minor hockey players. The ideas, philosophies, and exercises that began with my search to maximize the performance of my players have now filtered their way to thousands of coaches and all the players whom they influence. The positive feedback from readers about how the contents have improved their coaching and level of play only reminds me of the responsibility to continue to share information about the most current training methods.

I have progressively updated and unveiled the training program in pieces through articles. The scope and depth of advancements in hockey conditioning demand a new forum to offer the hockey-specific conditioning programs in one comprehensive package. As players become bigger, faster, and stronger, body contact becomes more forceful through high-speed collisions and more powerful combative forces. The focus on durability increases. The approach is to build a strong, reactive body that will withstand hockey impact and to develop the physical tools needed to get the upper hand during head-to-head confrontations. Players acquire the tools to win the battles.

At the same time, training programs are rounded out with an emphasis on improving skill and on-ice creativity. Fitness is the base, athleticism is the foundation, and enhanced hockey-specific skills and tactics are the goal. Efforts to improve training methods over the past decade have been all about increasing strength and speed in a way that translates to improved skills, tactics, and overall game performance, not just because a player has better fitness to fuel his skills but because the training has directly helped him become a better hockey player.

More professions are now integrating new training methods into their practices. I often find myself presenting lectures to conditioning coaches, exercise physiologists, personal trainers, teachers, physiotherapists, medical trainers, chiropractors, and kinesiologists. Earlier in my career, before the personal training industry started to flourish and before rehab specialists began adding movement exercises to passive modalities, I delivered all my presentations at coaches' conferences. I was the token fitness guy; most of the other sessions focused on team strategies and systems. Initially, many coaches used my talk to go out and get a coffee, to wait for the next presentation on team systems. Gradually, they became more interested. Nevertheless, many minor hockey coaches still devote too much time to coaching systems and not enough time to teaching their players how to be better hockey players.

Certainly, Xs and Os provide a framework for the on-ice plan, but hockey is really a game of organized chaos. No one knows what will happen from one second to the next. Opponents do not often cooperate with a team system, and the game breaks down to a series of one-on-one battles. The player who has the best physical tools and most creative toolbox will usually win.

The initial reluctance of coaches and players to buy into conditioning sprang from the view that sheer repetition on the ice would somehow improve skills. They also had a limited view of training. Training was what they saw in health clubs—cardiovascular fitness training and machine-based strength training—activities structured to produce general fitness and appearance benefits but offering limited value to on-ice action. For coaches set on improving individual players, these methods did not encapsulate the off-ice training style that could transcend conditioning to produce a direct effect on athleticism, movement skills, and hockey abilities. Training did improve fitness to give players greater endurance to fuel efforts but did little to directly affect hockey abilities.

Today, a player can improve his physical abilities off the ice and be better able to capitalize on the on-ice instruction. Several years ago I tested a small group of players on the ice. I used quantified tests for one-length speed, blue-to-blue quickness, red-to-blue stop-and-starts, agility, shot velocity, shot accuracy, and a subjective test of balance and combative balance. Players participated in a 6-week dryland training program during which they were not on the ice at all. At the end of the 6th training week, players spent three short acclimation sessions on the ice to get a feel for it again so that they could safely attempt best-effort on-ice tests. After 6 weeks of dryland training, all test results improved. Did I mention that all on-ice tests improved? Appropriately, today specialty skill-oriented and skating-specific hockey conferences focus completely on how to improve the individual hockey player.

In *Complete Conditioning for Hockey*, the updated hockey conditioning system focuses on linked system strength and power, multidirectional movement skills, and secondary fitness characteristics. By using an integrated strength model, hockey players are able to build lean muscle mass, size, and strength in a functional, whole-body manner that improves transfer to on-ice performance and better expresses the strength gained in the weight room in game action.

New hockey training programs draw heavily on the secondary characteristics of fitness, including dynamic balance, speed, agility, quickness, movement skills, muscle reactivity, and full-body reaction skills. This training applies muscular and physiological gains—in strength, aerobic fitness, and anaerobic fitness—to movement skills, the foundational movement patterns for athletic actions. When these are linked together in sequence, players can execute better skating moves, shots, passes, checks, stop-and-starts, pivots, turns, turn backs, and crossovers and play one-on-ones at higher intensity.

To accomplish this goal, coaches must train and teach players. The difference between coaching a drill and teaching a drill is significant. Coaching a drill involves running a drill, making sure that everyone is positioned correctly on the ice, making good decisions, jumping in at the right time. Teaching a drill requires having a critical eye to detect mechanical errors and having the ability to deliver purposeful corrective cues to help athletes improve technically within that drill. Why do coaches spend time forcing players to memorize Xs and Os and comply with a team system when players do not yet have the skating, puckhandling, and passing skills to get the job done? Often players don't even have the physical tools that they need to improve their skating. Paul Coffey, whose career was fueled on beautiful skating, used to say, "If you can't skate, you can't play."

In May 2005 at Sean Skinner's International Skating Summit, Dr. Jack Blatherwick, an exercise physiologist and world-renowned hockey researcher whose early works on overspeed training led the field, ended his presentation with a time–motion analysis of a typical minor hockey player. In a 60-minute squirt hockey game, players averaged 9.6 minutes of ice time, while their families averaged a 70-minute round-trip drive and a 3-hour total time commitment to net out the 9.6 minutes. The game-time assessment followed a below-average forward who touched the puck seven times over nine shifts. A defensive defenseman controlled the puck more—with 11 puck possessions averaging 2.6 seconds for a total puckhandling experience of 29 seconds. He was stationary most of the game, standing either at the offensive blue line or in front of his goalie, and skated fast only twice all game, racing from the far blue line back to his own net. In this game, the ref had the puck almost half the time.

Obviously, the better players have the puck more, but even top players who play a large number of games do not receive the athletic experience and skill repetition that they need to reach their potential. Dr. Blatherwick assessed a top forward in another squirt game, who played 11 shifts for an average of 58.4 seconds each, handled the puck 14 times for a total of 49 seconds, and took four shots. Herb Brooks used to say, "Give the game back to the kids." Perhaps a more fruitful game experience is needed, one that does more than replicate adult-structured games, one that would keep players on task and offer a higher volume challenge of their athleticism and puckhandling skills. Even at the college and professional level, according to a doctoral thesis by M.R. Bracko, players handled the puck on average for less than 3 seconds per shift. Of course, in minor hockey with players who still need to upgrade their skating and movement skills, this figure may be even smaller.

Game competition teaches positioning, timing, decision making, team play, tactics, courage, camaraderie, and other attributes. But young players receive little chance to improve their skills and athleticism. Even pro players are deconditioned at the end of a season, in poorer shape than they were when they reported to training camp. Then why play the large number of games, which do little for skills, skating, and conditioning? For young players in development, the volume of games needs to decrease and the structure of games—number of whistles, play stoppages, size of the ice, and other variables—needs to change to offer a better challenge to players' abilities. But for now, parents and hockey associations seem more intent on playing a prolike schedule of games. Even more confounding, they add *more* games, spending their time and money to travel to full weekend tournaments so that their kids can do more of the same and touch the puck a few times a game.

So how can we harness conditioning to approach player development differently? To build fitness, improve movement skills, and reach individual potential at any age, a player must train to develop the diverse skills of a decathlete. Hockey players require aerobic and anaerobic conditioning, speed, quick feet, quick hands, agility, reaction skills, balance, deceleration skills, multijoint strength, whole-body power, rotary power, and dynamic flexibility, each trained specifically for the unique characteristics of hockey. Consider carrying a stick, handling a puck, passing, shooting, bodychecking, dropping to block shots, warding off opponents, stopping and starting, continually switching between decelerating and accelerating, backward skating, moving laterally, pivoting, exiting turns, and constantly changing direction. Hockey has unique biomechanical, physiological, bioenergetic, and neuromuscular demands as well as challenging nutritional requirements.

The skating stride is a good example of the integration of conditioning and skill. A technically sound skater is mechanically efficient, so she uses less energy and delays fatigue. A poor skater uses much more energy and fatigues more quickly. A well-conditioned player will be able to skate longer without the fatigue that adversely affects skating technique. A poorly conditioned athlete will tire quickly, and performance of technique will deteriorate. Acquiring proper skating technique requires a base of strength, flexibility, speed, quickness, and agility. Ankle reactivity and whole-body balance greatly influence edging and aggressive on-ice maneuvers, and core strength helps players skate through defenders. Asymmetrical strength imbalances inhibit skating technique, and lack of joint mobility and movement skills interferes with complex skating patterns. Clearly, skill and technique acquisition or improvement must be integrated with physical conditioning for optimal player development.

The dramatic change overall in conditioning is represented in table 1. The left-hand column lists the typical athlete fitness program. Many recently retired NHL players will recognize this training program. The commonalities in leading-edge hockey conditioning programs are itemized in the right-hand column. *Complete Conditioning for Hockey* is a multidimensional program. In practice, we prescribe these elements at every Twist Athlete Conditioning Center, teaching them live to coaches and trainers at each location, implementing them with every athlete who walks in the door. For you, they are detailed throughout this book, defining the parameters of training for skillful hockey.

Table 1 Complete Hockey Conditioning

Previous conditioning plans	Modern conditioning plans
Emphasize aerobic cardiovascular fitness	Emphasize anaerobic fitness
Use $\dot{V}O_2$max testing	Use anaerobic and on-ice testing
Focus on linear movement, bike and track training	Incorporate unpredictable, multidirectional intervals
Feature stationary warm-up activities	Feature dynamic warm-up activities
Include forced, pre-ice stretching	Include gentle, post-ice stretching
Feature machine-based strength training	Feature whole-body integrated lifts
Include slow tempo, isolation exercises to overload muscles	Include multijoint, multiplanar lifts for explosive power
Include traditional situps and floor-based stabilization	Include standing core stabilization and exercises for rotary power
Develop linear acceleration speed	Improve deceleration and coupling between deceleration and first-step quickness
	Develop specific movement skills that link together for agility
	Include exercises that develop integrated balance for strength and transitional balance for change of direction
	Feature whole-body reaction skills and joint and muscle reactivity

Back in the days when hardly anyone trained and players were allowed a month to play themselves into shape, any pro player who participated in general strength and fitness training gained an edge over his out-of-shape training-camp challengers. Eventually most players participated in fitness training. Over the years, training became more hockey specific, creating another edge for those fortunate to be exposed to the new methodologies. Today, the new edge comes from adopting a training style aimed at increasing transference to on-ice actions, directly affecting on-ice abilities and driving hockey conditioning to new levels.

For young players, an interesting, challenging, and athletic style of training helps improve core hockey competencies, leading to self-efficacy—the feeling of "I can do it"—more success on the ice, and greater enjoyment of the game experience. Most important, if they keep training and keep playing hockey, they are more likely to participate in fitness and sport for life. Some of them will continue to move up the ladder. Even the best players in the world can improve their conditioning and physical abilities with this training system. What can *Complete Conditioning for Hockey* do for you?

A complete and up-to-date hockey conditioning program has evolved into the number one resource that world-class players consult to take their game to a new level. Likewise, coaches who desire to ice a competitive team and those who train individual players have a responsibility to provide the best resources possible. They also must know how to train their teams to execute the chosen strategies and systems. A team mandated to make quick transitions in the neutral zone, attack, and pressure with speed, with D-men who jump up into the play, would opt for a schedule of speed, first-step quickness, and anaerobic conditioning.

The expectations that I have for my athletes are that they never lose the drive to improve and that they carry an open mind and a spirit that allows them to succeed. These same attributes will help coaches, trainers, and parents provide the best resources for their players. For the players reading this book, young aspiring players and adult recreational players alike, the fact that you are taking initiative to learn for yourself bodes well toward what you can achieve on the ice.

I sincerely wish you tremendous success with *Complete Conditioning for Hockey*. If you have high expectations for yourself, if you love to compete—against both yourself and hockey opponents—then I fully expect that your heart rate will rise as you read each chapter. The light bulb will turn on as a plan unfolds to take your body and mind to a new level of hockey performance. The best part will be finishing and putting it all into action! Players and coaches, commit your mind, spirit, attitude, and body to drive through limits and discover new capabilities, on and off the ice.

Key to Diagrams

X   Player

△   Cones (pylons)

●   Puck

     Goal net

⟶   Forward skating

– – – →   Backward skating

— · — · →   Passing

·············→   Lateral crossovers

G   Goaltender

P   Passer

Chapter 1

Conditioning for Hockey Performance

On-ice skill development draws from five pillars of conditioning: balance; agility and reactivity; whole-body strength and power; speed and quickness; and anaerobic energetics. Focusing exercise creation and training guidelines on these five pillars has the goal of improving the five principal on-ice skills—skating, puckhandling, passing, shooting, and bodychecking—best expressed together as one-on-one tactics.

The five pillars of conditioning are the main categories of training in *Complete Conditioning for Hockey*. Each pillar has three main components: improving fitness, enhancing athleticism, and conditioning hockey-specific movements.

Improving fitness builds a foundation on which hockey-specific training styles and intensities can build. Fitness is improved with increased flexibility, proper nutrition, decreased body fat, increased strength and muscle mass, and elevated aerobic power. These factors affect health and immune function during a long season and usually help an athlete perform any activity better.

For hockey players, improved aerobic power aids endurance; decreased body fat allows faster, more efficient skating; and added strength and flexibility and a healthy diet help maintain an exercise regimen with reduced risk of injury. Because the aerobic energy system helps the body recover from bouts of anaerobic activity, the aerobic system should be developed first. Similarly, proper strength, lean mass, and flexibility are required before work can begin on strength capacity, explosive power, speed, quickness, agility, and reactivity.

Athleticism builds on fitness, putting the athlete more in tune with his body, with balance and coordination benefits during movement. Just as power-skating coaches modify body mechanics on the ice, a focus on athleticism improves body function off the ice. The best athletes make the best hockey players, and the higher an athlete's fitness and athleticism, the more he can capitalize on hockey-specific training. Athleticism comes from the secondary fitness characteristics—balance, agility, quickness, deceleration, speed, reactivity, multijoint strength, and anaerobic energy—through precise training that improves critical movement skills and body awareness.

The third category of hockey conditioning focuses on the sport-specific demands encountered on the ice. Exercises and drills must be selected and completed with specific exercise prescriptions so that the player's physical and physiological development best suits the game of ice hockey. Sometimes gains in strength, flexibility, or lean body mass can detract from hockey skills because the "improvements" are not appropriate for the demands of hockey. Meanwhile, other developments crucial to hockey success are sometimes overlooked. Hockey specificity takes improved athleticism and molds it into the exact requirements of on-ice game action.

The three categories feed the order of training in that fitness is a base of supply and recovery, providing readiness for more complex and intense exercise. Athleticism influences the results of hockey-specific training by improving the body's ability to coordinate more challenging movement and power exercises. When players are ready, the focus should shift to hockey-specific programs. The exercises and training guidelines recommended are designed to improve fitness and athletic skills. By design of training style, intensity, and complexity, the hockey-specific phase will continue to improve fitness and athleticism as a by-product of the demands of hockey-specific training. But the primary purpose of the exercise experience is to affect hockey skating, bodychecking, and tactical maneuvers common to specific game situations.

BALANCE

Fitness: When an unstable surface is introduced to an exercise, the additional balance challenge increases the number of muscle groups recruited, muscle activation within each group, and overall metabolic cost, eliciting higher heart rates for a given exercise. The body adapts with improved muscle endurance as well as the energy systems that fuel the heightened efforts.

Athleticism: Balance is all about coordination and body control. It improves the mind-muscle connection, making muscles more responsive to challenges and compliant to commands from the brain. Balance exercises focus on kinesthetic awareness, teaching players to be in tune to their bodies. Players learn to adjust mechanics and shift weight to load to a more advantageous position.

An oddity in health club settings is the row of televisions in front of treadmills, stair climbers, and bikes. If an exercise is *that* boring, perhaps there is a better way to train. More important, if an exercise requires that little concentration, what purpose does it serve? Skillful movement requires attention to exactly how the body is operating. Players must focus internally and discover how the body is working, make corrections, use the core effectively, and fire muscles in the right order with just the right amount of force. Athleticism comes from this precision. Precise control of the body leads to skill. Skill produces performance.

Hockey specificity: Hockey players require balance to perform aggressive edging when turning and cornering. Tight turns necessitate the ability to bring the body's center of mass far outside the base of support. Skillful skating uses single-leg balance while the skater pressures different parts of the skate blade. In a stop-and-start game, players who demonstrate excellent first-step quickness create space away from defenders and give themselves time to be patient and make good decisions. The quick start relies on braking into a well-balanced position to shift optimally into the start phase. Of course, shooting and bodychecking are also well served by establishing the perfect position of balance during the dynamic action needed to execute those skills. Balance enables players to produce the power required to generate a hard shot or a strong check.

AGILITY AND REACTIVITY

Fitness: Relative to running in a straight line or sitting and pedaling a bicycle, fast-paced agility patterns generate higher heart rates, maximizing cardiac output for aerobic power and passing the threshold into anaerobic work. The higher energy cost comes from loading the legs eccentrically to brake to prepare to change direction, absorbing deceleration forces. Multidirectional exercise not only suits on-ice requirements but also, from a fitness perspective, helps work the body equally, exercising different muscle groups and movement patterns.

Athleticism: Within the agility and reactivity pillar, a player improves specific movement skills such as lateral movement, open steps, drop steps, crossovers, backpedals, stride patterns, and loaded starts. These fundamental motor patterns, when linked together in sequence, are expressed as multidirectional movement, known as agility. Agility can be broken down into a series of individual movement skills. Each component must be biomechanically optimal for the whole chain of events to unfold fluidly.

Hockey specificity: Without improving power, speed, or quickness through physiological training adaptations, we can improve power, speed, and quickness right away by upgrading critical movement skills. Improving the biomechanics for multidirectional movement helps a player move more effectively and efficiently, thus being able to cover more ice in the same number of strides while expending less energy. By thinking like a power-skating coach, one can understand the improvability of agility. Adding reactivity makes muscles, joints, and the body as a whole more reactive,

© Getty Images

The athleticism of Ilya Kovalchuk of the Atlanta Thrashers gives him an advantage. His precise body movements allow him to play the puck skillfully even against difficult defenses.

elements critical to a high-speed, stop-and-start sport. Defensemen read the play and respond with mobility to take away lanes to the net, and forwards and offensive D-men who jump up into the play draw on agility to evade defensive D-men, outsmarting them to the net or selecting delay tactics to create space, giving them time to make a tape-to-tape pass to a teammate supporting the play.

WHOLE-BODY STRENGTH AND POWER

Fitness: Adding general strength and muscle mass is where it all starts. General strength is about tuning up the body and providing a foundation. Players are less susceptible to injury and can tolerate greater amounts of advanced hockey-specific training when they develop a base of strength throughout the entire body, taking care of any weak links in the kinetic chain.

Athleticism: Even in the NHL, I have observed aspiring players who report to camp with far too much upper-body bulk, which changes their center of gravity and interferes with fluid performance of skills. Training like a bodybuilder or like those whom you see in a health club serves one purpose—to develop bigger muscles. Bigger and stronger is good, but for hockey, a massive upper body relative to the core and lower body is counterproductive. Bigger and stronger is useful only if it is achieved with a lifting style that makes one a better athlete, not just a better weight lifter. The difference is considerable. Bigger, stronger, and smarter is the goal. While the athlete is getting bigger and stronger, the goal is to train movement, not muscle.

Hockey specificity: Hockey players need a strong core; big, powerful, quick legs; and a strong upper body without excessive mass that will inhibit puckhandling and slow them down. Strong legs, hips, and core topped with upper-body strength in pushing, pulling, and rotating patterns linked with forearm strength allow players to win battles along the boards, shoot hard, be strong in face-off positions, ward off opponents to drive to the net, contain opponents in the corners, maximize force during open-ice hits, and protect the puck. Specific strength exercises will transfer better to on-ice situations, especially when strength is trained as power with explosive lifting tempos. Power initiation is best transferred onto the ice with exercises that use body mechanics and joint angles similar to those used during game action.

SPEED AND QUICKNESS

Fitness: Higher tempo aerobic intervals and shorter high-speed runs produce more benefit than long, slow jogging. Continuous aerobic exercise drives up VO_2max significantly more when the work rate is intense. Shorter 90-second aerobic intervals using a high-speed pace (but a step down from top speed, which is pure anaerobic) improve fitness with characteristics that more closely match hockey. Improving fitness in a way that trains players to sustain high-speed efforts can be more beneficial than rehearsing slow movements at a set pace during a 30-minute jog or bike ride at a submaximal heart rate. Higher speed intervals elevate the heart rate to near maximum rates and improve the muscular endurance needed to sustain speed late in a shift.

Athleticism: Muscles must have the strength and physiology to sustain high-speed efforts late in a shift, as well as the neuromuscular readiness to coordinate such action. High-speed athleticism teaches the body's software to coordinate skillful movement at high speeds. Athleticism also uses body angles, stride length, and stride frequency to generate greater quickness and speed. Training the muscles contributes to speed and quickness. Teaching the nervous system to exploit optimal body mechanics contributes even more to speed and quickness. Training through a variety of movement patterns with specific movement skills ensures that players' speed and quickness will apply to more than a linear track sprint.

Hockey specificity: Like players in many team sports, hockey players rarely have the opportunity to move at their highest possible speed. But compared with running sports like football or soccer, hockey requires players to accelerate more rapidly to high-end speeds. First-step quickness helps create separation from defensemen or backcheckers. On the defensive side, quickness is crucial on the penalty kill to take away passing lanes and shots to the net and to jump on loose pucks. Top-end speed helps forwards get in fast on the forecheck, making it difficult for defensemen. Speed and quickness are highly trainable off-ice. The adapted muscles are then trained on-ice to establish specific neural pathways for quick, fast skating maneuvers. Many players can become fast off the puck; the most dangerous players are quick and fast while they handle the puck.

ANAEROBIC CONDITIONING

Fitness: Players draw on all three energy systems in a game, and indeed during each shift. But the aerobic system, known as the supply and recovery system, is most associated with fitness. Aerobic fitness gives general endurance for sustained exercise and helps keep the body healthy and the immune system functioning well over a long season. Historically, however, head hockey coaches placed too much emphasis on $\dot{V}O_2$max. Players often trained like triathletes. One well-known exercise physiologist who influenced many NHL coaches put out a hockey book that did not even contain a chapter on anaerobic conditioning! The program was based on aerobic bike training and strength training on selectorized weight machines. Recovery from this misguided training method took years. Many players made the mistake of doing too much continuous aerobic training, essentially training to be slow. Hockey conditioning was thought of in terms of fitness and an exercise to expend calories to lean up. In reality, conditioning is a base that players use to train more athletically and specifically for hockey.

Athleticism: As athletes progress from building a base of fitness to enhancing athletic ability, they need to condition the anaerobic energy system, because they depend on it for explosive movements and intense action. I liken goaltenders to quarterbacks. The goaltender needs to be a well-rounded athlete capable of leading his team for the entire game. Goaltenders' acrobatic game-saving plays illustrate athleticism. For all positions, the better the athlete, the better the hockey player. The better the athlete, the more he can capitalize on hockey-specific training. The use of anaerobic-fueled, athletic-oriented partner shadowing drills and high-speed agility drills trains attributes that players can harness for defensive mobility, transitions from forward to backward skating, and tight turns with high-speed exits. Creative offensive maneuvers during tight one-on-one checks require speed, agility, quickness, deceleration, power, and balance, but these attributes are trainable only through the anaerobic energy systems.

Hockey specificity: Hockey at all levels is about speed. This aspect is most evident in today's NHL, as it has been for years in college hockey, which has no center red line and features hungry players who play only twice per week. A closely contested game also uses strength, power, quickness, agility, and deceleration in short, intense shifts of best effort. These attributes draw on the adenosine triphosphate phosphocreatine (ATP-PC) system and the lactic system. Players develop the two anaerobic energy systems off the ice but ultimately need to condition them on the ice, where they can rehearse the exact skating mechanics. Anaerobic capacity is essential to allowing players to perform longer before fatigue deters proper skill execution.

Some players have gone to the other extreme and have applied 100 percent of their conditioning to anaerobic intervals. A superhigh VO_2max and higher anaerobic threshold will help a player sustain himself in a fast-paced game before he relies more heavily on the lactic system that feeds intense action but quickly shuts down the legs. Certainly, a pure sprint is anaerobic. But a well-positioned player can play a smart, high-tempo game with an equal draw on aerobic and anaerobic fuel sources. This approach is ideal because it preserves an anaerobic reserve during each shift that the player can draw on during game-breaking situations, such as blocking a shot at the point that bounces out over the blue line. The race for the puck and breakaway are pure anaerobic. Players need to have gas left in their tanks for those critical situations.

YOUR TRAINING DEFINES YOUR PERFORMANCE CEILING

"Compared with 20 years ago, today's players are in top condition. Players are bigger and faster because of their work ethic and their conditioning," says Chris Chelios, winner of the Norris Trophy as the NHL's best defenseman in 1989, 1993, and 1996. "There's only so much you can do on the ice. I think off-ice conditioning is the key. Most of my conditioning drills are for the legs. That's the most important component—to get your legs in the best condition you possibly can. Top players are in such good shape that if you don't work hard on your leg conditioning, you won't be able to keep up," stresses Chelios. "The season is so long and grueling, I can't emphasize enough your physical preparation."

Chelios skated for 23 years in the NHL and played on the world stage in his 40s. He competed for the U.S. national team, the U.S. Olympic team, Team USA in the 1991 Canada Cup, and seven NHL All-Star games. From this experience, Chelios recommends, "You have to train properly and professionally. You need really good coaches, because sometimes you can exercise and actually hurt your body or develop counterproductive to hockey. You need the right type of coaching to make sure you condition specifically for hockey."

Specific training of each of the components that make up the five pillars ultimately defines your performance ceiling. In the most critical hockey challenges—tournament elimination games, overtime periods, and playoff game 7s—some players will rise to the occasion psychologically. In that regard, leaders emerge, and players who mentally thrive on high-stress, clutch situations elevate their stature. But with a big game on the line, no one can magically become more fit overnight. From a physiological perspective, in their most important games, players never rise to the occasion—they sink to the level of their training.

Chapter 2

Tests for Hockey Fitness

Physiological assessments can be used to evaluate, rank, and compare players and provide an impression of a player's level of commitment. Test results help identify what fitness components each player needs to work on, providing players an objective evaluation of their conditioning and motivating them to improve their performance levels.

When scouting and preparing for the NHL draft, testing is a tool to help predict how good a player could become. Although a player may be currently of below average fitness, he may display exceptional (and natural) athletic movements in the speed, quickness, agility, balance, and lateral movement tests. I know that those players' bodies and minds can accept my coaching and develop to a much higher level.

If a coach wants to play a speed game with forwards who are quick on the forecheck and can wear down D-men by finishing their checks, he should first assess whether his current roster players can implement the desired system. The desired team system and the testing results together determine what exercises are needed. Mike Keenan likes an aggressive, up-tempo style of play, so he looks for excellent speed, solid standing strength, and top-end fitness to support the whole process. If his team is in a slump, Pat Quinn likes to retest to assess whether conditioning is part of the problem. If testing shows that conditioning is not the problem, Coach Quinn still gains value because he has eliminated one potential contributing factor and can then focus on other probable causes.

Midseason retesting is a good way to check whether players are maintaining their conditioning levels throughout the season. Retesting during the season can help coaches refine practices and workouts and determine the recovery needs of players. This information is especially important at playoff time. In the NHL, during some seasons we tested players at midseason, whereas in other years we decided to test 6 to 8 weeks before the playoffs so that we could use the results to individualize player conditioning and help them peak at the right time. Data from postseason testing can indicate what to emphasize in the player's off-season conditioning program.

Currently, I train players from numerous NHL, college, and junior teams during the off-season. I also train players from midget and bantam levels, most of whom stay in Vancouver for at least 8 weeks. We test players before they begin the off-season program and retest in process to track each player's progression toward individual training-camp goals, as well as to evaluate the effectiveness of my conditioning program.

Traditional physiological testing measures general strength and fitness, but hockey's new training methods specifically develop the physical tools that aid on-ice performance. Assessment should include the physical competencies that feed into skills and dynamic game action, as well as on-ice tests that involve skating proficiency because that is the environment in which testing results will be played out.

Ideally, the testing protocol should be specific to the demands of hockey. At Twist Conditioning, my team of coaches and sport conditioning specialists has worked hard to identify performance tests that reflect more than fitness. These tests determine the attributes that coaches desire in players—power, crossover speed, agility, quickness, lateral movement, fast feet, and balance. Curiously, for years hockey coaches referred to those attributes to speak positively or negatively about players, yet they did not scientifically train players to improve in those areas or test them. In each test, we determine a quantified result, such as time, distance, foot contacts in a set time, pounds of force, and so on. We also have a checklist of biomechanical movement skills that players must possess to perform the test optimally, so coaches make a subjective assessment of each player to indicate what the player can change in his body to produce better results. This approach is known as qualitative analysis, which is how a bench coach handles on-ice skills and how a power-skating coach determines what to teach a player. A standardized checklist provides an inventory of things that the athlete must do to be mechanically sound.

On-ice testing, although less scientific and reliable than laboratory testing, is valid because it measures conditioning in connection with skating technique and mechanical efficiency. The off-ice field tests offer simple ways to assess attributes crucial to game success. Because of the absence of scientific process, collectively these tests are known as field tests to indicate that they are more practitioner derived. Meticulous adherence to test protocols and well-trained testers are necessary if you hope to secure valid results.

Having said that, physiological lab tests are the most accurate and provide critical information. But they are beyond the scope of this book and beyond the reach of what coaches and athletes would be able to replicate themselves. For the past 16 years, Dr. Ted Rhodes of the University of British

Columbia has been overseeing the Vancouver Canucks' physiological testing, implementing tests for aerobic power, anaerobic power and capacity, strength, flexibility, and body fat. Dr. Rhodes is an exercise physiologist whose research greatly influenced the use of physiological principles in ice hockey training and the implementation of lab testing for NHL teams and central scouting.

I encourage readers to engage an exercise physiologist, perhaps at a local university, who has access to a standardized physiology lab. Valuable physiological energy system tests include $\dot{V}O_2$max, which is the volume of oxygen that players take in and deliver to their muscles in milliliters per kilogram of body weight per minute, and anaerobic measures of power and capacity, which test the sprinting energy systems for speed and speed endurance. These tests are the most valid and reliable measures of fitness. If a player does not have elite aerobic and anaerobic energy systems, no matter how skilled he is, he will fail to reach his goals and will definitely fail to display his best performance. Two lab-based tests that practitioners can readily administer are grip strength and body composition.

HOCKEY LAB TESTS

Grip Strength Test

Purpose: Measure hand, wrist, and forearm strength

Strength in the hand, wrist, and forearm is important during shooting and puck control, in being strong on the puck, and in being able to contain opponents physically. A handgrip

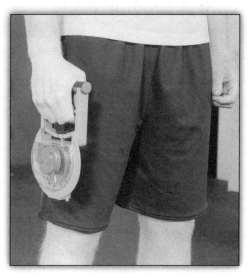

dynamometer produces a grip strength measure that correlates well with overall upper-body strength. The athlete holds the dynamometer in one hand at the side of the body. He grips as hard as possible for 2 or 3 seconds and then relaxes. The arm can move a bit as the athlete exerts force. The athlete makes two efforts with each hand; the highest score is recorded for each hand.

Anthropometry

Purpose: Measure lean muscle mass and body fat to determine general overall fitness

The relation of body fat to lean muscle mass, an indicator of general fitness, is extremely important for efficient movement and agility on the ice. Body composition is estimated through skinfold assessment. Subcutaneous fat folds are measured with a skinfold caliper.

We use six skinfold sites (biceps, triceps, subscapular, supriliac, anterior thigh, and medial calf). The results are summed to represent fat deposits. Various mathematical equations are available to estimate percent body fat, but because of the discrepancy between equation results and the skinfold sites used, we rely on just the sum as an indication of overall body fat. Skinfold assessments are highly susceptible to tester error, so the test administrator must be well versed in the test protocol. Significant variance often occurs in skinfolds captured by different testers. Consider using the same person to test all players, including retests. Avoid using plastic calipers, which only add to the inaccuracy.

Hydrostatic weighing is a more valid and reliable test that produces values for percent body fat and lean body weight. We also measure height and weight each time that we test athletes, before the tests of exertion begin.

ON-ICE FITNESS TESTS

Repeat Sprint Skate

DVD

Purpose: Evaluate anaerobic power and endurance, muscle endurance, skating speed and efficiency, and ability to recover

The repeat sprint skate test (RSS) is an on-ice assessment of anaerobic preparation (anaerobic power and anaerobic endurance), the endurance capabilities of the skating muscles, linear skating speed, recovery ability, and skating efficiency. The test consists of six maximal velocity skating sprints of 91.45 meters repeated every 30 seconds.

Players should be well warmed up for this test but not fatigued. The ice should be relatively clean and free of snow. To perform the test, the player starts behind the goal red line. On the whistle, the player sprints to the far red line and comes to a complete stop over the red line. The player immediately reverses direction and sprints to the blue line closest to the starting red line. The first timer (A) stands at the far red line and times how long it takes the player to sprint from red line to red line. The second timer (B), who is at the blue line closest to the starting red line, times the sprint from beginning to end.

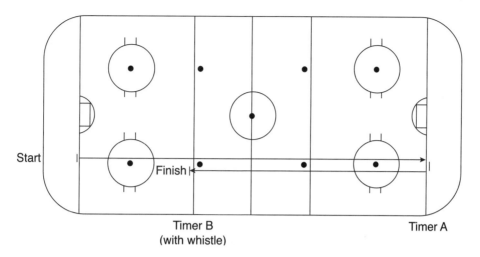

Timer B
(with whistle)

Timer A

Depending on the time it takes for the player to complete each full sprint interval, whatever remains of the 30-second sprint segment can be used for rest and recovery. For instance, if a player takes 18 seconds to sprint 91.45 meters, she gets 12 seconds of rest before the next sprint interval begins. The player must be ready at the red line for another sprint interval at the end of the 30 seconds. A 5-second oral warning is given before each repetition. There are three RSS measurements:

1. The speed index (usually the first complete length of the ice, from red line to red line) represents anaerobic power performance (ATP-PC system) and full linear speed ability.

2. The total time for the six repetitions represents the player's anaerobic endurance. One full repetition is from goal red to goal red back to the blue line at the original zone where the skater started. Add up all six reps for a total anaerobic capacity score expressed as total time.

3. The drop-off index, from the time difference between the slowest and fastest repetitions (usually the first and the last rep), is an indication of anaerobic fitness. If a player's drop-off time is short, the coach knows that the player has come to camp physically prepared. A long drop-off time indicates that the player is in need of improvement. Players should aim to keep their drop-off time within 10 to 15 percent of their speed index. To calculate drop-off index:

$$\text{drop-off index} = \frac{\text{slowest speed repetition time} - \text{fastest speed repetition time}}{\text{slowest speed repetition time}} \times 100$$

Here are some helpful tips on administering the test:

- All timers should start their stopwatches on the whistle. One timer (usually B) counts down the last 5 seconds to prepare the player and the other timer. The counting timer blows the whistle to start each sprint repetition.

- Players must begin with their feet behind the red line. The speed index sprint ends when one foot crosses the far red line, but the player must come to a full stop with both feet. The full repetition ends when one foot crosses the blue line at timer B.
- After players understand that a drop-off index is being measured, they may pace themselves to manipulate their times for a better drop-off index. To ensure a maximal effort, the speed index should be determined at a different practice with a one-rep speed test before the RSS test is announced. The RSS is administered another day, and the speed index is cross-referenced with the speed index measurement from the initial one-rep speed test. The times should be almost identical.

Blue-to-Blue Explosive Start Test

DVD

Purpose: Measure starting quickness and explosive acceleration

The ability to react and initiate movement, to be quick on the first step, and to accelerate rapidly are critical hockey abilities. To perform the test, the player starts with hips and shoulders in line with the blue line and both feet on the line. One coach stands behind the skater and slaps his stick on the ice to signal the start, eliminating any visual cues for the skater, and the player sprints blue line to blue line. The other coach or a testing assistant acts as the timer and stands even with the far blue line. The timer starts the stopwatch when the starter's stick hits the ice. The sound of the stick on the ice rather than a whistle is used to signal the start so that the timer can watch the stick move close to the ice as a visual cue to anticipate the start, making the start of the stopwatch less reliant on thumb reaction time to an audible cue. This method is especially valuable for a short distance test, in which delays in start times are magnified in the result.

The time is stopped when the skater's first foot crosses the far blue line. Time is recorded to the nearest 1/10th of a second. The final result is the average of three attempts. If one of the times differs greatly, tester error is the likely cause. Throw the test out and have the skater repeat a fourth sprint after a few minutes of rest. To provide adequate rest intervals between reps, all players should perform their first repetition before they attempt their second sprint.

The distance from blue line to blue line should be 60 feet (18.3 meters). If this distance differs in your arena, measure out 60 feet and mark the distance with cones to ensure that you use the standardized test distance. Use of a Speed Trap, which automatically and precisely captures start and finish, will improve test accuracy.

Stop-and-Start Sprint Test

DVD

Purpose: Measure explosive power, agility, quickness, acceleration, and deceleration

The stop-and-start sprint test is a modified pattern that grew from a dry-land T-test. This change-of-direction test assesses explosive power, the ATP-PC energy system, agility, quick feet, acceleration, and deceleration. These attributes are important in hockey for stop-and-starts, one-on-one confrontations, races for loose pucks, creating separation from defenders, and tactics that require high-speed directional changes. Have players warm up in another area of the ice to keep the ice between the two blue lines clean for the test.

This test uses two timers per skater; the result is the average of their times. To prepare for the test, the skater straddles the center red line, facing timer A. The player self-starts—the timers watch the player's feet and start their watches when one foot begins to move.

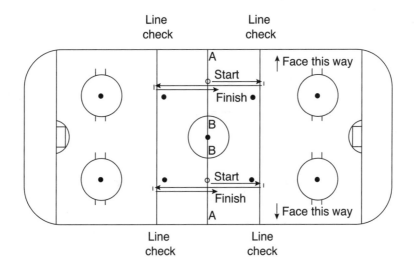

The player begins by sprinting to the left to the blue line, either crossing over at the takeoff or turning and skating forward—whatever style and strategy is preferred. At the blue line, the player must stop completely and face timer A. For the sprint to be complete, one of the player's skates has to cross completely over the blue line. Position a line checker at each blue line to ensure that the skater does this. If one skate does not cross the blue line, the line checker informs the timers, and the player repeats the test after a brief rest.

The player then skates to the right to the opposite blue line. Again, one foot must cross the blue line and the skater must stop completely, facing timer A. The player then skates left, back to the center red line. The timers stop the test when one foot crosses the center red line.

When measuring the test, the timers take positions on the center red line, one in front of the skater and one behind, so that they have a direct, straight view of the skater crossing the finish line. Both timers start their stopwatches at the same time and stop their watches as they view the skater cross the finish line. To be as accurate as possible, the timers must concentrate and watch the feet for initiation of movement at the start. Likewise, they have to be ready to stop their watches as the player approaches the finish line. The explosive nature of this test makes it a challenge to measure accurately, and the short distance amplifies the effect of any timing errors. Timers should first practice timing a self-start and a finish.

If the two timers' results are close when measuring the test (for example, 7.04 seconds and 7.10 seconds), the average of the two scores is used. If the two times differ greatly, say by as much as a half second, a tester error has occurred. When that happens and one timer realizes that he or she has made a mistake, then the other timer's score can be recorded. If the cause of the discrepancy is not clear, the skater should repeat the test after a few minutes of rest.

The shorter the test, the greater the distortion of results caused by tester error. For example, a timing mistake of 2/10ths of a second has little significance to times for a mile (1.6 kilometers) race that players may take 5 minutes to complete. In a short stop-and-start test that lasts 4 seconds, however, errors are amplified relative to the total test score, and player rankings are invalidated. For coaches who plan to implement speed, agility, and quickness testing and retesting throughout a season, and time sprints off-season, I highly recommend a wireless Speed Trap, which automatically detects the start and finish to an accuracy of 1/1,000th of a second. The device stores test times. To track results, you can identify athletes by number and then review their times on the machine or download them to a PC. The Speed Trap is simple to use and quick to reset for the next skater, so you can roll through a number of players as quickly as you can when using manual methods but with greater accuracy.

Rotate through all players and then repeat the test, this time starting in the other direction (to the right). Also, vary players' exact starting positions across the center red line so that players do not continually cut up the same strip of ice. For team testing, try dividing your team in two more groups. One group can rotate through a test, while another group or groups are elsewhere on the ice completing another test. You can organize testing to allow enough rest for players but not waste valuable ice time either, getting the entire team through a battery of tests in a shorter time.

Modified Iron Cross Agility Test

DVD

Purpose: Measure agility and movement skills

The game is won or lost on one-on-one battles. The ability to change direction quickly in tight spaces is critical for defensive coverage as well as evasiveness on offensive. Fluid movement skills allow a skater to get from point A to point B quicker while expending less energy. The test gives an indication of both quickness and efficiency, which both rely on skating skills. Screening players for a multidirectional sport, the test exposes weaknesses because the skating pattern requires forward, backward, and open pivots and turns to the left and right.

The test requires one person to record test results, one timer with a stopwatch, and two line checkers. Before the test, set up cones on both sides of the circle at the face-off hash marks. Athletes can have one warm-up trial. They perform this test for two trials, with adequate rest between trials.

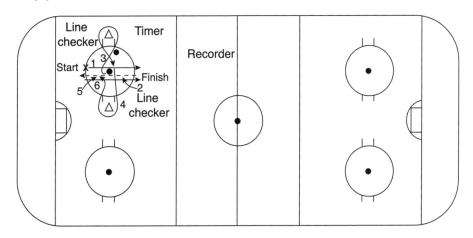

The athlete starts at the bottom of the circle on the line. The test begins when the athlete initiates movement. The athlete skates forward all the way to the top of the circle (a skate must break the circle), pivots backward at the top, and skates backward to the face-off dot. He open pivots to the left (touching the middle dot with his skate), skates forward to a cone, and tight turns around the cone, facing down ice. He skates forward across the circle to the other cone and tight turns, facing down ice. He then skates forward to the face-off dot and pivots backward. He skates backward to the bottom of the circle (breaking the circle with his skate), stops, and skates forward right through the top of the circle. The timer stops the watch as soon as a skate breaks the line as the athlete passes through the top of the circle. The better of two trials is recorded.

The line checkers must make sure that the athlete breaks through the top and bottom of the circle and that his skate touches the face-off circle. A trial may be disqualified if the athlete fails to touch the top or bottom of the circle, fails to get his skate through the face-off dot, or fails to turn around the cones.

WEIGHT ROOM TESTS

30-Second Balance Board Squat and Hold

Purpose: Measure balance and ability to retain an equally weighted hockey stance

Hockey players who can achieve a perfect position of balance are in the best position to generate power in any direction. If stationary on the ice—in the slot, off a face-off, or after stopping—a half-squat athletic ready position with legs equally weighted is the stance that would allow the player to move equally well in any direction, pushing off to skate forward, backward, or laterally left or right. Knowledge of how to assume this position after stopping gives a skater a tactical advantage over opponents who are not equally weighted or who linger when exiting the stop.

The test requires a designated testing Extreme Balance Board, a timer with a stopwatch, and a spotter (to identify and count board taps). The player performs the test for two trials, with adequate rest between trials. The athlete is not allowed a practice trial. The test should not be performed in front of any mirrors or reflective sources that provide visual feedback.

The athlete assumes a half-squat stance on the Extreme Balance Board. His feet are no narrower than hip-width and no wider than shoulder-width. The head and chest should be up, with the shoulders pulled down and back. Hands and arms can be anywhere, as long as they are not in contact with the body, but the goal is to keep the arms quiet.

The test begins when the athlete finds a reasonable center of balance. The athlete then gives the command "Go" to the timer, who starts the stopwatch. The spotter counts the number of times that the board touches the ground in 30 seconds. The spotter is in front of the athlete and lying on the floor to observe the board. If the player begins to rise out of the hockey stance, the timer must clearly cue him to get lower. Throughout the test, the timer should note the athlete's posture, muscular imbalances, and balancing technique. These notes may include subtalar

pronation; internal and external hip rotation; valgus or varus knee or hip alignment; pelvic misalignment, laterally or rotationally; tilting reflex forward and backward; shoulder posture (rounded); kyphosis, lordosis, scoliosis; use of front and back plugs to aid in balance; excessive shaking of the legs; upper-body compensation; or righting reflex laterally.

If the athlete successfully balances for 30 seconds without touching the balance board on the ground, he scores a perfect zero. The higher the score, the poorer the performance.

Single-Leg Lateral Bound Test

DVD

Purpose: Evaluate leg power and stability

Hockey is an independent leg activity. Although vertical jump is an easy measure of leg power, it is not the most relevant to hockey because the most advantageous skating position is low to power off laterally in stride patterns. If measuring triple-extension power, an indication of lateral power is more relevant to the movement patterns in the game. Although a vertical jump test assesses takeoff power, the single-leg lateral bound relies as well on deceleration ability determined on the lateral landing. Deceleration is key in a change-of-direction sport. Players must demonstrate their competency at deceleration before they train for acceleration.

The only equipment needed is lots of floor space, painter's tape (green with less adhesive), a measuring tape that is at least 3 meters long, and chalk. The test requires one person to record results and observe the athlete's technique and one person to measure.

Place a 24-inch (60-centimeter) piece of tape on the floor, with about 2 meters of space widthwise and 3 to 4 meters of space lengthwise. Mark a point in the middle of the piece of tape, 12 inches (30 centimeters) from either end. This will be the reference point for measuring the distance jumped. Measure and mark 1 meter perpendicularly from the reference point. This makes measuring a little easier.

After warming up, the athlete should perform one practice trial per leg but should be careful not to become fatigued. The test is performed for two trials per leg, with adequate rest between trials.

The athlete stands behind the tape, with the instep of the jumping foot flat on the ground and parallel to, but not on top of, the tape. The foot should be positioned so that the middle of the instep is aligned with the reference point (the 12-inch, or 30-centimeter, mark on the 24-inch, or 60-centimeter, start line). The nonjumping foot must be off the ground before takeoff.

After aligning properly, the athlete loads the jumping leg by triple flexing at the ankle, knee, and hip and simultaneously swinging the arms back for momentum. The athlete jumps and attempts to land solely on the other foot. With chalk or a piece of tape, the measurer marks the floor even with the part of the foot that lands positioned closest to the starting line. After the observer sees a stable landing on one foot that the athlete holds for approximately 1 second, the observer cues the athlete, who only then can use the jumping foot to stabilize. To allow accurate recording of distance, the athlete must not move the landing foot.

The measurer measures perpendicularly from the reference point out to the area where the athlete lands. He then measures over horizontally to the chalk mark or marking tape. He does not simply measure from the reference point directly to the landing point because that distance will not take into account any deviation from the lateral path that the athlete is required to travel. The distance is measured to the nearest centimeter. The better of two trials is recorded. Loading and generating power through triple extension across the ankle, knee, and hip integrated with trunk rotation and arm drive determine the bound distance, but the trial is allowed only if it ends in a stable landing, avoiding stutter steps, ankle inversion, lateral trunk flexion, hip rotation, or planting of the foot of the trail leg (takeoff leg). A trial is also disqualified if the jumping foot is misaligned or touches the tape before or during initiation of the jump, if the athlete deviates significantly from a lateral path, if or the athlete falls.

The observer notes the athlete's posture, jumping technique, and landing stability during the test, including balance at takeoff and landing; hip, knee, and ankle alignment in frontal and sagittal planes; arm position and use in the jump; trajectory of the jump, both horizontal and vertical; displacement; upper-body posture at takeoff and landing; and absorption at landing (triple flexion, sound of landing).

Tall players and shorter players are treated equally; no scoring adjustment is made for body height or leg length. This approach is consistent with other tests and true to the on-ice challenge, where players must find a way to be better than their opponent straight up, head to head.

10-Second Lateral Crossovers

Purpose: Measure agility and foot speed

Rapid and fluid footwork is required to manipulate the skates through a variety of patterns and use the skate edges well on the ice. The crossover pattern, in particular, is a common footwork pattern that players use when starting from a stationary position to initiate such actions as changing direction out of a stop; exiting a turn aggressively; skating out from behind the net, building up speed, and carrying the puck out of the defensive zone; cycling the puck in the corners; or shifting positions and taking away passing and shooting lanes on the PK.

The test requires one person to record results and observe the athlete's technique and one person to count the number of successful cycles (half cycles are counted). Testers need a rubber agility slat or painter's tape and a stopwatch. Place a 24-inch (60-centimeter) piece of tape on the floor, with about 2 to 3 meters of space on each side of the tape. The athlete has 1 minute of practice time to get accustomed to the motor pattern of the movement skill. The athlete should be careful not to become fatigued. The test is performed for two trials, with adequate rest between trials.

The athlete stands in athletic ready position on one side of the tape. The ankles, knees, and hips are slightly flexed, the core is engaged, the chest is up, and the shoulders are pulled back. The feet should be about shoulder-width apart and parallel to the line. The test begins when the athlete initiates the first movement.

If the athlete begins standing with the line to the left, she executes the following movement pattern. First, the athlete crosses the right leg up and over the left leg to the opposite side of the line, landing the right foot on the left side of the line. She then brings the left leg over the line and starts to position it beside the right leg. As the left leg touches down, the athlete lifts the right leg up (which helps her naturally load the outside left leg) and then steps again on the same side of the line. The athlete immediately lifts the left leg up and crosses it over the right leg to the opposite side of the line. She then brings the right leg over the line and starts to position it beside the left leg. As the right leg touches down, the athlete lifts the left leg up and steps on the same side of the line. She repeats the cycle from the beginning, crossing the right leg over the left leg to the other side of the line. The athlete performs these repeated lateral crossovers as quickly as possible, back and forth over the line, for 10 seconds.

After the athlete completes the trial, the test recorder records the number of half cycles that the athlete completed successfully within the 10 seconds. The better of two trials is recorded.

The observer notes the athlete's posture and movement skills including body positioning (positive angles and center of gravity placement), absorption (sound of foot contacts), upper-body inefficiencies (arm positioning), footwork and coordination, excessive rotation of the hips, and footprint consistency.

A trial may be disqualified if the athlete uses an incorrect crossover pattern or voluntarily stops for any reason. If any portion of the athlete's foot touches the line, she receives one warning. If she touches the line again, the trial is disqualified.

Linked System Squat to Push Throw Test

Purpose: Evaluate full-body power

Because hockey is a full collision sport, upper-body strength is vital. But a test of strength is applicable only if it evaluates multijoint power in a standing position. For the upper body, as well as trunk rotation, the push action is the most common strength pattern in hockey.

To test full-body power, the squat to push throw test uses a 12-pound (5.4-kilogram) medicine ball. The test requires lots of floor space, a designated testing 12-pound medicine ball, painter's tape, and a measuring tape. The single tester observes the athlete's throwing technique, marks where the ball lands, and records results.

Place a 24-inch (60-centimeter) piece of tape on the floor, with about 2 meters of space widthwise and 3 to 4 meters of space lengthwise. Mark a point in the middle of the piece of tape, 12 inches, or 60 centimeters, from either end. This mark is the reference point for measuring the distance of the thrown medicine ball. Place a piece of tape on the floor at the 4-meter mark and every meter thereafter. (Mark every half meter, if time permits.) Mark 10 to 14 meters, depending on the strength of athletes.

The athlete has one practice trial. He should be careful not to become fatigued. The athlete performs the test for two trials, with adequate rest between trials.

The athlete stands behind the tape with the 12-pound (5.4-kilogram) medicine ball resting on top of the start line between his feet. When the tester signals that he is ready, the athlete, in one fluid linked motion, squats down with his chest upright, picks up the ball from the floor, and throws it as far from the chest as possible. The athlete is permitted to jump over the line, but he must release the ball before his feet cross the line. The distance is recorded to the nearest 0.1 meter. The best score of two trials is recorded.

The observer notes the athlete's posture, jumping technique, and landing stability during the test. The observer should watch for hip, knee, and ankle alignment in frontal and sagittal planes; squatting technique (forward lean, curvature of the spine); fluidity of movement (any pauses or hesitation?); speed of execution; trajectory of throw, both horizontally and vertically; trajectory of jump, both horizontally and vertically; and force distribution with arms (does the athlete favor one arm?).

A trial may be disqualified if the athlete's feet cross the line before he releases the ball, if the athlete throws the ball in an asymmetric fashion (from a staggered stance or with one arm throwing significantly more than the other, or if the athlete pauses significantly during execution of the throw).

One-Arm, One-Leg Contralateral Tabletop Hold

Purpose: Measure core stability and endurance

Hockey strength training builds from the center of the body out to the periphery to establish the strong core needed for the legs and arms to produce maximum force. Because of the contact in hockey, core stability dictates a player's strength in a standing position, the strength that allows him to ward off opponents and absorb contact without breaking through the torso.

The test requires a yoga mat, a person to record data and observe the athlete's technique, a spotter (who can be an athlete), and a timer with a stopwatch.

The athlete performs this test for only one trial on each side. Generous rest should be given between trials to ensure that fatigue doesn't skew the athlete's performance. The first trial is on the left arm with the left leg up. The second trial is on the right arm with the right leg up.

The athlete lies prone on the floor so that the elbows and toes support the body. The elbows should be directly below the shoulders. The athlete lifts one leg and the contralateral arm (right arm and left leg for the first trial), making sure to keep them in line with the spine and parallel to the ground. The arm should be beside the head with the elbow fully extended.

The spotter stands beside the athlete and holds the athlete's hips so that the pelvis and hips are in a neutral position. This method ensures that the athlete can kinesthetically feel the proper position that she needs to stay in during the test.

The test begins when the athlete assumes the correct body position and the timer says, "On your mark, get set, go." On the "Go" command, the spotter releases the athlete's hips and the athlete attempts to hold the required position as long as she can. The time is recorded to the nearest second for both positions.

The observer notes the athlete's posture throughout the test. These notes may include lateral hip flexion; right or left winging of scapulae; pelvic rotation; neck posture; internal and external rotation of hip; lordosis, kyphosis, or scoliosis; and overall balance and weight distribution throughout the test.

To measure core stability accurately, testers need to be consistent from player to player. Unless testers are strict with technique, the test is useless. Players who fatigue will quickly flex the arm and leg in the air. The tester should cue a correction, and if the athlete can respond, keep timing. If the athlete reverts to the flexed position, the timing should end. Players without adequate core strength will rotate the forearm of the support arm toward the midline to create a stronger base of support. The tester should immediately correct this and discontinue the test if the athlete cannot comply. A trial ends if the athlete shows excessive rotation of the torso, all or in part, from shoulders to hips; if the athlete loses the neutral spine position (hyperlordosis, hyperkyphosis); if the athlete touches the floor with the hand or foot that should be raised; or if the athlete is unable to hold the extended leg and arm out straight from the body.

Supine Adductor Wall Test (Lying V)

Purpose: Evaluate flexibility

The adductor, or groin, muscle group requires strength and flexibility to accommodate the unique on-ice stride mechanics. The mode of locomotion in hockey imposes demands on a body that was made to walk, hike, and run. Athletes from sports like football or tennis at times push off on a 45-degree angle to cut and change direction, but that action is not their dominant mechanic of movement. Both full range of motion and equal flexibility are desirable. Players seem to have a natural tendency to be tight or hyperflexible, but everyone can improve flexibility. Flexibility imbalances certainly place skaters at risk of injury and limit fluidity of movement.

The test requires a sturdy wall, chalk, and a measuring tape. Mark a vertical line from the floor straight up the wall. An observer watches the athlete's technique and marks his result on the wall. The athlete performs the test for one trial.

The athlete removes his shoes and lies supine on the floor with his butt up against the wall so that his legs are going up the wall. The body midline is aligned with the vertical wall line, and the feet are together, one on each side of the wall line.

The athlete needs to relax completely, particularly in the hips and legs. Keeping the legs straight, the athlete allows his legs to fall *slowly* open as far as they will go. When the athlete has reached the most open V, the tester marks a spot on the wall adjacent to each ankle's lateral malleolus. The tester then measures the distance from each respective point down to the floor. This test gives a quick indication of whether flexibility is equal. Of course, a short leg and a long leg elicit different measures down to the floor, so players cannot be ranked on this test.

A more thorough measurement can be done to quantify range of motion. When the test is completed and the tester has marked the ankle position with chalk, the athlete can exit the test and assist the tester by holding a taut string or measuring tape from the ankle chalk mark to the centerline at the floor. From this, an angle measurement can be taken that is independent of leg length. Measure the angle from midline to the string line.

The athlete must repeat the trial if either leg bends at the knee; if either PSIS comes off the floor (indicates lateral rotation of the hips); if the athlete uses a ballistic movement to abduct the legs; if the athlete cannot hold the end point position long enough to establish a mark on the wall (about 10 seconds); or if the athlete stops voluntarily for any reason.

The tester notes the athlete's posture and technique during the test. These notes may include a large discrepancy between right-leg and left-leg angles and distances; low-back, head, and neck posture throughout the trials; restricted range of motion at the hip, knee, or ankle; or any indication of pain or discomfort by the athlete.

Chapter 3

Dynamic Warm-Up and Flexibility

What we put in our bodies affects our energy level, mental focus, health, and endurance. Some foods are better to eat the day before a game, and some are better right before, during, or after a game. Likewise, how a player prepares mentally, with pregame visualization and positive self-talk, affects performance. Could a physical preparation strategy improve play on the ice? Like off-season conditioning programs, nutrition, and mental training, certain pre-ice exercise strategies can prepare the mind and body for the challenges of a hockey game.

From the youngest players to NHL veterans such as Mattias Ohlund and Ed Jovonovski and past greats like Mark Messier, from new minor hockey coaches to veteran collegiate coaches, from Russian hockey experts to experts from Sweden and Japan, a common question concerns preparing for game time. While skiing recently, I was approached by a young player from Whistler. He walked up and introduced himself. He then asked, "So dude, I mean Coach Twist, what's the real deal with warming up? My coaches make me stretch, and I just want to get on the ice and go. On the mountain, I get off the lift and start to carve some turns. In the weight room, I just start to lift. Can you talk to my coach?"

Although the player was hoping that I would talk his coach out of requiring warm-ups, I would instead advise the coach of the value of a different style of warming up. And this is what I told the snowboarding hockey player at Whistler. Entering a game, what are your goals? What do you hope to experience in that game? Many players aim to have a strong game in which they feel athletic and skillful, strong but fluid, mobile yet explosive. Pre- and post-ice routines that incorporate dynamic warm-up, joint mobility, static stretching, and myofascial release will help set up the muscles to support those goals.

To start well in a game, the player needs to enter the first shift ready to exert explosive power and display rapid agility from the get-go. The pre-ice (and similarly, preworkout) routine plays an important role in readying the player's mind and body to exert best efforts skillfully. Historically, players would drop down and bang off a few 10-second stretches at center ice as part of their prepractice warm-up. Players do brief on-ice stretches with good intentions, but the result is little more than a preskate ritual that at best does nothing but could be causing damage. Stretching cold muscles and entering an aggressive stretch for a brief time, made awkward by bulky hockey equipment, can leave the muscles tighter than they were before stretching.

To get the best start at the drop of the puck, static stretching alone is not the way to go. The goal of pre-ice exercise is to wake up the mind, warm the muscles, and link the mind and muscles so that when the brain commands the muscles to move skillfully and explosively, they comply. The goal is to have a responsive system that is prepared to react quickly. Static stretching defeats the purpose. Stretching is still important, but the timing changes. Players should stretch after a workout or practice when they are warm and tired and when muscles are in need of stretching.

Think of static stretching. The goal when stretching is to turn off the mind, shut down the system, and let muscles relax. Stretches are held in a static position like a statue. How can stretching like a statue prepare the mind and body to move explosively during complex athletic actions? It can't. Research shows that in workouts following static stretching, strength and speed are lower. Moving from a stretch-hold position to a sprinting condition can easily lead to injury. You will notice that world-class sprinters warm up, stretch, and then move through a dynamic movement-based warm-up in a progressive preparation to exert their best effort.

A dynamic warm-up is the recommended preactivity, and static stretching should occur after the activity, when the muscles are tired and need recovery, and when the mind is also fatigued, ready to shut down and relax. The purpose of a dynamic warm-up is to prepare the body for intense workout or on-ice demands, create a cohesive mind–muscle link, and ensure that the muscles will be compliant to explosive, complex movements before intensity increases.

The body is constructed of more than 600 muscles and 206 bones. Tendons connect muscles to bones. Each muscle crosses over a specific joint in a way that causes the bones of that joint to move when the muscle contracts (shortens). The command to contract comes from the nervous system. The nervous system tells the muscles how to move, and the muscles act on the bones to generate mechanical movement. Part of the pre-ice routine focuses on preparing the software, making sure that the software and hard drive (muscles) are communicating. But remember that in a game, no matter how smart the software, muscles work better if they are well warmed up.

For smooth, coordinated movement on the ice, muscles need to contract and relax at just the right time. Muscles are pliable tissue, and temperature influences extensibility. A pre-ice routine that increases the deep muscle temperature is part of the performance recipe. A warm muscle that has moved through a full range of motion and woken up with proprioception and movement challenges will be more extensible on ice and will contract and relax quickly, facilitating high-speed skill execution. A cold muscle restricts movement and is easily injured. Quick movement of a cold muscle can result in a muscle tear or strain.

Yet even a warm muscle has limits to its range of motion based on flexibility. Because movements in hockey are unpredictable, with players constantly reacting to sudden changes on the ice, muscles should be able to move easily through all possible motions—even those unexpected movements that a player makes when she is hit or falls from an awkward position. Stretching remains important. Its timing changes, and it becomes part of a flexibility program. To gain the freedom of movement that hockey players seldom achieve, a mix of static stretching, joint mobility, and myofascial release can help get the job done.

Flexibility training can increase a muscle's range of motion. Good flexibility is important for fluid movement, long skating strides, and injury prevention. Static stretching helps tune up the body so that the player has equal range of motion throughout the body, eliminating asymmetries. Uneven muscle flexibility can come from preferentially shooting off one side, stopping more often on one side, loading up one leg more than the other to generate power striding forward, leg length discrepancies, and past injuries that led to compensational patterns in the body.

Eliminating asymmetries helps agility, quick direction changes, skating speed, and shot power, and prevents the common pattern of slowly setting oneself up for injury over time after performing a high volume of asymmetrical movement. Flexibility imbalances are passed on to other joints and muscles, resulting in structural compensational shifts that can gradually set up a player to be injured. To improve on-ice performance, players should focus on achieving balanced flexibility rather than excessive range of motion. They must be in tune with their bodies, sensing what muscles are more restricted, applying more stretching volume to tighter body parts.

A regular post-ice flexibility program increases the extensibility of muscles, improves the range of motion around joints, and reduces the risk and severity of injury. I recommend that players follow this program just as they do strength training or on-ice drills. The post-ice flexibility program needs to be purposeful, structured, and habitual. Intervention is needed to balance the body in pursuit of equal flexibility. A tuning-up program is best achieved when flexibility training is scheduled postworkout and postgame, when joints are well lubricated and muscle temperature is high, thus facilitating muscle pliability to allow easier and deeper stretching.

At this time, players are also mentally and physically tired, more likely to spend the appropriate amount of time for effective stretching, happy to shut down the body to accommodate a relaxed stretching session. When players stretch before activity, they are often impatient and unfocused, always shortening stretch hold times. After finishing all weight room work and on-ice physical exertion, they are more likely to chill out and hold each stretch longer, which is crucial to eliciting changes to range of motion.

Post-ice and postworkout, players will appreciate the relief given by myofascial release, which reduces delayed muscle soreness and helps muscles recover from exercise. The state of the fascia also moderates overall flexibility. Muscles, bones, nerves, veins, and organs are wrapped in a dense sheath called fascia, like a spider web that holds everything together. Fascia is normally pliable, but after injury to the body the fascia becomes scarred and tenser, restricting movement. A program to release the fascia is critical for collision sport athletes who have sustained injuries and direct blows to the body that create dysfunction through tighter fascia. Static muscle stretching is much more effective in improving flexibility after the athlete attends to the tight fascia.

Consider also just how much flexibility a hockey player needs. Yoga, for example, is a tremendous fitness activity that provides many benefits to the mind, body, and spirit. Some of my players participate in yoga to aid recovery, unloading from intense hockey workouts while working on dynamic flexibility. Yoga is a positive activity, but in truth, yoga attracts flexible people who can excel in that activity, just as football attracts big, strong athletic bodies and marathon running attracts lighter weight, slow-twitch, high-endurance athletes. So what about hockey players and stretching?

Although it is common dogma that any flexibility is good flexibility, coaches have more to consider when determining what scope of flexibility improvements they are aiming for. Excessive flexibility may counteract efforts to improve strength and power and leave players predisposed to injury. Muscle stiffness and reactivity contribute to the ability to change direction aggressively, stop on a dime, accelerate explosively, and withstand body contact. Although no one knows the precise optimal mix of flexibility and strength for any sport, including hockey, players need enough to help tune up the body. Tight muscles are counterproductive, but the flexibility of a gymnast, dancer, or yoga instructor is not the hockey player's goal.

Special care should be demonstrated with young hockey players, a percentage of whom will already be hypermobile and predisposed to injury. Most youth players should get into the habit of postworkout stretching, but coaches should keep an eye out for those who are already capable of extreme ranges of motion, which may need strengthening through that range as opposed to placing more stress on joints to accommodate even greater stretch.

The specific flexibility gained through static stretching, yoga, or Pilates, all completed at a slow pace, are not completely transferable to top-speed movements. Simply put, the great flexibility demonstrated in static hold postures cannot be harnessed during rapid, explosive movements. Muscle range of motion and joint mobility need to be applied to progressively increasing speeds so that the range of motion achieved can be harnessed in high-speed movement. For this reason I advocate postactivity static stretching to increase muscle range of motion, and dynamic flexibility through joint mobility to ensure range of motion in a standing position, with movement, working the joint at varied angles. The static stretching is always static. The joint mobility starts at slow speed and progresses in speed over a large number of flexibility workouts.

HOCKEY-SPECIFIC DYNAMIC WARM-UP

The purpose of a dynamic warm-up is to prepare the body for the demands of the activity it is about to perform. This could be a workout, a hockey practice, game, or other sport activity. A good dynamic warm-up raises core muscle temperature, which increases muscle elasticity, increases the rate of agonist muscle contraction, and increases the rate of antagonist muscle relaxation. (Agonist muscles contract to contribute to the movement; antagonist muscles oppose the agonist muscles and must relax to allow movement.)

The dynamic warm-up enhances movement integration for the skills and drills of the training session, increases dynamic range of motion, enhances muscle compliance, stimulates motor unit activation, and creates joint stabilization to help protect from injury. Representing its role in turning on the mind and muscles, preparing the body's software for game action, a dynamic warm-up is also referred to as nervous system activation. Pre-ice exercise helps prevent injuries and excite all the sensors, receptors, and minibrains throughout the body that work to produce balance and coordinated quick stops and starts. The goal is to activate muscles and prepare them to contract quickly. A progressive, athletic, movement-based, dynamic warm-up provides physiological and psychological benefits for the athlete engaging in a subsequent workout, game, or practice (table 3.1).

Bottom line, players who spend their pregame time stretching may have less strength and lower speed in the game. The key to good workouts, well-executed practices, and high-energy games is being prepared to move well and think well. Dynamic movement-oriented exercise routines begin with slow and simple movements and, after muscles begin to warm, progress to faster, reactive, complex movements. The goal is to wake up, warm up, focus, feel loose and athletic, and become ready to move explosively. Achieving this goal requires a planned dynamic warm-up that goes through a number of progressive steps.

Table 3.1 Physiological and Psychological Benefits to a Dynamic Warm-Up

Physiological benefits	Psychological benefits
Activates the nervous system for kinesthetic awareness and balance	Activates the mind
Increases muscle and connective tissue temperature	Establishes mind–muscle compliance
Increases blood and nutrient flow to muscles and joints	Increases alertness
Enhances joint mobility and stimulates synovial fluid in joints	Focuses the athlete's mind on training and competing
Stimulates efficient energy system production	Increases aggression
Prevents premature onset of lactic acid and fatigue	Decreases fear of injury
Executes game-specific motor programs	Pumps up the athlete or helps reduce stress

FIVE QUICK TIPS

1. Don't stretch before a game.
2. Use movement and balance to warm up to play your best.
3. Start slow and easy with simple exercises.
4. Finish with faster movements, changes of direction, and highly reactive complex exercises.
5. To put you in the right mental state to play your best, perform drills that are fun and challenging with teammates.

The player who hopes to have a personal best game, to move explosively with great precision, must do more than just walk out from the dressing room, skate out to center ice, sit in a circle, and do a few 10-second stretches. Specific pre-ice exercises packaged and ordered into a routine can prepare both mind and muscle to be their best in an unpredictable, high-speed, stop-and-start environment, in which the most powerful, reactive, and fluid players are the most effective and dangerous. Here are some practical tips to implement pre-ice and preworkout.

Structure drills to be fun and a little competitive. Against the hockey tradition of routine and ritual, change the dynamic warm-up program frequently to stimulate the desired results. Before games, use the dressing room, lobby, hallway, meeting room, Zamboni bay, or any other location that you can secure to have space for movement. Players can warm up when they are half dressed to minimize the time delay between warming up and stepping on the ice. The timing and the process put their minds in the right place, getting them thinking about competing in the game!

A useful dynamic warm-up should last at least 12 minutes and could be as long as 30 minutes. The end goal is for players to be warm and a little sweaty, with the mind pumped up and ready to go, and the whole body feeling awake and athletic but not fatigued. When introducing warm-ups for the first time, have players think about how they usually feel during the first practice drill compared with 30 minutes into practice, or how they feel in their first shift of a game compared with late in the first period. Often players report that in the latter instances, they are mentally more into it and physically more on top of their game. Players usually recognize the advantage of beginning the practice and game in that optimal state and getting a jump on their opponents.

To put this into practice, table 3.2 summarizes the warm-up program stages, purposes, and exercises to include in a dynamic warm-up. The program starts with balance and proprioception drills for a low-impact method of activating many muscles and turning on the mind. These drills safely challenge the small stabilizer muscles, which are crucial to reactivity and physical confrontations. Balance brings focus. Players must think and concentrate to coordinate their bodies through each drill.

Table 3.2   Dynamic Warm-Up Inventory

Program	Purpose	Exercise inventory	Details
Balance and proprioception	Activate many muscles through low-impact movements Increase heart rate and muscle temperature Turn on mind and muscles, core dominant Increase mental focus and muscle activation including stabilizer muscles Increase responsiveness	1. Extreme board squats 2. Extreme board push-ups 3. BOSU tuck holds 4. BOSU jump landings 5. BOSU hockey ready stance knock-offs	Keep ankles steady, load legs, set core. Have a solid posture and quiet arms. The goal is to land or load smoothly and stably, under control. As you progress, hold positions deeper (more leg strength) and pause longer at midposition to challenge point of balance. Once warm, increase tempo.
Movement skills	Use and warm lower-body musculature Lengthen and shorten each muscle during movement	1. Cool walking 2. Slow jog 3. Butt kickers 4. Backpedal 5. Zigzag bounds 6. Open Steps 7. Drop steps 8. Lateral shuffles 9. Sumo squats 10. Crossovers/unders	The style of this phase is slow, gentle, full range of motion. No need to speed; take time to execute well.

(continued)

Table 3.2 *(continued)*

Internal reactivity	Stimulate joint mechanoreceptors and stabilizing muscles Ready ankle, knee, and hip for precision skating	1. One-leg balance squat, eyes closed 2. One-leg jump and land 3. BOSU one-leg balance 4. BOSU split lunge to one-leg balance 5. BOSU lateral load	Each exercise lands or loads into a ready position (half squat). Hold, be patient, play with the balance challenges.
External reaction skills	Use dynamic, unpredictable read-react drills Elevate heart rate and prepare for first-step and lateral quickness	1. Reaction ball games 2. Follow leader runs 3. Partner mirror agility 4. Tennis ball drop starts 5. One-leg partner mirror	Move into athletic ready position before each drill repetition. Rely on legs and footwork.
Quick feet	Prepare the mind and feet for rapid turnover and explosive action	1. Figure-eight mirror drill 2. Rapid-fire line drills 3. Two-foot line repeats 4. Two-in-one out hurdle drill 5. Ladder shuffle	Stay on balls of feet. Make a quick coupling off ground with rapid-fire repeats.
Whole-body strength	Link lower body into core and upper-body activation Prepare to harness body as one unit Rehearse using the body as a whole to produce power moves	1. Partner BOSU high-fives 2. Standing towel pulls 3. Standing stick pushes 4. Standing stick holds with footwork 5. Squat jumps (with soft landing)	First brace the core. Load the legs before extending through the legs, core, and on to the upper body.

Players next go through specific movement skills in which they move large muscle groups through slow, linear movements and progress toward faster, more dynamic multidirectional movements as the warm-up continues. They begin with easy movements and progress to faster actions that require thinking to coordinate. My athletes begin by walking up on their toes to wake up their calf muscles and ankles. They move up the body until they have worked each muscle group. The movement skills sequence begins in a straight line and progresses through angled patterns, lateral movement, and crossovers before advancing to multidirectional drills. This sequence adds quick feet, stop-and-starts, and reactive demands. The progression of the movement skills follows:

1. Linear movement (walk forward, jog, perform butt kicks, backpedal)
2. Angled movement (45-degree lunge, bound holds, open steps, drop steps)
3. Lateral movement (lateral shuffles, sumo squats)
4. Crossover patterns (crossover and cross-under pushes, carioca)
5. Multidirectional change (known patterns plus unpredictable patterns) and movements of increased tempo and responsiveness (add reactivity), which are accomplished in the internal reactivity, external reactivity, and quick-feet stations

The dynamic warm-up finishes with whole-body strength exercises to help link the body together, activate muscles from toes to fingertips, and sequence the muscles in the order that they will need to fire for shooting and bodychecking. Players benefit when they step on the ice feeling strong and durable.

Make it clear to athletes that the objective of each exercise is not just to get to the finish line faster but also to focus on the quality of each movement repetition. They must execute with purpose. To get started, minimally select two exercises from balance, internal reactivity, external reaction skills, quick feet, and whole-body strength. Players complete the entire movement skills phase. In general, the more time that you spend on pre-ice exercise, the better the result. Just be sure that players are warmed and activated, but not fatigued.

HOCKEY-SPECIFIC FLEXIBILITY

Your hockey flexibility program consists of specific exercises that target muscle groups and movement patterns related to on-ice characteristics. The flexibility program includes three types of exercises: joint mobility, which can also be used pre-ice; static stretching; and myofascial release.

JOINT MOBILITY

After completing a dynamic warm-up, players may opt to move specific joints through a wide and varied range of motion. Blending movement skills with dynamic joint mobility frees the body so that it can execute skills with greater fluidity. But I would first implement joint mobility post-activity, before static stretching. After players have acclimated and enjoy more fluid range of motion, joint mobility exercises can become part of the preactivity program. Think of the speed and control that a martial arts instructor displays when warming up, moving limbs through a full range of motion, especially across the hip joint. The movement is quick and precise, under control. This is the goal. In a hockey player's program, joint mobility always begins slow and controlled. Then, after a player is more experienced and displays more freedom of movement, he progresses to faster movements around a joint.

Joint mobility exercises may expose tight muscles that can be attended to with extra stretching in the postactivity program. The tight muscles may be evident from a restricted range of motion, lack of fluidity (forced movement), or when the rest of the body compensates or changes position (cheats) to allow the one joint to gain movement. Again, this identifies a need for extra stretching for the body part that is limiting freedom of movement. That discovery is valuable. You have likely just prevented an injury from happening 40 games from now, proactively preventing a player from missing many games.

Rainbow Squats

Focus: Quadriceps, hamstrings, groin, glutes, low back, shoulders

From a wide stance, slowly shift your center of mass laterally and lower into a lateral squat, loaded up over one leg. Next shift to the other side, following an arc pattern so that you come up out of the squat and lower laterally onto the opposite leg. Your goal is to be wide and low. Initially this will feel laborious. Many players are unable to secure the wide, deep range of motion, but they eventually enjoy the sense of moving quickly and effortlessly into position.

After your mobility has improved, add shoulders and low back by holding your hockey stick behind and above your head with straight arms, using a wide overhand grip. The position of the hockey stick should stretch your shoulders and back. Tight hamstrings, low back, or groin will prevent you from holding the stick overhead with a straight trunk. Instead, your arms or trunk will fall forward. Repeat 10 times on each side.

On-ice: Follow the same procedure in place.

High Leg Swings

DVD

Focus: Hip flexors, extensors, adductors, abductors, lower abdominal muscles

Stand upright and balance on one foot. Keeping your trunk upright and core strong, slowly swing your opposite leg forward and back in a smooth arc. Next, swing the leg away from the midline of your body and then bring it back right across in front of your body. After you improve your range of motion, try to shift from swinging the leg to contracting muscles actively to control the leg through the same movement pattern. Perform 10 leg movements each way.

On-ice: Complete forward and backward leg swings while gliding down the ice balanced on one leg. Side-to-side leg swings are better performed while holding on to the boards with one hand for support, although you should strive to perform this exercise with no balance assistance.

Outward Rotations

DVD

Focus: Hip flexors, abductors, outward rotators

Stand on one leg. Bring your knee up above waist height and then outwardly rotate your hips so that your leg moves around to the side of your body. Your knee should be parallel to your shoulder. Note any differences between the left side and right side, especially the outward rotation. Avoid lateral flexion (trunk tilting sideways at the waist) or trunk rotation, two common compensatory patterns that will help move the knee through that pattern with tight, restrictive hip muscles. Also try reversing the flow of movement. Perform both ways 10 times for each leg.

On-ice: Complete the drill while gliding down the ice balanced on one leg.

Trunk Rotations

DVD

Focus: Lower back, abdominal muscles, shoulders, chest

Hold your stick behind your upper back, with knees flexed. Slowly and smoothly rotate left and right. Then hold your stick behind your back while leaning forward at the hips. Again, slowly and smoothly rotate. Observe differences between rotating to the left and to the right. Perform 20 rotations upright and 10 leaning forward.

On-ice: Complete both ways while gliding around the ice balanced evenly on two skates.

Arm Patterns

Focus: Shoulders

Stand upright with knees slightly bent. Keep one arm relaxed at your side. With the opposite arm, complete forward circles. Keep your arm straight and close to your body as it circles. Your arm should be very close to your head as it circles up top. Use a slow, smooth motion in a big arc. Unwind that circle pattern, circling backward. Repeat with your other arm. Perform 10 circles each way with each arm. Watch for excessive truck rotation that you may need to allow the full shoulder range of motion. Repeat the sequence and repetition count, on both sides of the body, for the following arm patterns:

Bring your right arm straight across to wrap the right hand around the left shoulder (*a*). Then unwind that straight-across pattern to open up with the right hand, level with the shoulder, far outside away from the trunk.

Bring your right hand across the trunk toward your left pocket. Wrap the right hand around the left hip (*b*). Unwind that diagonal pattern to finish with the right hand high overhead, outside the body.

Bring your right hand down to your right knee and then unwind that up-and-down pattern, bringing your right hand straight up overhead.

On-ice: Complete two to three reps of each pattern on-ice while gliding. You can hold your stick in your relaxed arm or try it in the active arm for light loading.

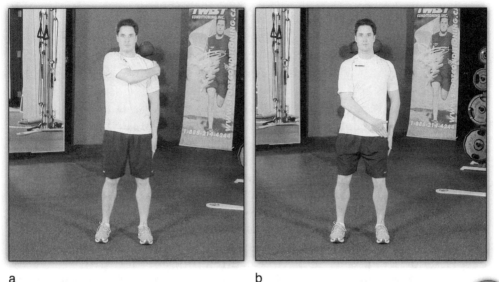

a   b

Wide Stickhandling

Focus: Arms, abdominal muscles, low back

Stand in an athletic ready position on top of an Extreme Balance Board, with knees slightly bent. Hold a hockey stick. With or without a wooden stickhandling ball, take the stick through an exaggerated puckhandling pattern. Move through wide loops in a slow, smooth motion. With feet planted on the floor, you can also hold the stick upside down and use a 5- or 10-pound (2.27- or 4.54-kilogram) Olympic weight for some light loading, placing the end of the stick in the middle of the weight. Use a slide board–like surface to move the weight through the same stickhandling pattern. Note the increased hip and core activation. Try the ball stickhandling and 5-pound (2.27-kilogram) plate stickhandling on one leg, atop the platform side of a BOSU, which requires you to balance and shift your weight as you would on ice.

On-ice: To a achieve a similar effect on the ice, execute similar exaggerated-range stickhandling with wide C-cuts from right leg to left leg. Build up some speed and then enter into large, wide-arc C-cuts, handling the puck both inside and outside the body. Take your time; think smooth C-cuts and wide puckhandling.

HOCKEY-SPECIFIC STRETCHING

To do static stretching, athletes select a muscle and gently move across a joint until they feel a comfortable stretch on the muscle. They then stop and hold that position for a short time. They are stretching the muscle in a static, or stationary, position. For athletes who lack flexibility in certain areas, static stretches are great for isolating muscles. They are easier to learn than proprioceptive neuromuscular facilitation (PNF) stretches and safer than ballistic stretches.

To clarify, players do PNF stretching with a partner. For a hamstring stretch, the partner moves the athlete's leg into position to stretch the hamstring. Then the athlete contracts the hamstring, trying to push the leg back down, while the partner resists the movement. Next, the athlete relaxes the muscle, allowing the partner to move the leg deeper into the stretch. PNF stretching typically uses a stretch, contract, relax, and stretch deeper sequence. PNF is an advanced stretching method with an aggressive approach; care is needed to make sure that players do not stretch too aggressively, forcing a stretch beyond the capabilities of the tissue. In conjunction with joint mobility and myofascial release, I prefer gentle static stretching to hold more precise stretch ranges in an effort to tune up the body.

Despite all the potential benefits of a stretching routine, many of the players I've coached say that they have tried stretching but that their muscles end up feeling tighter or even strained. I tell them that warming up and stretching didn't cause their discomfort—improper warming up and stretching caused it or, if they stretched before workouts, the timing of their stretching caused them to feel worse. To stretch successfully, players must do it correctly. After players learn to stretch properly, they are sold on the merits. For successful stretching, players must adhere to the following 10 guidelines for static stretching:

1. Stretch postactivity, when muscles have a higher deep core temperature, which improves the elasticity of the muscle.

2. If you end a workout with tight legs and heavy lactate accumulation, a 5- to 10-minute cool-down will help flush the legs and put them in a state more conducive for stretching.

3. Isolate the muscle to be stretched with strict technique. Do not cheat by altering the exercise slightly just to stretch farther.

4. Move slowly and smoothly through the stretch. Fast movements will cause the muscle to contract to protect itself. Receptors within muscles and tendons can sense the rate of lengthening. If the receptors sense a rapid lengthening, they will tell the muscle to contract to protect itself from lengthening too fast.

5. Do not overstretch. Most athletes try to stretch as far as possible, straining to move farther into the stretch. This may seem sensible, but the receptors in muscles and tendons also sense how far you are stretching the muscle. Straining a joint beyond its range of movement only

causes the muscle to contract to protect itself from being stretched too far. Stretching across a contracted or tight muscle ultimately leads to formation of inelastic scar tissue. You need to stretch a relaxed muscle, not a contracted muscle. Hold the stretch in a comfortable position. You should feel only slight tension in the muscle, which should subside as you hold the position. If the tension does not subside, back off to a more relaxed position.

6. Hold the stretch in a static position where you are comfortable and relaxed, without needing to contract several muscles just to hold the position. For example, lying in a doorway with one leg straight up the doorframe allows you to stretch the hamstrings from a relaxed position. This technique is much different from standing on one leg on the ice to balance while holding one leg on the boards.

7. Hold each stretch for a minimum of 30 seconds, optimally up to a minute. The longer you hold an easy stretch, the more likely it is that the muscle will relax and loosen. A longer stretch helps you achieve results at the muscle–tendon junction, which is avascular, receiving lower oxygen and nutrient supply.

8. Inhale before you move into a stretch. Exhale as you move into and through the stretch. Continue to breathe normally and freely as you hold the stretch. If a stretched position inhibits your natural breathing pattern, you are obviously not relaxed and are likely straining. Ease up until you can breathe naturally. Take full, relaxed breaths. Never hold your breath.

9. Progress to development stretching. The initial easy stretch should relax the muscle. If your muscle was comfortable during this stretch, move another half inch (1.25 centimeters) for a longer stretch. Move farther into the stretch until you again feel slight tension. The tension should subside. If it doesn't, back off to a more comfortable position. As with the initial stretch, as you increase the range of motion and progress deeper into the stretch, exhale slowly.

10. Hold the stretch to about half the perceived tension that you would feel in an aggressive, best-effort stretch that you might perform during team testing.

STRETCHING EXERCISES

Begin a hockey flexibility program with calf stretches, working through the 13 exercises in order. This takes you through a total of 21 stretches, accounting for the single leg and single arm exercises. Hold each stretch in a comfortable position for a minimum of 30 seconds. Complete each stretch twice, adding volume to particularly tight regions. Unload from the stretched position before repeating the same stretch. You will have greater success if you think of stretching as a full program, as opposed to banging off a few stretches.

The hockey flexibility program consists of two sets of each of 13 off-ice exercises. Allow adequate time to relax mentally and physically and move through at a focused pace. If any body part is uncharacteristically tight, complete the next stretch twice, return to the tight muscle group, and repeat the stretch. This sequence will help set up the tight muscle to be receptive to a deeper range. Continue through the complete sequence of stretches.

Standing Calf Stretch

Focus: Calves

Stand facing a wall. Place your hands on the wall and one foot on the floor near the wall. Move your opposite foot behind you, placing the toe down and slowly lowering the heel to the floor. Keep your body upright and hold for a stretch. To increase the degree of the stretch slightly, press your hips forward. The farther your rear foot is from the wall, the greater the stretch. To reduce the degree of the stretch, place your toe closer to the wall.

Kneeling Leg Stretch

Focus: Ankles, shins, light quadriceps

Kneel with your buttocks on your ankles. For an easy stretch, keep your hands on the floor in front of your knees, with weight forward. To increase the stretch in all three areas, sit more upright, with your hands on the floor at your sides. To progress the stretch further, place your hands on the floor behind your ankles, with your weight shifted backward.

Seated Hamstring Stretch

Focus: Hamstrings

Sit on a bench with your left leg stretched straight out, with your foot hanging over the edge. Place your right foot on the floor beside the bench. Move into the stretch by moving your chest straight ahead a few inches (8 to 10 centimeters) toward the left leg. Keep your head up and your torso straight—do not roll your torso just to stretch farther. Hold the stretch in a comfortable position. Repeat for the right leg.

Lying Quadriceps Stretch

Focus: Quadriceps

Lie on your side. Grasp the ankle of your top leg, pulling the heel toward your glutes. To stay comfortable and relaxed, extend your lower arm out

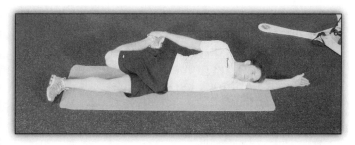

along the floor or position pillows under your head, keeping the neck and spine in a neutral position. Roll over to repeat the stretch with the other leg.

Lying Groin Stretch

Focus: Groin

Lie with your back flat on the ground, with the knees flexed and feet together in front of you, close to your body. Let gravity pull your knees toward the floor. Pulling your feet in closer to your glutes will increase the stretch along the groin

muscles. To shift the stretch to the high groin and musculotendinous junction, elect for a seated position, with your back straight up against a wall. To increase the stretch, position your feet closer to your body but do not push your elbows into the knees—the groin region must be relaxed to stretch. Your elbows are placed on your knees for posture positioning only, not to apply pressure.

Split Knee Hip Flexor Stretch

Focus: Hip flexors

Place your left knee on the ground with your right foot flat on the ground out in front of your body. Make sure that the laces of your back foot are against the ground. Start with a straight trunk. Shift your weight forward as you drop your hips toward the left foot. You may notice a stretch on the glutes at this stage. Next, place both hands on the floor, inside the front leg, even with your front foot, and lower your hips farther to the ground. Repeat with your right foot back and left foot forward.

Lying Hip Rotator and Gluteal Stretch

Focus: Hips and glutes

Lie on your back with your right leg bent and the foot on the wall or against a post. Place your left foot across your right quadriceps, close to the right knee. Press your pelvis into the floor and shift your body closer to the wall to accelerate the stretch. Gently pushing forward on the left knee will deepen the gluteal stretch. Repeat on the opposite side. Pay particular attention to flexibility imbalances between left and right sides, which will affect fluidity of lateral movement and crossovers on one side.

Lying Knee to Chest Stretch

Focus: Lower back and glutes

Lie on your back. Lace your fingers behind your left knee and pull it to the chest area. Keep your right leg flat on the ground even if you cannot move the left knee all the way to your chest. Hold the bent leg in a comfortable position. Repeat on the other side. After you can  easily pull the leg in close to your chest, keep it just as close to your chest while you pull it across to the other side of the body.

Abdominal Push-Up Position Stretch

Focus: Abdominals

Lie face down on the floor in a push-up position, with your hands on the floor at your sides. Push up so that your arms are extended and your torso is in the air but keep your hips and legs on the floor. Hold for the stretch.

Standing Rotation Torso Stretch

Focus: Abdominals, lower back

Stand facing away and about 2 feet (60 centimeters) from a wall. Assume a shoulder-width stance, with knees slightly flexed and with solid posture. Hold your arms out in front of you while you slowly rotate. Try to place both hands on the wall directly behind you. Allow your elbows to flex slightly because they naturally will find a comfortable position. Repeat, moving in the opposite direction.

Overhand Grip on Frame Stretch

Focus: Upper back

Place both hands on a waist-high ledge or frame. To accommodate your precise height, set up an Olympic bar across a squat rack. Stand back with your feet flat on the ground and bend over at a 90-degree angle at the waist. Stay bent over while lowering your hips backward toward the ground.

T-Stretch

Focus: Chest

Stand in a regular-sized doorway and place your elbows on the wall, just slightly higher than the shoulders. Place your forearms and hands flat against the wall, with elbows flexed to 90 degrees. Lean into the doorway to stretch the chest muscles.

Wall Stretch

Focus: Shoulders

Stand at an angle to a wall. Place one hand high on the wall and lean into the stretch. To advance the stretch, rotate your upper body away from your hand. Repeat on the other side. Adjust the precise hand position to vary the stretch.

MYOFASCIAL RELEASE

Fascia is a tough connective tissue that spreads over the body in a web from head to foot without interruption, wrapping the body just under the skin. The fascia covers and penetrates tissues. In a perfect, healthy state, the fascia is pliable and allows the covered and penetrated tissue to move freely. Trauma and inflammation, common among hockey players, leads to a binding down of the fascia in which the fascia adheres to soft tissues. A problematic cycle develops because a tight fascia, scarring, and adhesions significantly restrict muscle function, which in a hockey game can lead to muscle injuries. Myofascial release frees the fascia, helps break down old scar tissue, reduces muscle tightness, and releases trapped nerves.

The method is simple and intuitive, using small balls and foam rollers that the player lies over to apply sustained pressure to the fascia. Think of it as a self-massage that uses your body mass over the top of a ball or foam roller. The roller and small balls have a specific density that creates the desired change in the fascia. Kelly Roberts, a peer in the fitness industry, passed on a memorable cue: rock and roll. Roll over the ball very slowly to help release the fascia. When you sense more significant or painful fascia restrictions, slowly rock back and forth over that particular area, spending more time there.

For players who have muscle tightness that does not fully respond to stretching, small ball or foam roller release may be the missing link to getting them over challenging flexibility hurdles. Myofascial release works to free up tight fascia so that muscles have all their freedom of movement available. Sample exercises are shown in the photos. The technique is intuitive in that once you begin, the process relies largely on feel. Active release balls come in a variety of sizes, allowing for varying pressure from soft to deep. Foam rollers are available either cut in half or full (round). You need the round foam to accommodate the rolling of the body over the top. Both work well, but for road trips, the small balls are convenient because they are more portable.

Myofascial release exercises.

Chapter 4

Base Conditioning

Unlike a car that has one engine and one fuel tank, your body has several engines, each of which draw on different fuels to feed it. The different energy systems require different training styles and affect how well a hockey player can perform on the ice. Hockey players desire speed, quickness, strength, power, a fast forecheck, a strong backcheck, and the ability to win races for loose pucks at the end of a shift. To play like this on the ice, hockey players should not train like long-distance athletes *or* elite sprinters. Hockey players must be able to sprint well, but more important, they must be able to sprint repeatedly. They need to be explosive, with specific endurance to take them through a shift, a period, and an entire game.

A hockey player's body has different energy systems that work together to fuel hockey performance. The aerobic system provides energy for low- and moderate-intensity exercise and helps the body recover from fatigue. The anaerobic systems produce energy quickly to meet the demands of intense action, such as taking a slap shot, sprinting on a breakaway, or stopping and starting while penalty killing.

AEROBIC CONDITIONING

Aerobic fitness, the dominant energy supply for marathon runners, fuels low-intensity, long-duration exercise. In hockey, aerobic fitness is known as the oxygen system and a supply and recovery system because it supplies energy (oxygen) for submaximal efforts and helps players recover on the bench after intense, sprint-paced work.

But the submaximal efforts that oxygen can fuel are relative and highly dependent on aerobic fitness levels. The ability to supply oxygen to fuel increasingly intense effort is determined in NHL testing by measuring the rate at which the body can breathe oxygen into the lungs, transfer oxygen from the lungs to the heart, deliver the oxygen through the blood to the working muscles, extract the oxygen from the blood to the muscles, and use the oxygen in the muscles for energy production. Aerobic fitness is expressed as $\dot{V}O_2$max, the maximum volume of oxygen that can be taken up and used by the body (ml $\cdot$ kg^{-1} $\cdot$ min^{-1}).

Supply

Hockey players train aerobic fitness so they can skate longer and at a higher pace. A full-out sprint is always anaerobic, but a well-trained aerobic system allows players to utilize oxygen to fuel higher intensities before having to rely more on anaerobic fuel, which would result in accumulation of lactic acid and fatigue. Aerobic exercise helps raise the lactate threshold of muscles, the point at which lactic acid accumulation exceeds its utilization and removal. Lactic acid build-up, a by-product of the anaerobic sprinting energy system, indirectly interferes with working muscles and leads to fatigue, evident when players must get off the ice for a shift change. Excellent aerobic fitness that can handle high-intensity skating helps postpone fatigue.

For a given game tempo, an extremely fit player will draw much of his energy from aerobic supply, compared with a deconditioned player, who will have to dip into his anaerobic supply sooner. By raising lactate threshold, athletes can perform at higher intensities aerobically without having to meet energy demands anaerobically, delaying accumulation of lactic acid (figure 4.1) and preserving valuable glycogen stores needed to produce anaerobic energy for full-out sprints.

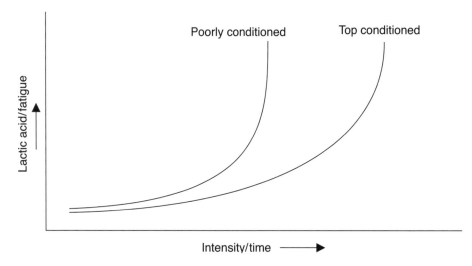

Figure 4.1 The relationship between level of conditioning and fatigue. Better conditioned players can compete at a higher intensity with less lactic acid accumulation and compete longer without fatiguing.

Recovery

A player relies on the aerobic system when he comes off the ice from his last shift and sits on the bench, out of breath, breathing hard, and trying to take in more oxygen. The more ice time a player has—the longer the shifts and the shorter the bench time—the more important the aerobic system is for recovery. Defensemen like Ed Jovanovski who cover a lot of ice and play close to 30 minutes a game must have a high aerobic supply and quick recovery to meet the challenge of playing every second shift.

Similarly, aerobic fitness that can speed recovery after intense bouts of exercise helps players sustain peak outputs throughout a dryland training workout, allowing greater workout intensity. Between sprint intervals, among strength sets, and during lengthy play stoppages on the ice, players should keep the legs moving to facilitate recovery by the oxygen system. Aerobic fitness also increases the efficiency of the body's cooling system, which is helpful in sustaining and repeating workout and on-ice output. Training aerobically also helps decrease body fat, so that a player carries less extra mass on the ice, making skating movements more energy efficient.

Aerobic Training

Even today's big players like Mattias Ohlund have $\dot{V}O_2$maxes over 60, and they also produce outstanding anaerobic scores. To achieve scores like these, players can improve aerobic fitness in three ways: through submaximal continuous exercise; through high-intensity, intermittent aerobic exercise; and by contributing some of the energy and through the process of recovery from long anaerobic sprint intervals that max out heart rate.

Hockey conditioning programs begin with general exercises at a continuous pace at 75 to 85 percent of maximum heart rate for 30 to 60 minutes to improve the ability of the heart to deliver oxygen to the muscles for energy. As the off-season progresses, programs feature more specific exercises and intermittent aerobic sessions, using a series of higher intensity exercise bouts that last for 2 1/2 minutes (interspersed with 2 1/2 minutes of active rest) to cause further improvement in oxygen supply and the ability of the muscles to extract oxygen from the blood. These effects drive up the anaerobic threshold. Players then adopt increasing volume and frequency of anaerobic sprint training. Table 4.1 gives exercise guidelines for designing an aerobic conditioning program.

Off-ice aerobic exercises can include running, stationary cycling, spin classes, road biking on hills, stair climbing, and treadmill running. Machines that provide quantified feedback on speed, load, level, and duration; heart rate monitors that show time and heart rate; and GPS devices that show speed, distance, heart rate, and other quantifiable measures all provide structure to workouts. The structure is highly replicable, allowing players to repeat or take a workout challenge up one step at a time in a progressive overload of the aerobic system.

Table 4.1 Aerobic Conditioning Variables

	Continuous aerobic conditioning	Intermittent aerobic conditioning
Intensity	75% to 85% of maximum heart rate	5 beats below maximum heart rate
Work time	30 to 60 minutes	2 to 2.5 minutes
Work-to-rest ratio	NA	1:1
Reps and sets	NA	6 to 12
Frequency	3 times/week first half of off-season 1 time/week second half of off-season 1 time/week in-season	1 time/week first half of off-season 2 times/week second half of off-season 1 time/week in-season*

*On or off ice

For aerobic fitness, I also take players running on mountain trails that feature moderate and steep inclines, roots, rocks, sharp turns, obstacles such as logs and creeks, and a variety of graded descents. They train for power on strong leg extensions to run uphill, they speed hike and run up undulating trails, and they use strong, coordinated deceleration to handle steep descents with aggressive braking and lightning footwork. The uneven, changing terrain develops good ankle, knee, and hip stability; fast feet; and reactivity that will help with strong edges and durability on the ice. I find that the more athletic the aerobic experience, the more players will enjoy it.

Two common aerobic training questions deal with aerobic training versus strength training and the effects of in-line skating. Will too much low-level continuous aerobic conditioning counteract efforts to build strength and power? Traditional aerobic training preferentially trains slow-twitch muscle fibers through controlled tempo movements. The slow-speed, slow-twitch emphasis may counteract efforts to train fast-twitch fibers for explosive power. Marathoners demonstrate this effect. The high volume of daily aerobic training that they do produces a thin, small body custom made for efficient long-distance running at submaximal levels. Such a body is not made for strength, power, speed, quickness, and agility. The legs of a marathoner look quite different from those of a 100-meter sprinter.

But that example demonstrates extreme aerobic training. Hockey players who train for 30 to 60 minutes at an intense pace as part of their overall conditioning program do not set themselves up to compromise their strength gains. A hockey player's goal is to be a superior anaerobic player who is strong, powerful, and capable of speed and quickness. Jogging five times a week at a casual pace does not contribute to these goals. But in the new NHL, with changed rules to increase flow and speed and with modern conditioning coaches who emphasize the speed and power anaerobic characteristics, some players have gone the other direction and train only anaerobically. Players also use aerobic energy in a fast-paced flow game, more than they do in a fight-through-checks, hook-and-hold, stop-and-start game, which is more dominantly anaerobic. The bottom line for all players is that intense, faster paced aerobic intervals build a key part of hockey-specific fitness and do not detract from strength and speed development. I have coached players who rank near the top in aerobic, anaerobic, and power output tests all at the same time.

The second question concerns in-line and treadmill skating. Do these exercises hurt or help ice skating? Both in-line skating with wheels on pavement and skating uphill on a moving treadmill use a similar movement pattern to the forward on-ice stride but employ different mechanics, which, if trained too frequently, can alter on-ice skating mechanics. Both methods can be beneficial if a player uses them as one exercise in an overall program, but they can be detrimental if the player uses them as the program itself. The specificity of in-line and treadmill skating can enhance oxygen extraction capabilities of the skating muscles and leg endurance in a deep stance, both of which are valuable. But both types of skating use a slightly different technique that can ultimately interrupt on-ice mechanics and make players feel awkward on ice if those modes dominate their programs. Any kind of skating for a long duration causes muscular fatigue, which can result in a complete breakdown in technique. Skaters have more trouble handling long durations than do runners, for example, who can more easily maintain satisfactory mechanics. For this reason, I recommend treadmill skating more for anaerobic intervals.

AEROBIC

Figure-Eight Skate

Purpose: Build aerobic fitness and oxygen extraction capabilities of skating muscles

Move the net posts even with the face-off circle hash marks so that the distance from net to net is 160 feet (49 meters). Skate continuously around each net and through the center in an elongated figure eight. Complete as many laps as possible in 2 1/2 minutes. Then rest while teammates complete an interval. Repeat several times.

Circle Skate

Purpose: Develop aerobic fitness and oxygen extraction capabilities of skating muscles

Start at the goal line in the corner and skate around circle 1. Skate down the boards and around circle 2. Skate diagonally across the ice and around circle 3. Skate down the boards and around circle 4. Skate diagonally back to the starting position. Continue for 2 minutes. Rest for 2 minutes. Complete six reps. For two of the reps, skate backward through the course.

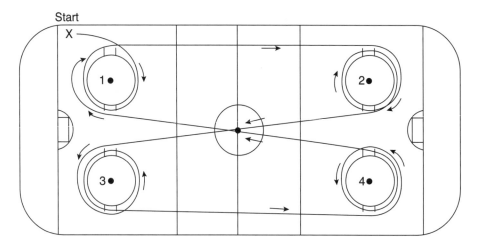

ANAEROBIC CONDITIONING

When people think of fitness and endurance, the word *aerobics* is often mentioned, but the aerobic system is not the most important hockey energy system. Sprinting, speed, quickness, strength, and power are all anaerobic actions. The anaerobic energy system fuels most intense game efforts. High-speed breakaways, stop-and-start penalty killing, bodychecking, races for loose pucks, shooting, and full-intensity shifts rely on anaerobic conditioning.

People love to watch Todd Bertuzzi drive to the net, whether through a player with strength and power or around a player with high-speed agility. Bert sets himself up to enjoy these performances by training his sprinting system all summer. He mixes up his training, opting for track sprints, stair running, ladder drills, as well as enjoyable, competitive partner drills that involve speed races. The goal is to prepare himself to skate at his top speed, whether in the first period or late in a shift in the third.

Think of the anaerobic system as your sprinting fuel tank—available immediately but quickly depleted. Players need to engage in intense anaerobic conditioning to extend the time that the anaerobic system can supply high-paced energy and expand the ability to replenish this hockey fuel. Because hockey is a stop-and-start sport involving repetitive multidirectional sprinting situations, players must be able to react to a situation and explode into action by exerting maximum effort over short distances. A well-trained anaerobic system is also needed to handle the workload and intensity of higher levels of training. Anaerobic conditioning is structured as repeated sprint intervals.

The first anaerobic energy system, known as the adenosine triphosphate phosphocreatine (ATP-PC) system, provides an immediate form of energy. This system fuels bursts of maximum-intensity exercise for up to 10 seconds. Explosive starting, bodychecking, and shooting fall into this category. After 10 seconds of intense action, continuation at an intense level depends on anaerobic glycolysis, which is the second anaerobic method of energy supply. This method is also referred to as the lactic acid system or anaerobic lactate system. This system draws on muscle glycogen or blood glucose stores (carbohydrates) for energy.

Anaerobic glycolysis provides an important energy supply for hockey shifts. Anaerobic glycolysis can produce energy for as long as 120 seconds, depending on intensity, but it peaks at 30 to 45 seconds. For that reason, the typical hockey shift lasts for 45 seconds. Intensity will drop off during shifts that last much longer than that. Players fatigue from temporary fuel depletion, and their legs become heavy from the build-up of lactic acid, a by-product of the anaerobic glycolysis energy system, which accumulates

© Getty Images

Chris Pronger averages close to 30 minutes a game. At this level and intensity, both the aerobic and anaerobic systems are pushed to their limits.

in the muscles and the blood. Stopping and starting, sprinting, fighting through checks, and battling one-on-one for the puck require intense efforts that together over the course of a hockey shift produce lactic acid in both the upper and lower body. With lactic acid accumulation, muscles take longer to contract and suffer a decreased rate of relaxation between contractions, which leads to slower movement and stiffness or burning in the legs at the end of a shift. Because lactic acid indirectly hinders the ability of the muscles to move, its build-up adversely affects skill and technique.

During a game, the two anaerobic energy systems and the aerobic energy system are active for every shift. If a player needs a high rate of energy supply for explosive acceleration or a quick shot from the point, the ATP-PC system is drawn upon. Intense action of longer duration uses anaerobic glycolysis. The aerobic system fuels submaximal efforts and between-shift recovery (figure 4.2). Although each of the three systems has its specialty, at no time does any one energy system provide the entire supply of energy needed for a movement. Rather, the three energy systems are drawn on at the same time, and the extent to which each responds depends on the intensity and duration of the activity, the player's fitness level and skating efficiency, and the game situation. General variables such as style of play, role on the team, positional variations, or ice conditions mediate energy demands. Specific situations also define the energy expenditure—killing a penalty, being quick on the forecheck, bodychecking, or playing the point on the power play each use different relative contributions of the three energy systems.

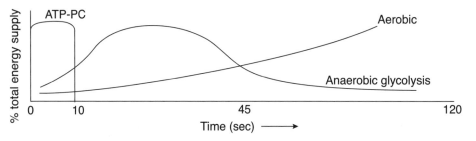

Figure 4.2   Relative contribution of the three energy systems over time.

The effect of anaerobic conditioning—or lack of it—is pronounced. When fatigued, players tend to straighten their legs and have little "jump" in their stride. To compensate, players alter their skating technique by skating taller, thus producing less stride power and making themselves more vulnerable to being knocked down by opponents. To handle sharp pivots, high-speed crossovers, explosive acceleration, and crushing blows, players need to maintain a deep knee bend, with hips low and the knee over the front foot. By improving anaerobic conditioning, players can maintain this position for longer periods.

Anaerobic conditioning raises the lactate threshold, allowing players to compete at a higher intensity longer before the accumulation of lactic acid exceeds its removal. The energy production system becomes more efficient, because a given work intensity produces less lactic acid. Intense anaerobic conditioning also promotes toleration of lactic acid; players become accustomed to the feeling of lactic acid build-up in fatigued legs. Training develops the mental strength needed to keep playing for a few more seconds, a critical capacity when a player is stuck in her end for a long time killing a penalty or when a player blocks a shot at the point at the end of a shift and suddenly has a breakaway opportunity. Table 4.2 gives exercise guidelines for designing an anaerobic conditioning program.

Table 4.2 Anaerobic Conditioning Variables

	ATP-PC	Anaerobic glycolysis
Type	Sprint intervals	Sprint intervals
Intensity	Full out	Full out
Work time	10 seconds	30 to 60 seconds
Work-to-rest ratio	1:5	Begin with 1:4; progress to 1:1
Reps and sets	Begin with 8 reps, 1 set; progress to 8 reps, 2 sets	Begin with 6 reps, 30 seconds; progress to 12 reps, 60 seconds
Rest between sets	3 minutes	5 minutes post (easy relief pace)
Frequency	1 time/week first half of off-season	1 time/week first half of off-season
	3 times/week second half of off-season	3 times/week second half of off-season
	1 time/week in-season*	2 times/week in-season*

*On or off ice

Sprint Intervals

Full-out, high-intensity, high-speed intervals followed by a rest or active relief interval is the best way to build the anaerobic systems. For anaerobic glycolysis, players should build up to a 60-second work interval to prepare for a best effort during a 45-second shift. To prepare properly for the extreme demands of hockey, however, players need to condition at a higher intensity than they will face during a game. In the most critical game, players do not rise to the occasion; they sink to the level of their training.

Moreover, several wild cards come into play in hockey conditioning. No one yet knows the final metabolic cost of a hockey game. What is the energy cost of performing a strong bodycheck? Containing an opponent against the boards? Fighting through checks and illegal hooking and holding to drive to the net? Skating on poor, snowy ice at the end of a period?

Playing overtime and back-to-back games? Using a more physical style of play? Performing at playoff intensity? No one has fully quantified the additional energy costs of these situations, but we all know that they add to anaerobic demands.

Four key training variables can be manipulated to improve anaerobic conditioning: duration of each sprint; intensity (defined by the load, speed, heart rate, and effort); density (amount of between-sprint recovery); and volume (total number of sprints by time). These variables are listed in order so that as you progress, you know which variable to change next to stimulate further improvements.

Step 1. Begin with six 30-second sprints with a 1:4 work-to-rest ratio.

Step 2. Add volume. Increase total workout time by increasing the number of intervals, to a maximum of 12.

Step 3. Add intensity. Increase resistance (bike load, run with parachute, tandem tow).

Step 4. Add intensity. Gradually increase speed.

Step 5. Alter density. Decrease the length of rest intervals until the work-to-rest ratio is 1:1.

Step 6. Lengthen duration. Increase the length of the interval by 5 seconds, maintaining a 1:1 work-to-rest ratio.

Step 7. Continue progress by lengthening sprint intervals (and the corresponding rest interval) with the end goal of 60 seconds of work followed by 60 seconds of rest.

Workout to workout, remain at a certain stage and retain the same structure, if speed drops too greatly. At step 7, if a player has trouble graduating to a longer interval, return to a 1:2 work-to-rest ratio to enable him to complete the longer sprint. When the player can handle the volume of longer sprints, begin to whittle down the rest times until he achieves a 1:1 ratio.

Drills should also be structured specifically to develop the ATP-PC system. Speed (page 157), quickness (page 126), and agility (page 143) drills can incorporate shorter intervals and longer rest periods to yield optimal development of the ATP-PC system. Anaerobic glycolysis drills result in enough muscle fatigue and leg discomfort that they force players to adhere to a between-sprint rest period—players need and want to rest. But ATP-PC sprint intervals require greater coach control.

To develop the ATP-PC system, athletes must work under full-out conditions and then allow enough time for the energy supply to replenish itself to fuel the next sprint repetition. Additionally, bouts must be short (less than 10 seconds) to condition this system. If sprint intervals are not done full out, if they are too long, or if rest intervals are too short, the player will not build the ATP-PC system. To achieve these conditioning gains, rest intervals are critical. Players are so accustomed to pushing themselves to full fatigue that they are not satisfied with very short sprints followed by long rest periods. If they sprint for only 5 seconds, coming nowhere close to fatigue, they don't understand why they should take a 25-second rest, especially because coaches always push them in the opposite direction. Coaches should overload their athletes at times, but ATP-PC quickness training is quality training, not quantity training.

Confined-Space Skill Integration

An advantage of running athlete development camps instead of a team is being able to focus on how to improve individual players instead of how to structure a team, what systems to use, what lines to match. Around 1995 I implemented a series of small-space scrimmages into my pro camps to give players an experience similar to the less structured pond hockey of days gone by, but in a tighter environment that requires quick decision making.

Confined-space skill integration refers to small-space scrimmages in which players are always on task, either attacking or defending, often played three on three, two on two, or even one on one. Players are continually in a one-on-one battle to fight for the puck or find open space to receive a pass. The varying game surface sizes and net positions require thinking and the ability to recognize and react to situations on the ice without making the chesslike adjustments that players are told to memorize with full-ice five-on-five systems.

My coaches and I discovered that players of all ages had more fun, worked harder, and competed more intensely when playing in small spaces. The scrimmages challenged their footwork, hands, and minds, forcing their skills to keep pace and handle the incessant one-on-one battles. After enhancing their physical toolbox through hockey-specific dryland training as detailed in this book, all players demonstrated improvement from in-tight scrimmages.

The metabolic demand of small-space scrimmages is immense. Efforts are highly anaerobic. We time the duration of shifts and determine the number of players waiting in the line based on what work-to-rest ratio we want to prescribe. For example, active players may compete two on two for 30 seconds, with eight other players in a lineup, producing a 1:2 work-to-rest ratio. To drive up anaerobic conditioning and integrate quickness, agility, and explosive effort, I inform players that they will get their full shift unless their tempo drops off, at which time I will whistle down the drill and switch to the next players in line. Players learn that they must maintain a certain effort to play their full shift.

Training the muscles and systems that influence their performance for their specific functions in hockey games, both routine and unexpected, means that the strength, power, speed, and quickness achieved will be usable. The goal of hockey specificity is to make training as transferable as possible to game action. Because the body is a highly integrated structure, not a series of parts that function independently, the mind and muscle must develop together to coordinate explosive movement, stabilization, balance, and skill execution. Confined-space skill integration builds hockey-specific anaerobic endurance and challenges players to remain reactive and agile from the start to the end of every shift. The games impose extreme challenges, overloading the player's body, vision, mind, and complete skill package, and driving up his sprinting energy systems.

In-Season Anaerobic Conditioning

Star players such as Markus Naslund work out right after most games. Nazy finishes the game and changes into his shorts and running shoes right away to do full-out bike sprint intervals against heavy resistance followed by a full-body multijoint strength lift. The lift is structured with whole-body supersets to produce top-end heart rates for 45 to 60 seconds at a time, using explosive movements that also draw on the anaerobic system. This schedule of off-ice anaerobic training allows the most recovery before the next game.

Noteworthy is my effort to remain off bikes during summer training but use bikes in-season. When with the Vancouver Canucks, we went over 3 years without a groin injury and had extremely low man-games lost per season. Part of this results from training that stresses the body specifically to what an actual game imposes. Training does not just replicate game demands; it specifically improves the physical tools that players can draw on for better and safer on-ice performance, preventing the groin, hip flexor, and back injuries that plague many players. In-season, it is also valuable to be able to unload from daily on-ice demands—lateral movement, deceleration, hockey strides, body contact, heavy core activation—and perform some conditioning without taxing the body as it is on ice.

Postgame sprints work well. After a game, Nazy's legs are already warmed up, and tired if he played a lot of minutes. That circumstance is perfect because he wants to train the ability to get full speed out of his legs when they are tired. He will sprint for 30 to 60 seconds as fast as he can under heavy resistance and then rest for 30 to 60 seconds. He does six to eight sprint intervals before cooling down and moving on to his multijoint lifting routine. When I traveled to coach him in Sweden, he liked to complete multiple sets of heavy weight, high-rep leg strength exercises to the point of anaerobic failure.

In minor hockey, in-season sprinting can occur after practices. Off the ice, resisted running overloads the legs and challenges the engine that fuels high-speed work. Coaches can also accomplish this on the ice, with enjoyable drills that include relay races or partner races for pucks. Coaches also use resistance tools such as parachutes to apply resistance and overload, forcing players to stay low and skate hard with long strides as they lap the ice.

Players themselves can squeeze in a couple of sprint repeats at the end of practice as teammates are hurrying off the ice. A few minutes of extra effort each practice can add a lot of benefit over a season. If players want to improve on the ice, they need to build the tools to fuel top performance. And if they improve, their playing time increases, adding to their work volume.

Whenever possible, players should skate and train at sprint intensity and drive up sprint endurance capability so that they can play the whole game at a fast tempo. Remember, most players lose fitness through a season. To get an edge, players should train to be better each month, peaking when it really counts in the playoffs. Players who perform well are often rewarded with more game time, but if they do not have the sprinting fitness to handle the extra ice time, their results will drop off, pushing them back to square one. Players need to build their bodies so that they are ready to take advantage of opportunities.

QUICK IN-SEASON TIPS

1. Squeeze in a few extra sprints at the end of a practice or workout. Always do a little more.
2. Mix up skating, biking, and running sprints for well-rounded development.
3. Aim for high speed. Turn your legs over quickly, especially at the end of each sprint interval.
4. Sprint against resistance to drive up the anaerobic long-sprint system.
5. Strive for a 1:1 work-to-rest ratio so that your legs are able to recover quickly and be ready for another sprint.
6. Use an active rest phase, in which you skate, run, or bike slowly.

OFF-ICE ANAEROBIC EXERCISES

Anaerobic workouts are less about selecting distinct exercises and more about manipulating training variables (sprint duration, intensity, density, volume) to make many different exercises suitable for anaerobic development. I select drills for anaerobic workouts from the speed, quickness, and agility drill inventories and structure training based on the training guidelines in table 4.2. Use the seven-step progression (page 58) to construct challenging but appropriate anaerobic training sessions for each player.

ON-ICE ANAEROBIC EXERCISES

Quick-Start Relays

Purpose: Improve the ATP-PC energy system and explosive starting abilities

Divide players equally so that about five players are at each of the four face-off circles. For 5-yard (4.6-meter) sprint relays, half of each group line up at the face-off dot and the other half line up at the edge of the circle. On the whistle, the first player sprints toward his teammate. The next player up in the opposite line maintains a stationary ready stance until the first player touches glove to glove. The second player sprints to the next player in line and so on. Five players per group make a 1:4 work-to-rest ratio. Each player completes eight reps, racing against the other groups. To use the relay competition to heighten skating intensity, try four reps followed quickly by a second relay race of four reps. After eight reps total, players rest and repeat. Try using three distances: 20 yards (18 meters), from blue line to blue line; 10 yards (9 meters), from center red to blue line; and 5 yards (4.6 meters), from the face-off dot to the edge of the circle. In different races, use four different stationary starts—forward, backward, and sideways (left and right start).

Pair Race

DVD

Purpose: Develop the anaerobic glycolysis system and practice performing skills under a partially fatigued condition

Two players (A and B) start together at the face-off dot. A second pair of players (C and D) start from the diagonally opposite corner. On the whistle, all four players begin. Players stop at the center red, skate back to the blue, and the go on down the ice. After players cross the center red line, they get a pass from the last two players in line at the boards. The

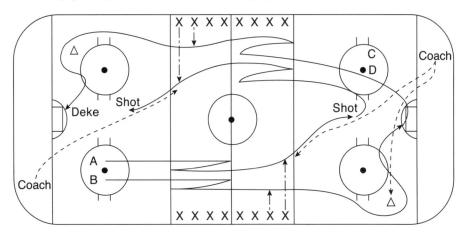

lead skater—the first one to cross the center red line (in this case player A)—shoots from the top of the slot. The trailing skater has to attack right to the net for a deke, skating straight down the boards and moving across the low slot. After shooting, players immediately turn up ice and complete the same pattern down the opposite side. This sequence emphasizes the first sprint—the trailing skater ends up with a longer skate down both sides of the ice. The next two pairs of players start at the face-off dot on the coach's whistle.

Line Skate Drill

Purpose: Develop the anaerobic glycolysis system and lactic acid toleration

Split the team into thirds, lined up across the goal red line. On the coach's whistle, one-third of players sprint to the blue line and back. They then immediately sprint from the goal red line to the center red line and back to the start. Next, they sprint down to the far blue line and back to the start. To finish, players skate right down to the far red goal line and back to the starting goal red line. When players stop, they should face the same side of the ice each time so that they get equal practice stopping and starting left and right. Players rest for two turns while the other two-thirds of the team complete the drill, for a 1:2 work-to-rest ratio. Repeat six times or a volume of reps that best complements the overall practice demands.

Gut Check Drill

Purpose: Increase lactic acid toleration, build mental toughness, and develop the anaerobic glycolysis system

Players start on the goal red line. They sprint to the second face-off dot (arrow 1), make a full stop, and sprint back to the original dot (arrow 2). They make a full stop and then sprint past the second face-off dot right

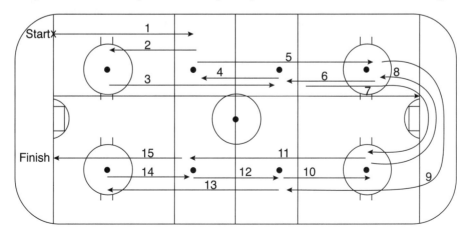

on through to the third face-off dot (arrow 3). They make a full stop and sprint back to the second dot (arrow 4) and so on, skating two down and one back, right around the ice. They stop and start facing the middle of the ice to work both sides equally and to face the play.

Note: In the illustration, arrows on the diagram are spread out to provide visual clarity. When skating, players stay in line with the face-off dots.

Two-Lap Sprints

Purpose   Develop the anaerobic glycolysis system

Move nets up to the hash marks. Players skate two laps and then rest. If you have 20 players on a team, line up 10 on each side of the ice in the neutral zone. The first two players in line pair up and are ready at the center red line. On the coach's whistle, the first pair from each side sprints two laps. After the first pair completes one lap, the second pair in line joins in and pushes the first pair to maintain their speed through the second lap. The goal for the skaters in the first pair is to avoid being passed by the second pair. The third pair gets ready to join in on the second pair's second lap. The fourth pair joins in on the third pair's second lap. Continue cycling through pairs. This setup gives a 1:1.5 work-to-rest ratio. For longer or shorter rest periods, group players accordingly.

Position- and Shift-Specific Drill

Purpose: Develop the anaerobic glycolysis system through position-specific skating patterns, with a hockey-specific recovery setup

On the coach's whistle, the players in the first wave hop over the boards to complete one full-speed lap around the rink, exiting the lap at their position locations, where they complete 30-second stop-and-start patterns. Goaltenders skate from the post to behind the net and back again, move post to post, and then drop down and get up, alternating sides for 30 seconds. Defensemen skate from the midslot to the corner, backward to the front of the net, forward to the face-off dot, and backward to the slot for 30 seconds. Forwards forecheck to the end boards, skate over to the side boards, and then sprint to the top of the slot, continuing for 30 seconds. With the lap, these sequences net about 45 seconds.

On the second whistle, players skate hard over to the bench and sit down, while the players in the next wave hop the boards and begin their full-speed lap.

CONFINED-SPACE SKILL INTEGRATION DRILLS

The following modified scrimmages demand anaerobic supply by setting up an environment of persistent one-on-one tactics, removing space to skate off the play, and forcing players to be on task offensively and defensively at all times. Coaches are accustomed to questioning a player's work ethic. Perhaps our drills are just not that inspiring. Confined-space scrimmages stimulate players and force them to try harder. They have no place to hide.

Players experience more time with the puck, a higher volume of shots, and gamelike practice for stickhandling, puck protection, footwork, tight turns, defensive mobility, body contact, hockey sense, puck support, and more aggressive jumping into the open and commanding the pass from teammates. They rehearse all this at anaerobic intensity. Remember Dr. Jack Blatherwick's concern discussed in the introduction—that young players experience little opportunity for skill development in an actual game. Confined-space scrimmages keep them on task, all game, practicing skills under pressure.

Three of the confined space drills—three-on-three, safe zone scrimmage; two-on-two no-passing scrimmage; and two-on-one transition scrimmage—are three of my favorites from *Small-Area Games* by Paul Willett.

Two-on-Two Circle Scrimmage

Position two nets at the hash marks of one face-off circle. Coaches are ready outside the circle with a pile of pucks. If a loose puck travels outside the circle and after a goal is scored, coaches yell, "Puck" and immediately inject a new live puck into the circle. There is no down time. After 30 seconds, coaches whistle in new players, who jump on the puck and continue the process. Coaches may choose to modify or slightly enlarge the playing surface by marking it off with cones. The same game can be played with one net; players turn from defense to offense by passing the puck to the coach and getting open to receive it back. This setup frees up a net and goalie to run a separate two-on-two circle scrimmage and roll through all players on the ice more frequently.

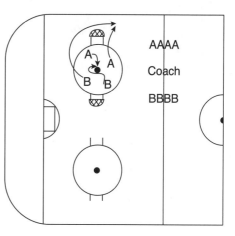

One-on-One Circle Scrimmage

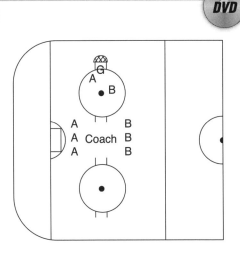

Position one net and a goaltender on the outside edge of a face-off circle. In this drill, the emphasis is on one-on-one tactics in a tight space with puck protection, good stick positioning, and physical play. A player is either attacking or defending the net. Whoever has the puck is on offense right away. Goaltenders will face a higher volume of shots. Coaches inject pucks after goals or when the puck escapes the playing area. Two new players must be ready to jump in on the whistle to inject fresh players every 30 seconds.

Three-on-Three, Board-to-Board Scrimmage

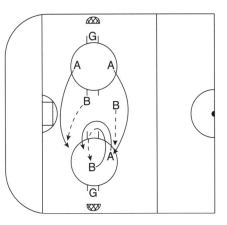

Nets are placed along the side boards, and play is from the blue line in. This setup leads to quick attacks, turnovers, and rapid transition from offense to defense. You can opt to require that each player touch the puck before a goal can be scored, forcing players to work harder to get open. The first team to 3 points wins. To increase intensity from the get-go, start two on two and establish that when a team scores their first goal, their third player can join the play. This variation places more importance on scoring the first goal. Play 45 second shifts.

Three-on-Three, Nets Back to Back Neutral Zone Scrimmage

Set up in the neutral zone with nets back to back at center ice, so that goaltenders stand facing the offensive zones. The puck and players must stay between the two blue lines. This setup puts skaters in a cycling pattern—shooting off the cycle, passing off the cycle, or dropping the puck behind to the support provided by a teammate. The first team to 3 points wins. If goaltenders score, the team is awarded 2 points. You can also position a stationary offensive player from each team, one on each side along the boards at the center red line, across from the nets, who is available for give-and-go passes. The passers must remain at the boards.

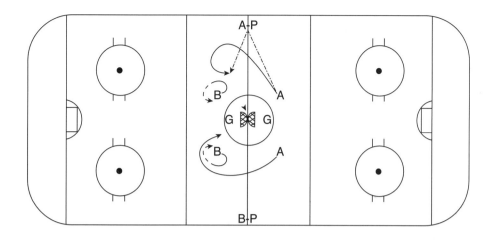

Three-on-Three, Safe Zone Scrimmage

Players compete two-on-two across the ice in one zone. Nets are positioned at the face-off hash marks closest to the boards, which leaves room to skate behind the net. A stationary passer from each team is placed in the offensive corner; this player can work a give-and-go with two skating teammates, leading to a shot on net. Players have to pass to their teammate in the corner before shooting on net. The safe zone designates that the corner passer cannot leave the corner and cannot be pressured.

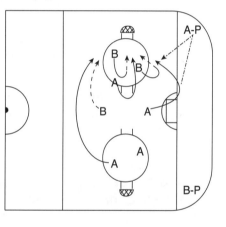

This drill requires skaters to hustle to find open space and compels defensive players to cover them and take away the pass.

Two-on-Two, No-Passing Scrimmage

The game is played from boards to boards in one zone. The nets are out from the boards on the face-off hash marks. Players are not allowed to pass the puck; they must carry it until they lose it or attempt a shot. Teammates must support the puck by getting in position to pick up a loose puck or by helping to create space and open lanes for the puck carrier. Defensive players work to close gaps and create turnovers.

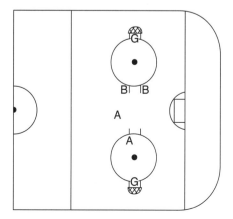

Two-on-One Transition Scrimmage

Nets are placed at face-off hash marks to play boards to boards. Teams have two players, but one player from each team must stay on the offensive side of the ice at all times. This always plays out as a two-on-one at either end. When a turnover occurs, the defender has to try to skate the puck out or pass up to her teammate, who may have to delay to create time for the trailing teammate to jump up with the play. On a turnover, the offensive player nearest her end drops back to defend, and the remaining teammate must stay in her offensive zone.

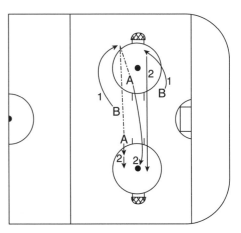

Progressive One-Zone Three-on-Three Scrimmage

This scrimmage is a modification of coach Willet's progressive three-on-three, boards-to-boards drill. One net and goaltender remain at the regulation crease position. One offensive player skates the puck into the zone against one defensive player, protecting the puck or attacking the net for 10 seconds. At 10 seconds, another player from each team enters the zone. At 20 seconds, another player from each team enters. Play continues three on three until 45 seconds have elapsed. When a goal is scored or the defensive side clears the puck from the zone, the coach injects a new puck by passing to an offensive player, who must create space and get open. When these six players are up the next time, they switch offensive and defensive sides. The first team to 5 points wins.

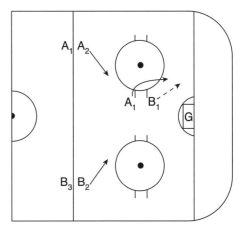

Chapter 5

Strength and Power

Hockey requires great leg strength, particularly eccentric strength needed to negotiate turns at high speeds, stop instantly, and change directions on a dime. Explosive power is needed to fuel accurate, high-velocity shots; come out of the blocks quickly during races for loose pucks; and accelerate to top-end skating speed. Strength, stability, and explosive power are applied during physical battles on the ice, in front of the net, and along the boards.

Both absolute strength (total muscular strength) and relative strength (strength in relation to body weight) are important to on-ice performance. Hockey requires absolute strength, because players must have the mass and strength to move others and withstand contact. Relative strength fosters quickness, agility, and speed.

Strength-trained muscle, joint stability, and reactivity help the body apply more force when performing multidirectional on-ice tactics. Opponents impose body contact to impede a player's efforts to gain ice, so the same attributes also protect the player when receiving and absorbing hits and obstruction from all sides. Hockey is a collision sport, with big open-ice hits and battles along the boards, testing every player's durability. This kind of action is most notable during the playoffs, when pro players compete every second night at elevated intensity. Teams that advance face a war of attrition.

As you will discover in this chapter, strength affects all other training components, such as speed and balance. Above all, strength influences explosive power, which is the ultimate on-ice expression of a good strength base.

LINKED SYSTEM TRAINING

To execute successful shooting and body checking, players need integrated coordination of their entire bodies. The body is a unit of linked systems that work together to coordinate athletic actions. Typical strength training, however, attempts to develop the body with a piecemeal approach, isolating specific muscle groups. Worse yet, strength training is often done with the body completely unloaded. The player sits stationary on a weight stack machine while moving one isolated body part through a controlled range of motion. The starting and ending points of movement are predefined, and the load is balanced. Often the exercise requires only single-joint action in one plane of movement. Bodybuilders designed these exercises with a focus on muscle size and appearance. But optimal on-ice movement occurs at explosive tempos through a linked system called the kinetic chain.

Within the kinetic chain, each joint, group of muscles, and nervous system connection affects the movement of the next joint and group of muscles in the chain. From the top of the head, down the neck, upper back, and shoulder girdle to the core muscles of the trunk and hips, and on down to the knees and ankles, any breakdown in stability, muscle activation, body alignment, or firing sequences will result in mechanical problems along this chain of movement.

Linked system training is the key to building skillful coordinated on-ice movement, eliminating all the weak links in the kinetic chain. This kind of training is especially important for hockey players, most of whom come from a traditional exercise background (which does not link body movements together) and have experienced injury in their hockey careers. Weak links lead to muscle imbalances and repetitive technical flaws that affect hockey mechanics and, over time, set up the body for injury. Whole-body lifts that draw muscles from toes to fingertips aim to correct these weak links and imbalances. Some exercises are purposefully designed to prevent players from working around their weak links, forcing the weak parts to contribute and catch up.

The body responds to common hockey injuries to the knees, adductors (groin), hip flexors, and low back by inhibiting neural activation to help protect the injured area, altering firing patterns and creating compensation shifts in which other parts of the body have to bear more of the load. Passive modality-based rehab and isolation rehab exercises will return players to game action prone to further injury and certainly unprepared to perform at their best. Hockey players must reestablish the mind–muscle links, reactivate the lines of nerve–muscle communication, and regenerate the coordinated strength that, all together, facilitate skillful, whole-body on-ice actions. Whether players are peak training in the off-season or undergoing midseason back-to-play reconditioning, hockey strength training follows similar rules.

Hockey performance requires coaches to look beyond traditional strength-training philosophies. Traditional lifting philosophies start from the outside in. How do athletes look? What is their body composition? Are they big enough and strong in their overall muscle size and definition? What can they bench press? Get bigger, stronger, and leaner. Look for evidence in the mirror and weight-room strength tests. The focus is building the athlete from the outside in.

By building from the inside out, an athlete can not only achieve gains in strength and size but also greatly improve the specificity of the strength developed and enhance transferability to on-ice performance. Philosophically and mechanically, this approach relies on a training style that focuses on movement, not muscle.

Some key lifting guidelines remain constant. Heavy loads with a focus on intensity and time under tension still drive strength improvements. My players lift heavy weights to momentary fatigue. Their lift schedule is periodized from hypertrophy through to explosive power phases. But there are additional ways to challenge and overload a muscle and different methods to achieve greater hockey skill and on-ice performance. Put away the weight scale and the mirrors to focus on the techniques best suited to an athletic, unpredictable sport.

Training from the inside out prioritizes these parameters:

- Using 360-degree core stability in a standing position to strengthen the deep muscles that establish posture and gait patterns.
- Building from the center of the body out to the periphery. A strong speed center influences all subsequent strength training.
- Teaching muscles to stabilize and contract in the correct order. For example, walking downstairs (hence deceleration) requires the left gluteal muscles to fire and stabilize a single-leg position before the right leg strides and lands. Although people can walk without doing this, and similarly can perform other athletic actions incorrectly, they pay a price: deficient mechanics and compensatory patterns that decrease strength and power and lead to injury.
- Enhancing the minibrains that influence joint and muscle responsiveness, especially in single-leg positions.

Toe-to-Fingertip Linked System Strength

The goal in hockey is to be strong on your feet and generate explosive power during wrist shots and slap shots. Whole-body power is also drawn on during body contact, whether an open-ice hit or effective containment in the corner. Lifting movements that cross the ankle, knee, hip, core, and upper extremities build strength while teaching the muscles to fire in the correct order. Sequential muscle firing sums forces through the body, transferring more power that can be applied to hockey forces, such as lateral movement, open-ice hits, and races for loose pucks.

This training effect itself becomes a skill that applies to skating acceleration as well as fighting through checks and driving to the net while warding off defenders. The aim is to lift heavier weights but also learn hockey-specific, multijoint mechanics; timing of power initiation; preloading; and positive angles that will express the most power during hockey actions.

© Jeff Zelevansky/Icon SMI

A powerful, skillful player like Jaromir Jagr of the New York Rangers is able to attack the net explosively.

Neural Overload

During strength training cycles, the inventory of variables available for progressive overload include load (weight), intensity (percent of one repetition maximum and perceived exertion), time under tension (slow lift tempo), frequency (more times per week), and volume (additional sets).

Neural complexity is another overload variable, challenging players to solve the puzzle of how to coordinate mechanics to succeed at an exercise. In this process, they learn how to activate the correct muscles that allow them to stabilize loading points before powering through concentric contractions. Many neural factors play an important role in optimizing lifting effects.

The power of neural input to strength training is evident in many single-limb research studies in which specific muscles of the left arm or leg are trained while the right side of the body receives no training. All studies report strength improvements in the left side, of course, but also in the right (untrained) side due to neural innervation, which can be referred to as bilateral transfer. Neural-based strength improvement is also evident at young ages when kids strength train during a stage of growth and maturation when they do not have the circulating hormones for muscle hypertrophy. At the end of a training phase, their bodies look the same, their muscles are the same size, but their strength levels are up; this change is a neural adaptation.

Postpuberty, when hockey players improve strength, muscle hypertrophy accounts for some of the gains, but an electromyogram would also show increased muscle activation, which means that the nervous system is doing a better job of recruiting muscle fibers to complete the lift. The goal in *Complete Conditioning for Hockey* is to train so that neural contributions are not just incidental to the function of recruiting fibers to move a load through a simple pattern. Exercises can be structured in many ways to optimize neural adaptations, taking hockey strength and power to new levels.

As strength improves in a traditional isolation strength setting, the activation level needed to recruit and command muscles to contract actually decreases. Because the individual muscle fibers are stronger, fewer are needed to lift a fixed amount of force. But if we increase the amount of activation, more force is generated and strength improvements occur more rapidly. The trick is to increase muscle size and strength, and then manipulate training variables to force the nervous system to dial up the maximal number of fibers to go to work.

Integrated Instability

Research done by Dr. Greg Anderson has verified and quantified the contribution that balance training has on muscle activation. Integrating an unstable environment into hockey strength training for a given load allows the player to continue to overload the neuromuscular system, essentially using more muscle groups to stabilize lifting postures and drawing on more muscle fibers to move the same load. The mechanisms of balance are detailed in chapter 6.

Within the scope of a strength program, adding instability helps expose and train weak links in the body, helping it handle combative forces. For a collision sport played on thin edges on ice, integrating balance and strength has obvious applications. Neural overload affects the amount of strength generated or force that can be applied. Similarly, a neurally coordinated body will better handle whole-body skills in high-power actions. This quality is referred to as neuromuscular coordination.

Coordinated Strength

If the goal is to develop strength that is transferable to intense hockey games, a player must learn to be in tune with his body during training itself. The emphasis is on quality training versus quantity training, using exercises that demand focus on body control and changing body mechanics to find the most advantageous power position. After initial improvement, quality movement can also be attempted within a dense volume of fatiguing exercises, thus training coordination under fatigue.

Players should learn how to set the correct positions and manipulate the kinetic chain during dynamic actions to ensure that the muscles fire in the right sequence, at the right time, with just the right amount (gradation) of force. Motor unit synchronization helps coordinate the activity of multiple muscles. We are not concerned with who can win the bench press competition in the weight room; it is all about who can best express strength gains on the ice, up on their skates. In the end, the goal is smart muscles. Attaining this goal requires a specific curriculum to remap the brain and unify firing patterns, thus enhancing stabilization and kinetic chain motion to produce maximal power during complex maneuvers.

Coordinated strength also emphasizes the role of the core in controlling movement. Players are encouraged to train from the inside out to establish a base of strength in the speed center—hips, abs, and low back. Core strength contributes to

- standing balance during movement, direction transitions, and contact;
- application of strength (pushing to check, warding off to protect the puck) in a standing position;
- control of tight turns;
- stabilized core so that legs can produce force to skate aggressively; and
- transfer of power from the legs to the arms during skating and checking.

Think of this as "core-dinated" strength to remember the importance of building a strong and functional core to produce coordinated movement on the ice. The body must be able to stabilize the appropriate joints to produce the leverage necessary to generate power. Stabilization is trained at slow speeds to build the base and then trained at explosive speeds for power.

Lift Tempo

The power that players can harness on the ice depends on the strength of the muscles, the coordination of the neuromuscular system, and the speed at which they can execute movement. Nothing on the ice is done slowly. To compete on the ice, players must display explosive power. This requires both strength and speed (strength + speed = power). The best way to build a foundation of muscle size, strength, and stability is through controlled tempo and heavy loads. Players should do this by selecting exercises that assemble the body into an integrated machine, as opposed to exercises that isolate body parts that cannot be harnessed during complex, high-speed, one-on-one maneuvers on the ice.

The controlled-tempo lift phase provides the eccentric strength needed for safe and effective deceleration and core stability. This will be built on with fast-tempo lifts. Ultimately, the athlete must be able to initiate power explosively and handle aggressive deceleration forces. The sequence of lift tempo changes is important in laying the foundation of strength that power will build on, and in progressing the training sensibly and safely to more aggressive lift outputs. Players should spend enough weeks at steps 1 and 2 to add muscle mass to their frames and make significant gains in the amount of weight that they can lift.

Step 1. Train strength and stability at controlled speeds throughout the entire range of motion, when both raising and lowering the weight. Pause midway for a peak concentric contraction. The tempo should be as slow as 2:2 and can even go to 2:4 (4-second negative).

Step 2. Maintain a controlled, full-range-of-motion eccentric phase at a 2-second pace, with more force behind the concentric lift phase, taking 1 second to raise the weight. Even if the athlete has established a strength base and is in a power phase, he will need acclimation to new exercises introduced to the program in this power-up, control-down step to learn and adapt to new movements safely.

Step 3. Progress to using a fast eccentric phase, but still pause and get set before initiating power into the concentric phase.

Step 4. Plyometric integration is the finishing touch for harnessing strength gains into maximal power. At this stage the fast eccentric lift phase is immediately coupled into the power initiation phase. Try to eliminate the pause between the eccentric and concentric phases. Cue players to trigger the hips to generate the most power from the fast coupling.

Step 5. Continue eccentric–concentric coupling and strive to increase the overall lift velocity for a given load.

Step 6. Vary and shorten the range of motion for eccentric loading.

Eccentric loading becomes a quick and short preload. On the ice, power initiation occurs at a variety of joint angles. Consider leg drive, for example. Sometimes a player is in a deep position during powerful skating; other times he may just load the legs to a partial range of motion before coupling into power to deliver an open-ice hit. I call this stage multiple-joint angle power initiation training. Using a cue of "load and go," instruct players how far into the eccentric range they should lower before they explode in the opposite direction. Power initiation from coupling is joint angle specific. Try to train coupling and power initiation at a variety of joint angles. Players will need the full arsenal on the ice!

Triple Flexion and Triple Extension

Visualize the biomechanical cycle to prepare for and release a wrist shot. In your mind, see a hockey player loading her back leg, pushing off aggressively from a skate edge into the ice, extending the back leg with plantar-flexed ankle, triggering the hips and rotating the core, and following through to load the front leg as the shoulders and arms snap the stick to transfer all power behind the puck. This is a literal expression of linked system kinetic chain power, transitioning from preloaded triple flexion to triple extension to summon power forces seamlessly in a line of force production from toes to fingertips.

For multijoint lifts that transfer to skating mechanics, shooting, and body contact, emphasize triple flexion and triple extension. This approach optimizes the toe-to-fingertip sequence that I refer to as linked strength, thus improving training specificity for striding in hockey or warding off players on the backcheck. It harnesses leg, hip, and core power toward what are seemingly upper-body actions.

During triple flexion, players are cued to share the load among their ankles, knees, and hips. Landing, loading, or planting the foot occurs outside the body, producing a positive angle from ground to foot to hip. A player's center of mass should shift over the back leg as he lowers his body weight onto the same leg. This shift is used during upper-body lifts as a preload, setting the body in the correct position to optimize strength and power moves.

Thinking about a skater's stride phase helps visualize triple extension in action. In training, I cue athletes to power through the legs and ensure full triple extension and summation of power by teaching them to release their heels during the lift. A heel release ensures that power is developed across the ankle, improving strength performance and replicating on-ice stride extension. All muscles along the kinetic chain contribute to force production, even during upper-body lifts. With back-leg heel release, the hips are free to trigger power and the core is able to rotate through a greater range, both of which are key to the transfer of power through the body. By unlocking the base of support from the ground, the player feels more athletic and fluid, more willing to drive power from the legs.

Muscle Balance

Having comparable strength in opposing muscle groups—for example, in the hamstrings (back of the upper leg) and in the opposing quadriceps (thigh)—reduces the possibility that a quick contraction of a strong muscle will tear a weak opposing muscle. Balance of strength in the legs is important. If a defenseman's left leg is stronger, he will tend to favor it. When backing up (gliding) on the ice, he will have more body weight on the left side. If he must suddenly cut laterally to the left to cut off an opposing forward, he will experience a critical delay before he can explode to the left because he must first shift more weight over to the right leg so that he can push off to the left! This brief delay will result in losing one-on-ones and races for loose pucks.

With the same asymmetry, during linear acceleration he would produce a stronger push-off with the left leg than he would with the right. The right would be a weaker stride, which would alter technique and waste valuable time. This player will not continue accelerating at the same rate until he can plant the left foot back under his body for another powerful push-off.

HOCKEY-SPECIFIC STRENGTH TRAINING

Specific strength-training methods match the science of lifting with the biomechanics of hockey. The following guidelines will help you construct strength workouts and design a weekly program.

Lift Organization

Lift organization defines what body movements are exercised and the lift patterns, planes of movements, and types of lifts to include.

Push, Pull, Core Stabilization

Upper-body strength and closed kinetic chain core stability contribute to containing opponents, fighting through checks, and protecting the puck. For strong skating, a stabilized core allows the legs to generate more force and move the body up the ice without swaying away from the pure line of intended travel. Strong shoulders and arms lead the legs. Push–pull lifts can be accomplished in prone or supine positions for core integration, or in standing postures with legs and hips integrated to produce whole-body actions more similar to what players use to produce strength on the ice. Even while a player is pinning an opponent against the boards with the arms, the torso is contracted to stabilize the effort, while the legs continue to balance the body and drive toward the opponent. These lifting patterns can be done in sequence: a push set followed by a pull set followed by a core set. The opposing push–pull patterns can be accomplished in a superset but still allow over 95 percent strength output on both lifts. The push and pull lifts already challenge core stability, so it fits this workout day. The core is also activated during dedicated core-emphasis exercises in kneeling, supine, prone, and standing positions.

For core strength, gone are the days of doing hundreds of sit-ups, curl-ups, crunches, and other floor-based abdominal exercises. The focus is on performance, not the six-pack look. Core stability exercises are more postural in nature, building strength 360 degrees around the torso and linking in the hips, as well as within each of the push–pull lifts. Challenge core stability by applying forces from tubing (BOSU lateral two-foot jumps with Slastix tubing, page 112) or partners (partner knock-offs, page 86), integrated instability (kneeling stability ball balance with lateral shift, page 112), or holding prone postures, lengthening levers with compromised base of support (stability ball hockey stick push-ups, page 110). These types of exercises demand strong isometric contractions but also develop a highly reactive core able to contribute to regaining balance after being bodychecked. A hockey player doesn't need just a strong core; she needs a highly responsive core that will contract quickly as she anticipates the hit, protecting the spine and making her more difficult to knock off the puck.

Legs–Shoulders–Core Rotation

Leg strength is important to skating strides, acceleration, turns, and stops. It contributes to first-step power for a strong push-off and anaerobic endurance for repetitive strides. For a hockey player, "It is more important to develop mass in the lower body," says Lorne Goldenberg, a respected expert on developing pro players and veteran of several NHL teams. "By lowering the center of gravity, players have the strength to bend their knees more to make tighter turns. A hockey player with a big upper body and no legs will fall over in tight, high-speed turns."

Primary leg movements include squats, split squats, lunges, lateral moves, strides, and cross-under patterns. Exercises are done with both feet planted, on one leg, or by shifting from leg to leg. Off the play, skaters spend most of their time gliding on both feet, but when they are on task challenging for the puck, players use a single leg over 80 percent of the time. They stop and balance on one leg, push off with a single leg, and shift body weight to one leg for agility moves around defenders. Even during two-legged actions, players often transfer weight back and forth from one leg to the other to use their edges strategically, such as when handling tight turns or building speed when skating backward. For aggressive edging, players need excellent and equal strength and coordination abilities in the legs.

Primary shoulder exercises include multijoint lateral raises, multijoint posterior deltoid and rotator cuff lifts, front raises, and shoulder presses. The shoulder joint offers the most versatile joint angles, which helps stickhandling and various puck skills, but with that capability also comes greater susceptibility to impact damage relative to other joints. The shoulder links push, pull, and ward-off movements to deliver hits, battle for pucks in the corner, clear the slot, and absorb forces from opponents. Shoulder function is drawn on during shooting. Slap shots and wrist shots rely on a strong, full range of motion. Snap shots require power initiation with short range of motion. Backhand shots rely more on posterior shoulder action.

Shooting uses torso rotation through the transverse plane. While shooting or delivering shoulder checks, a player squats laterally, loading up his outside leg, extending his back leg, and pivoting off the toe, which allows him to rotate through the legs and across the hips while applying force outside the body's center of gravity. A shot-specific rotary power exercise is still a whole-body strength move that incorporates a weight shift from back leg to front and a hip drop to drive up phase. This type of rotary training also transfers well into ward-offs, shoulder checks, and aggressive entering and exiting of turns. Because of the involvement of the legs and core for shoulder lifts, and the legs and shoulders for rotary power lifts, these three are combined on one workout day.

To train rotary power safely, begin with a strength emphasis and controlled speeds to build torso strength. Gradually progress to quicker rotary movements that focus on power initiation:

Step 1. Develop proficiency in static supine and prone ball exercises.

Step 2. Progress to standing closed kinetic chain isometric holds.

Step 3. Move on to rotary patterns with slow and controlled tempos, learning to shift weight to use legs and hips.

Step 4. Add slow eccentric loading and a definitive pause, followed by powerful power initiation through the rotary pattern.

Step 5. Add a fast eccentric catch and a definitive pause, followed by powerful power initiation.

Step 6. Add a fast eccentric catch immediately followed by powerful power initiation.

Step 7. Vary the range of motion.

From step 1 to step 6, players must demonstrate technique, strength, and then endurance before they move up one step. Skipping stages can lead to training injury. But not achieving step 6 will leave players predisposed to on-ice injury. So players must do it right—taking baby steps along the way to ensure that they do well at one stage before they advance to more demanding training protocols.

At stages 6 and 7, the cue "trigger the hips" connects players with the action of snapping the back hip to help initiate explosive movement, transferring angular momentum through full-range-of-motion rotary power. Medicine balls and heavy strength tubing (Slastix tubing) make torso plyometric actions possible, during which the player does not have to decelerate toward the end of the range of motion as he does with weights. Remember, after training for rotary power to elevate shot velocity, players need to practice raising their arms and sticks above their heads!

Sets and Reps

Weight training is organized by sets and repetitions (reps). A rep is one complete range of motion under load for a particular exercise. A group of reps makes up a set—the number of reps performed without resting.

The more intense the workout, the greater the strength development. The load for a given exercise is best determined by the number of reps, the rest time between sets, and the speed of movement. In general, hockey players should work within 4 to 15 repetitions. For a 10-rep set, estimate the weight that will cause fatigue on the 10th rep.

On the low end, performing 6 to 12 slow repetitions is an effective way to grow muscle size and strength. Sets of 4 to 8 repetitions are appropriate for powerful lifts, and sets of 12 or more repetitions target muscle endurance and power capacity. Rest time between sets affects the amount of weight that the player can lift on the next set. The longer the rest interval, the higher the quality of lift, allowing better technique and a heavier load, driving up strength gains. The shorter the rest, the more the lifter is taking existing levels of strength and power and working to build capacity.

Hockey Lifts

Supine lifts are parallel to the floor with the player facing the ceiling. Supine lifts often involve pull movements up to a bar for the back or push movements with dumbbells or against partner resistance. Core stability begins in supine positions.

Prone lifts are done from a push-up position with the player facing the floor. Prone lifts often require balance or abdominal contraction in conjunction with chest and arm work.

Multijoint lifts are whole-body exercises that generate force across the ankle, knee, hip, and sometimes the shoulders.

Cross-body exercises shift power from the left leg to the right arm or vice versa. An athlete can be stable on two feet and execute a cross-body lift, shifting his body weight over to one flexed leg before extending the leg and transferring his weight across the body to the opposite arm.

In contralateral lifts, the player lifts from a single-leg position, requiring the opposite leg and arm to work together to produce the required force. In contrast, for a unilateral lift, the athlete lifts from a single-leg position but uses the arm on the same side.

Combination lifts are a blend of more than one type of lift. For example, a strength exercise could begin with a contralateral movement and finish in a unilateral hold. Integrated lifts are a blend of more than one component of training. For example, a lift could integrate strength and balance.

Lift Mechanics and Positive Angles

Some exercises use supine or prone positions; others purposefully place the body at a biomechanical disadvantage, such as on a narrow base of support, to build strength and stability; but the final touch to help transfer strength to the ice applies positive angles to exploit the body's mechanics and generate the most force. When preloading eccentrically, the foot–ground position relative to the hip should create a positive angle to produce more force. Positive angles can be used with strong edges to apply more force in the correct direction to get the upper hand on the ice during ward-offs, when containing in the corner, or when driving through an opponent in the slot. Using positive angles increases eccentric balance and concentric power simultaneously during combative expressions of power, such as fighting through a defensive check. It is both a tool to move more load in the weight room and a dryland opportunity to lay down motor engrams of advantageous on-ice mechanics. Lifting with positive angles teaches the player how to adjust her body to be strong on her skates, no matter what direction a check comes from.

Prelift Prep

A three-step posture checklist will shift you into a safe, strong beginning position for most exercises. Before each set, assume an athletic stance with feet shoulder-width apart, knees flexed, legs loaded, hips low, chest up, and core and midback set. This is your power base.

Set your core before lifting by drawing in the abdominal muscles about 7 percent. Then brace the core, contracting around the torso to achieve a corset effect. You will also set your midback by pulling the shoulders up, back, and down, relaxing the traps but squeezing the shoulder blades together. Think of pulling the rhomboids down and back. This positions your shoulders in a strong position, ready for shoulder, back, and chest contributions.

Breathing

Holding your breath while lifting a weight increases blood pressure and poses potential heart problems. The high blood pressure can cause you to feel dizzy or faint, not a good situation while holding a weight!

The common instruction for breathing during strength training is to exhale on the positive phase (lifting a weight) and inhale during the negative phase (lowering the weight). But this assumes that you are exerting effort to lift the bar and then just letting the bar lower with gravity. Giving resistance on the negative phase requires great effort and develops a lot more tension in the muscle fostering strength and size gains. A better method is to exhale during both effort phases and to pause briefly at the top and bottom to inhale. For more explosive lifts, breathe out during the positive phase and inhale during the negative phase. Sometimes it is more natural to take several short breaths during a lift, and the degree of exertion may demand this. The main rule is to avoid holding your breath.

Power Cleans

DVD

Purpose: Build whole-body strength and power through the legs, hips, back, arms, and trapezius, and train multijoint muscle sequencing

Squat and grasp the bar with a shoulder-width, overhand grip, arms outside your knees. Position your shoulders over the bar and maintain a flat back. Begin the upward movement by extending your knees and moving your hips forward. Keep the bar close to your body throughout the lift. Keep pulling the bar up the quadriceps and then explosively extend your ankles, knees, and hips in a jumping movement. At the end of the jump phase, shrug your shoulders and pull up with your arms, leading with your elbows. To finish, rotate your elbows around and under the bar, rack the bar on the front of your shoulders, and lower your hips and knees to absorb the weight.

Weight Plate Stickhandling

Purpose: Develop abdominal, hip, and low-back rotation strength and teach the body to shift weight for shooting and puckhandling, link arms for puck protection, and handle forces outside the body

Put a 10- or 25-pound (4.54- to 11.43-kilogram) Olympic plate on slide board material or similar flooring. Stand upright with your knees slightly flexed. Hold a hockey stick upside down, placing the end in the hole of the Olympic plate. Slowly move the plate through a wide figure-eight movement. Then move the plate left to right, moving it as far outside the body as possible. Next shift the plate back and forth rapidly within the width of your stance.

Standing Lateral Raise

Purpose: Build shoulders

Stand upright with your knees slightly bent, holding dumbbells at your sides. Lift the dumbbells up and out at your sides until the dumbbells are higher than your shoulders. Slowly lower the dumbbells back to your sides.

Squats

Purpose: Develop legs, glutes, back

Stand upright with the bar balanced on your back, using a wide overhand grip. Your feet should be shoulder-width apart and parallel, with toes pointed out slightly. Maintaining a straight back, with your head up and neck neutral, focus your eyes on a point slightly higher than head level. Begin to lower the weight by dropping your hips into a seated position and flexing your knees. Your weight should be on the middle to back of your feet. Your knees should remain over your feet; if you glance down they should not be out far past your toes. Lower the bar until your quadriceps are parallel to the ground. Then raise the bar by straightening your hips and knees.

Hockey Lunges

Purpose: Strengthen hamstrings, quadriceps, groin, gluteal muscles, calves, abductors, hip extensors, hip flexors

Hockey lunges are similar to walking lunges, but you stride out at a 45-degree angle (an angle similar to the push-off on the ice) with your leg outwardly rotated and your body weight over the single striding leg, just as you do on the ice. When landing, the foot should be in line with the leg to protect your knee. Planting the foot in line with the leg (out at a 45-degree angle) also puts that leg in a position to push off the next stride at a 45-degree angle.

Lateral Crossover Box Step-Ups

Purpose: Build gluteal muscles, hamstrings, quadriceps, groin, and abductors

Standing away from and sideways to a stable box, complete a sumo side lunge to step in closer to the box. With your outside leg, step over the inside leg up onto the box. Pushing off with the foot that remains on the ground, bring the inside leg up on the box. Try to keep your shoulders and hips facing square throughout this movement to challenge your flexibility around the hips. Use a light weight and take as long a stride as possible; exaggerate your range of movement.

Medicine Ball Shoulder-to-Shoulder Pass

Purpose: Build upper-body explosiveness and torso and shoulder power

This exercise is similar to a medicine ball chest pass, but you pass the ball from your right shoulder to your partner's right shoulder. Then you complete a set passing from your left shoulder to your partner's left shoulder. When catching the ball, absorb it with trunk rotation and slight knee flexion to develop power in the abdominal muscles and low back.

Advanced athletes can catch and throw the ball with one arm only (for example, when passing from right shoulder to right shoulder, the left hand provides no catching support). This focuses more on the rear shoulders, abdominals, back, and legs to assist the action.

Medicine Ball Rotary Passes

Purpose: Build rotational power

Stand back-to-back about 12 inches (30 centimeters) from a partner. With rapid rotation, pass the ball off one side and rotate over to receive it on the other side. Complete the exercise clockwise and then counterclockwise. Advanced athletes can rotate farther to meet at the back for a 360-degree pass motion.

CORE STABILITY

Ball Holds

Purpose: Build standing core strength that will absorb contact without breaking at the waist

Stand in an athletic ready stance, core braced. Face a partner or coach. Hold a Swiss ball. As your partner pushes against the ball, hold steady, resisting the pressure from your partner. Try to keep the ball as still as possible as you maintain your ready stance.

Partner Knock-Offs

Purpose: Build standing core strength that will absorb contact without breaking at the waist

Anchor into an athletic ready stance, with your core braced. Have a partner push you on the shoulders—sideways, front, and back. Begin with 3-second sustained pushes so that you can recognize where the force is coming from and how to counteract it. Later, have your partner strengthen the push and increase the frequency.

Up, Up, Down, Down

Purpose: Link upper-body stability and arm strength to trunk and pelvic stability for on-ice combat

Begin by getting into a prone plank position, with forearms on a stability ball and core engaged. Pick up your right arm and place your right hand on the ball, followed by your left. While doing this movement try to keep your hips from rotating side to side. Reverse the movement that got you up there, placing your right elbow where your hand was by using your left arm to lower yourself with control. Last, lift your left hand off and place your left elbow where your left hand was. Repeat for the desired number of reps.

Standing Rollout

Purpose: Develop core strength in an aggressive forward lean position, specific to skating postures

This exercise adds more overload to an already strong core. Stand in a deep squat stance, with a stability ball in front of you. Place your fingertips on the down slope of the ball (the side closer to you), shift your body weight from the legs, and transfer your weight to load over the hands on the ball. Brace your core and roll the ball forward. Pause and hold before returning backward.

Two-Ball Instability Rollouts

Purpose: Strongly activate the shoulders, back, abdominal muscles, and hips to link them together for hockey actions that require a reactive core

Set the heels of your hands on the top outside of a stability ball in front of you. Place your knees on a ball behind you. Set the midback. Shift some of your weight onto your hands and work to hold this position without exiting the balls. React to any deviations in balance by pulling back to a centered position. Progress to extending your arms and legs to create more separation between the balls.

CORE ROTATION

Medicine Ball Double-Rotation Passes

Purpose: Build rotary plyometric action for wrist shots, slap shots, and leading the body into aggressive turns

Partners set up four strides apart with knees flexed, core set, feet shoulder-width apart, and head turned to see the partner. Catch the medicine ball and rotate to lower it to your back knee. Rotate across the body, stop, and return again to the back knee. Finally, rotate back across and release a powerful throw to your partner.

Medicine Ball Shoulder-to-Shoulder Pass

Purpose: Develop strength in the shoulders and back; link the strength through the legs, hips, torso, and upper body; and train the body to absorb forces

Stand facing your partner, about three paces apart. Keep your feet shoulder-width apart, with knees slightly flexed and abdominal muscles contracted. The pass line goes from your right shoulder to the partner's right shoulder. Receive the ball by cushioning the pass reception with your entire body. The ball comes into your hands, your arms bend to draw in the ball closer to your right shoulder, your core rotates, your hips drop, and your body weight shifts onto your right leg, which flexes at the knee. This is a whole-body catch. The pass back reverses the flow. Begin the pass by pushing your foot into the ground, extending your leg, rotating your hip and torso, and finally extend-ing your arms to thrust the ball back to your partner. The arm move-ment is more of a direct push from the shoulder, similar to a shot put, rather than a baseball throw. Repeat the set, throwing from left shoulder to left shoulder.

Single-Leg Ball Rotations

DVD

Purpose: Improve hip mobility and strengthen independent leg inward and outward rotation to develop the strong, mobile hip action that is key to edging and skating mechanics

Set up in a push-up position, with one foot on a stability ball. Move the knee of the free leg down and around the body as the leg on the ball rotates to the inside. Unwind this movement and continue past the neutral (setup) position, moving your free leg up and over your body. The goal is to touch your foot to the floor on the opposite side of your body.

Prone Ball Holds With Knee Drive

Purpose: Tie abdominal strength to hip flexors for the recovery stride phase to link the hips into core rotation.

Assume a push-up position, with the heel of your hands on the upper outside of a stability ball. Keep up, with hips low and knees flexed, as you would in an aggressive forward start stance. Load your body weight onto your arms and engage the core. With a Slastix Hip-Thigh Blaster attached to the ankles, slowly bring the knee of one leg straight up as close to your chest as possible, pause, and return. Alternate legs. Next, pull the knee in and over to the opposite elbow. Begin with a slow, controlled tempo and pause for a half-second hold at the midposition. After you have developed strength to handle this, increase the speed of movement, driving the knee to the opposite elbow before holding.

Woodchops With Hold

Purpose: Develop rotary strength in the core

Attach a Slastix strength tube to a stationary object such as a weight machine. Stand in athletic ready position at about a 45-degree angle to the stationary object, grasping the tubing in both hands. Shift your weight sideways and downward to flex and load up your inside leg, bringing the Slastix handle to your inside knee. Moving from your core, pull the tubing out and across your body and away from the stationary object, pushing up from your legs. Hold for a few seconds. Under control, return to the starting position and repeat.

Push–Pull to Rotation

DVD

Purpose: Integrate push–pull patterns into rotary holds to help transfer rotary power to shooting and physical confrontation

Begin in an athletic position in a split stance—the front foot is contralateral to the pulling arm. Set up your pressing arm with the elbow up and the hand holding the Slastix grip at the shoulder. For your pulling arm, the hand grips with the palm facing in and the elbow is tight to your body.

Simultaneously push and pull while pivoting on your feet. Make a rowing and pushing movement with your upper body. With one arm performing a rowing motion and the other a push, the whole body rotates and pivots in the same direction as the pulling arm. The pushing arm finishes extended at shoulder height, while the pulling arm finishes with the elbow tight to the body and the hand at hip height. Through rotation and pivoting, the front foot becomes the rear foot (finishes on toes) and the rear foot becomes the front foot. With your whole body, return to the starting position by reversing the pivot, the pulling action, and the pushing action.

Hockey Stick Rotations

DVD

Purpose: To develop rotary strength in 180 degrees of motion

Begin in athletic position, holding a hockey stick in front of your body at arm's length, with elbows slightly bent, hips forward, and trunk rotated to one side. Your partner stands chest to chest with you in athletic position, holding the hockey stick and facing you. Initiate movement at the hip, rotating the trunk 180 degrees toward the center. The legs, hips, and core drive the movement. Your partner counters the resistance and follows the rotary path of the movement. Regain your core stability before the next application of rotary force.

LEGS

BOSU Step-Up to Shoulder Press

Purpose: Develop leg power and improve balance while training the shoulders

Place a BOSU dome side up on a stable platform. Hold a dumbbell in your right hand. Put your left foot on the top of the BOSU and push yourself up, lifting your right knee and pressing the dumbbell up with your right hand as you step up onto the BOSU. Try to maintain your balance and slowly lower the dumbbell back to the shoulder, under control. Under control, step down and repeat for desired rep count. Switch legs and work the other shoulder.

Crossover Lunge to Side Angle

DVD

Purpose: Train strength in the crossover pattern and challenge hip mobility

Load up the Olympic bar across the shoulders, with feet shoulder-width apart, chest up, and core set. Stand centered directly in front of the Power Plyo in a balanced athletic position.

Keep hips and shoulders square. Drop the hips and cross the right leg in front of and across the left leg (lateral crossover step). Land the right foot on the left panel of the Power Plyo in a deep position, keeping the toes pointing forward. Keep the chest up, core set, and the hips and shoulders square (facing forward). Find a momentary state of balance. Push up through the right heel, triple extending the ankle, knee, and hip, back to the starting position. Find a momentary state of balance before initiating the crossover lunge to the opposite side.

Leapfrog Lateral Jumps

DVD

Purpose: Develop dynamic single-leg power and overload stopping positions with hooking-like forces

Begin in athletic position, balanced on one leg. Keep the chest up and set your core. Flex your standing knee. The Leapfrog is belted around your waist with the distal end of the Leapfrog secured around the base of a squat rack. Turn laterally from the secured end of the Leapfrog. You bound laterally from the distal end of the Leapfrog.

For the power-out phase, find a momentary state of balance. Initiate movement with the arms, driving across the body. Triple extend the ankle, knee, and hip with a lateral bound. Land on the lead leg in triple flexion of the ankle, knee, and hip, with upper-body control (chest up, core set). As the stretched leapfrog pulls on you, find a momentary state of balance and hold before initiating the next bound back to the starting position. The movement tempo is important. Land, stick, and hold the bound out. Quickly couple the return to the start position with another power-out bound.

Gliding Discs for Adductors

Purpose: Improve balance and develop dynamic single-leg power for skating

Stand on two gliding discs, holding a hockey stick in your left hand. From an athletic ready position, extend the right leg through a stride pattern while the right arm moves forward. Aim for a long stride and low body position. To activate adductors (groin), dig your toes into the ground and slowly pull the leg back in to athletic ready stance. Alternate legs.

SHOULDERS

BOSU PSU Squat to Shoulder Press

Purpose: Develop toe-to-fingertip linked system strength and use strength from a deep stance

Begin on the BOSU, with platform side up and feet evenly spaced. Stand in a low athletic position. Hold the dumbbells at shoulder height with palms turned forward. Find a momentary state of balance. Initiating with the legs, come out of your squat position by triple extending at the ankle, knee, and hip while simultaneously performing an overhead shoulder press. Find a momentary state of balance. Link the lowering phase of the dumbbells by lowering back into your starting position by triple flexing at the ankles, knees, and hips.

Single-Leg, Opposite-Arm Lat Raise

Purpose: Build cross-body patterns important in ward-offs and puck protection

Begin in low athletic position, balanced on one leg. Hold one arm in tight to your body, with a 90-degree bend at the elbow (maintained throughout movement), holding a dumbbell.

Initiating with the leg, perform a lateral raise with the arm while simultaneously triple extending at the ankle, knee, and hip, finishing on your toes. (This is the rising phase of the squat.) The elbow and wrist finish the phase parallel to or slightly above shoulder height. Simultaneously bring the arm back to starting position while maintaining the 90-degree bend at the elbow and lowering back into a squat position, triple flexing at ankle, knee, and hip.

Lat Jump to Lat Raise

Purpose: Link dynamic lateral leg movement to upper-body shoulder power

Begin in athletic position, balanced on one leg. Keep your chest up and core set. Flex the knee of your standing leg. Hold one arm in tight to your body, with a dumbbell in hand and the elbow bent at 90 degrees (maintained throughout movement).

Initiate with the arm. Perform a lateral raise with the arm while simultaneously triple extending at the ankle, knee, and hip during a lateral bound. Triple flex the ankle, knee, and hip on landing. The elbow and wrist finish the phase parallel to or slightly above shoulder height. Keep the chest up and the core set throughout the movement. Simultaneously bring the arm back to the starting position while maintaining the 90-degree bend at the elbow and bounding back to the start leg. Triple flex the ankle, knee, and hip on landing. Keeping the chest up and the core set.

BOSU PSU Superslow Lat Raise

Purpose: Overload cross-body patterns critical to on-ice success segment by segment, exposing weak links

Begin in a low athletic position on the BOSU, with platform side up. Hold the Slastix strength tubing handle across the body at the rear knee.

Initiating with the legs, perform a slow-tempo lateral raise with the arm while simultaneously triple extending at the ankle, knee, and hip. The elbow and wrist finish the phase parallel to shoulder height. To lower simultaneously bring the arm back to the starting position while lowering back into a squat position at a very slow pace, triple flexing at ankle, knee, and hip.

MJ Rotator Cuff

Purpose: Balance hockey-dominant lateral and forward shoulder strength patterns so that the shoulder girdle has posterior strength when receiving hits along the boards

Begin in a low athletic position. Extend your arm, holding the Slastix toner grip in your hand. Set your core and scapula, keeping your chest up.

Initiate movement with the legs, triple extending at the ankles, knees, and hips while pulling the arm backward until the elbow is at 90 degrees of flexion, parallel to shoulder height (*a*). Finish the movement by pulling the hand upward, externally rotating at the shoulder joint while retracting the scapula (*b*). Keep the chest up and core set. Simultaneously lower into the low athletic position (low phase of the squat) through triple flexion of the ankles, knees, and hips, while internally rotating the shoulder. Lower the hand parallel with the elbow and shoulder and extend the arm back to the starting position. Keep the chest up and core set.

a   b

Front Raise Repeats

DVD

Purpose: Develop pop-in shoulders and legs for powerful open-ice hits and explosive muscle capabilities

Begin in low athletic position. Hold dumbbells at knee height, with palms turned toward the body. Initiating movement with the legs, triple extend at the ankle, knee, and hip while simultaneously performing a front raise. Flex at the shoulder. The ending position is on the toes, with the dumbbells slightly higher than shoulder height. After a brief pause in the top position, lower the weights back to the starting position, linking the lowering phase of the dumbbells with triple flexion of the ankles, knees, and hips. Repeat immediately for the desired reps or time.

Extreme Board Arm Curl–Shoulder Press Combo   *DVD*

Purpose: Link legs, hips, and arms to shoulder strength capabilities and train the legs to stay in a balanced hockey stance while the upper body works

Begin in athletic position on an Extreme Balance Board, feet apart to create balance. Set your core and hold your chest up. Hold the dumbbells at shoulder height with palms turned in toward your chest.

Find a momentary state of balance before simultaneously performing an overhead shoulder press with one arm and a biceps curl with the other arm. The ending position is in the athletic position with one arm completely extended above one shoulder and the other arm completely extended below the other shoulder, with the palms turned out. Keep the chest up and core set. Find a momentary state of balance before simultaneously flexing both elbows, bringing both hands back to the starting position with palms facing in. Keep the chest up and core set.

CHEST

Olympic Rock Singers With Lat Step   *DVD*

Purpose: Develop linked system strength outside the midline, ability to absorb forces, strength to contain opponents

Begin in athletic position. Hold an Olympic bar at arm's length directly in the midline of the body. Set your core and bend your arm slightly at the elbow. Keeping the elbow up, step laterally to the side, loading the leg through flexion of the ankle, knee, and hip (lowering phase of the squat) while simultaneously flexing the arm at the elbow until the hand is in line with the chest.

Initiating movement with the legs, perform a pressing motion, extending at the elbow while simultaneously triple extending at the ankle, knee, and hip and stepping laterally back to the starting position. The bar and body will travel from the midline, laterally, and then return to the midline.

Multijoint Stick Push

Purpose: Bring leg power behind upper-body push strength and the aggressive angle used for body contact and to fight through checks

Face your partner at approximately arm's length. Both of you grasp the hockey stick between you with an overhand grip. Stand in athletic position, with arms extended directly in front of your shoulders at arm's length and with shoulders set. Your partner should stand in athletic position as well, with arms flexed at the elbow so that the hockey stick is slightly in front of the chest, with shoulders set. You and your partner perform the exercise with a cooperative press–resist combination. One partner presses the stick, while the other provides appropriate resistance.

With your partner performing a pressing motion, provide sufficient resistance to overload your partner but keep the stick moving by flexing at the shoulder until the hands and arms are overhead. With your partner providing resistance, perform a multijoint pressing motion by extending simultaneously at the ankle, knee, and hip while pushing the stick up and away from the body. Reset by lowering back to the starting position before initiating the next push.

Drop Step to Slastix Tubing Push

Purpose: Improve single-arm push strength assisted by hip power, to power upper strength from aggressive edges and weight preloads on ice

Begin in athletic position on the BOSU, with dome side up. Hold a toner grip at shoulder level, with elbows up and core set. Keeping the elbow up, simultaneously step laterally and back 45 degrees off the BOSU with the same leg and arm, loading the rear leg (triple flexing through the lower body) into a low power position. Initiating movement with the legs, push off the back leg while simultaneously performing a press action with the arms and stepping back onto the BOSU, matching the feet. The arm should finish extended in front of the body in line with the shoulder.

Dual-Arm Chest Push Repeats (Fast Feet)

Purpose: Quickly develop linked system pushing strength with fast coupling to get pop on hits

Begin in athletic position. Hold toner grips at shoulder level, with elbows up and core set. Initiating movement with the legs, perform a press action with the arms while simultaneously performing a short jump forward by triple extending at the ankle, knee, and hip. Keeping the elbow up, simultaneously bring the arms back to the starting position by flexing at the elbows and jump back by triple flexing through the lower body. Repeat phases immediately for the required repetitions.

TRX Push-Ups

Purpose: Develop strength with stabilization for effective strength when up on the skates

Grip the TRX handles in either a prone (palms turned down) or neutral (palms turned in) grip. Lean forward onto the toes into a prone plank position (core set, hips level), with the arms extended out in front of your body. Retract the scapula.

Find a momentary state of balance before slowly flexing at the elbows, lowering the body into a push-up position. Keep the scapula retracted and the core

set. Maintain hand position. Find a momentary state of balance before pushing back up to the starting position, slowly extending the elbows and driving the body up, keeping the hips level and the core set. Step back into the squat rack and start with a body position closer to parallel with the floor.

Two BOSU Power-Overs

Purpose: Develop explosive upper-body power and core stability

Position two BOSU side-by-side. Start in a prone plank position, with one hand centered on top of a BOSU and the other hand on the floor. Hips are level, the core is set, and the scapula is retracted.

Starting in a deep push-up position (elbows flexed to 90 degrees) with the left hand on the floor and the right hand on top of the first BOSU, power up into full elbow extension. At the top of the movement, pop the hands across to the right.

For the next push-up, both hands are on the tops of the BOSU. Flex the elbows into a deep push-up and power up into full elbow extension. Travel across the BOSU in a push-up and pop-off manner until the right hand is on the floor and the left hand is centered on top of the BOSU. Repeat the push-up motions and popping back and forth across both BOSU. Repeat for the desired number of repetitions. Keep the hips level and the core set.

BACK

Supine Pull-Ups With Towel Grip

Purpose: Develop back strength linked with trunk and forearms to be strong with the stick

Drape towels over an Olympic bar. Grip the towels in a neutral grip (palms turned in), with hands shoulder-width apart. Position your body in a plank position, with hips level with the shoulders and heels, the core set, and the heels in contact with ground. Retract the scapula.

Initiate movement with the arms, flexing the elbows while retracting the scapula and pulling your body up toward the Olympic bar. Slide the elbows past the ribcage while maintaining level hips. If possible, attempt to make chest contact with the Olympic bar at the base of the sternum. Keep the core set. Lower your body by extending at the elbows. Return to the starting position, maintaining level hips and keeping the core set. To progress the movement, prop up the heels on the edge of a bench or on a stability ball.

Squat to Row

Purpose: Develop linked system pull strength and balance out the on-ice push movements

Begin in low athletic position. Hold toner grips, with arms extended and with core and scapula set. Initiating movement with the legs, simultaneously come out of your squat by triple extending at the ankle, knee, and hip while rowing the Slastix toward the ribcage by flexing at the elbow. Finish on your toes, with your hands at sternum level and scapula retracted. To return to the starting position, simultaneously lower your back into a low athletic position (low phase of the squat) while extending at the elbow.

Partner Towel Rows

Purpose: Strengthen forearms with core, hips, and back as the prime pulling mover

Face your partner with enough distance between you to extend one arm fully in front. Maintain a low athletic position, gripping the end of a towel in each hand, with one arm extended straight out in front and the other arm flexed at the elbow next to the ribcage. Keep the chest up and core set. Your partner is in the same position, with arms opposite yours, chest up, and core set.

Keeping the chest up and core set, attempt to pull your extended arm back with a rowing motion, flexing at the elbow and sliding past the ribcage while your partner applies resistance (countermovement). Simultaneously, you are applying resistance (countermovement) for your partner, who is pulling his extended arm back, flexing at the elbow, and sliding past the ribcage. Repeat the action with alternating arms for the desired number of repetitions.

Single-Leg, Opposite-Arm Row

Purpose: Develop pull strength while challenging cross-body stabilization and single-leg balance

Begin in athletic position, balanced on one leg. Bend forward to 45-degree flexion at the hip (maintain throughout exercise). Hold a dumbbell in the hand opposite the balancing leg. The dumbbell should be directly below your shoulder. Set your core and shoulders. Keeping the elbow in tight, row the dumbbell toward the ribcage by flexing at the elbow, finishing with the dumbbell at sternum level. Lower the dumbbell by extending at the elbow back to the starting position.

TRX Pull-Ups

Purpose: Develop toe-to-fingertip linked system pull strength and build mass for body contact

Grip TRX handles in a neutral grip (palms turned in) or prone grip (palms turned out) and extend the elbows. Lie in a supine plank position, with heels on the floor. Set your core, with hips in line with the ankles and shoulders. Retract the scapula.

Initiate movement from the arms. Flex at the elbows while retracting the scapula. Pull the body up toward the hands. Slide the elbows past the ribcage while retracting the scapula and keeping the core set. If possible, finish the movement with the hands at or near the midpoint of the chest. Lower the body back to the starting position by extending the elbows. Maintain level hips and keep the core set. To progress the movement, prop up the heels on the edge of a bench or on a stability ball.

Chapter 6

Balance

Many fitness and exercise science books speak of balance in terms of body equilibrium—the ability to maintain the body's center of gravity within the base of support. In ice hockey, however, skating maneuvers depend on shifting the center of gravity *outside* the base of support. I teach my athletes balance skills to help them extend the limits of balance, so that they can shift their center of gravity farther outside their base of support, allowing them to skate more aggressively under control.

Hockey also requires stability—the resistance to disruption of equilibrium. Players can improve their ability to withstand bodychecks, wardoffs, and incidental body contact. During tight turns or crossovers, if they lose an edge and their mechanics break down, they are trained to regain balance instead of fall.

Consider a high-speed collision sport that relies on movement mechanics supported only by a thin skate blade over ice. One has to wonder why hockey players have not forever embraced structured balance training. Perhaps we did not understand that balance is highly trainable. Balance training overloads the variety of software that the muscles rely on to detect, read, and process biomechanical adjustments. We can also teach this software to compute accurate responses and command the muscles to get the job done right. This system of minibrains that sense shifts in body position and muscles that react with corrective actions is called proprioception. The result is greater control and efficiency of movement.

Visual feedback is an important part of the information loop used to process body awareness and changes to body position. But the human body is also armed with myriad sensors and receptors that collect proprioceptive data and determine each segment's position in space. These minibrains are located in muscles, tendons, ligaments, and joints, positioned to assess the relative position of each lever, deviations in the center of mass, body sway, speed of muscle lengthening, and a host of other moderators of posture and mechanics. These minibrains can be overloaded, trained, and improved. They can be challenged through structured exercise that will require them to read the situation to maintain balance or produce corrective actions to regain balance. When body parts change position, the information is detected and sent to the brain, which acts like a computer to determine what movement is needed to select a more skilled body position.

With training, minibrain sensors become more sensitive. They identify deviations sooner, thus shortening the neural response loop. Information is processed quicker, and response accuracy improves. The muscles receive precise, accurate instructions appropriate to the on-ice challenge.

PERFORMANCE BALANCE

Hockey features speed and impact played out on slippery terrain, making falls a given and rapid body adjustments a requirement. A highly trained proprioceptive system keeps players on their feet, able to capitalize on a body more reactive to unpredictable events. More specifically, balance helps transfer training results to hockey-specific strength, movement speed, and reactive agility.

Balance for Strength

A skater's perfect position to apply optimal power is his perfect position of balance. Even massive football linemen would get an edge through balance training. Likewise, hockey players need whole-body stability to battle well and avoid injury. With training, they can automatically assume a more stable position before applying or absorbing force.

Balance drills are also designed to improve joint stability by removing weak links in the body. Players often load up weight on the bench press and feel strong in the weight room. But in a standing position when applying force against an opponent, they are only as strong as their stabilizing muscles. And they need to find the most advantageous position, the most stable position, from which they can apply the most force. Balance drills train any weak links in the body, creating a stronger full body, one that can perform well in a standing position.

Although a balanced stance and a linked body increase the force that a player can create in a standing position, which helps when battling for the puck or blasting a slap shot from the point, skilled movement is not always about producing the most force. For optimal skill execution, some muscles must contract powerfully, other muscles must stabilize, and still others need to relax. Some of the working muscles need full-out efforts; others need to apply a small amount of force. Becoming in tune with the body to learn how to apply just the right amount of force enhances skilled and fluid movement.

Scott Niedermeyer of the Anaheim Ducks is one of the NHL's top skaters. A well-balanced skater is able to attack from a position of power.

Unstable training also helps develop ankle, knee, and hip strength. Strong, reactive ankles contribute significantly to achieving more aggressive edging, dramatically sharpening skating skills. Strong knees that can handle multiple position changes are also part of this. Improving ankle, knee, and hip joint integrity by training in unstable environments helps prevent common MCL, ACL, ankle inversion, and groin injuries.

Dynamic one-leg strength and balance is the common bond to hockey performance and an important foundation on which all other training builds. The better an athlete's single balance, the more he is prepared for advanced workouts. The most important feats of strength and balance will be required in unstable situations such as driving through traffic to the net or cycling in the corner and protecting the puck under tight check.

Balance for Movement

A player who hopes to improve acceleration must first work on deceleration and mechanics to achieve perfect transitional balance. Stopping under control into a perfect balanced position decreases the incidence of injury and sets up the player for proficient acceleration in the opposite direction. An important transition occurs between the eccentric loading (the stop) and the concentric contraction (the start). Transitional balance aims for proper weight distribution while activating all the deceleration muscles to brake into a perfectly balanced position, with knees flexed, center of gravity low and over the braking leg, and aggressive body lean. Essentially, players decelerate into the perfect starting mechanics.

Being in a perfect balance position is also important to each stride, whether executing linear power strides, crossing over, or skating backward. Achieving perfect balance on each stride will result in more movement per stride and less expenditure of energy, a powerful combination.

Balance for Reactive Agility

Balance is critical in a multidirectional sport such as hockey in which athletes are on one leg 80 percent of the time and change direction constantly. Well-trained balance and deceleration feed into first-step quickness. Improved deceleration becomes the illusion of quickness. Adding balance into the equation produces better movement. Quickness and agility are two key attributes that differentiate between top-level and lower-level players.

High-speed reactive agility becomes increasingly critical as players move up to higher levels. Each graduation to a higher league brings the challenge of having less time to make decisions, less time to cover a set amount of ice, and less time to execute skills and tactics. Opposing defenders are better skaters, more skilled, smarter, and better positioned; they get on their players sooner. Tighter competition space against more qualified opponents makes reactive agility an important asset.

At its core, hockey is already a game of organized chaos. A highly trained proprioceptive system makes the body more reactive to unpredictable events. Balance training improves muscle responsiveness and develops tremendous body awareness and coordination. Quite simply, reactive agility is dynamic balance expressed as fluid maneuverability.

PERFORMANCE BALANCE

1. Perfect point of balance = optimal position for power.
2. Movement balance = less energy expended per stride.
3. Transitional balance = optimal position for first-step quickness.
4. Reactive balance = optimal maneuverability.

TRAINING BALANCE

The key rule is that a player must be out of balance to train balance. For this reason, to train performance balance, we select only training tools and exercises that players cannot master. When a player perfects a balance exercise and is able to remain stable through every rep, she is no longer improving balance. She requires new exercises that keep her slightly unstable. Accessories such as stability balls and BOSU fit a hockey balance program because they accommodate an endless variety of exercises. A player needs to be able to select a more advanced drill to present a new level of difficulty. This progression improves the mind–muscle link, producing smart muscles that can perform complex moves.

For all ages and levels of players, balance training is fun because it has a pure element of play and athleticism. Trying to coordinate the body to succeed at a balance challenge is interesting. Players learn to focus and become more in tune with their bodies, an important shift for team sport athletes. Compared with individual sport athletes, hockey players push themselves very hard but tend just to *do* exercises. Track athletes, on the other hand, *execute* exercises, listening to their bodies, trying to perfect mechanics. With balance training, hockey players are forced to pay attention to the intricacies of their muscles, focusing on how the body can coordinate the required actions, building from the inside out.

To acclimate your players to the unstable environment, begin balance training with simple exercises that are safe and achievable. Coaches should know a regression for each exercise and be prepared to teach the exercise in segments. For example, players should learn and perfect the landing with pause holds before they perform the entire exercise sequence. Each player's preexercise checklist includes setting the core and midback (page 81), assuming an athletic ready stance (page 80), and checking proper foot position.

Most hockey players know how to fall. They get plenty of practice on the ice. Certainly, participating in balance training is much less risky for a hockey player than it is for a runner or the average fitness participant. Still, any player using a new training tool should be taught an exit strategy, so that he knows how to get off the equipment safely if he is not able to regain balance.

Performing a strength exercise such as a push-up in an unstable environment draws on additional muscles and increases muscle activation, increasing metabolic demands. Players must dial up many more muscle fibers in an attempt to handle the unstable condition.

For players just starting to get back into shape, upper-body, core, and leg balance exercises work well. They can easily sustain an elevated heart rate and expend more calories while participating in low-impact exercises that automatically help tune up the body, all of which are important features when they are resuming a program.

The level of difficulty in coordinating body mechanics to execute the exercise indicates balance intensity. This neural complexity places higher demands on the nervous system. Higher balance intensity produces greater muscle activation, a higher heart rate, and greater effort and focus.

Hockey players typically have good athleticism, like to be challenged, and learn quickly. As players improve, coaches need an inventory of drill progressions to provide their athletes with new challenges. Without adding load, speed, or displacement to the equation (for overload), balance training can be aggressively but safely progressed by increasing the level of instability or, by other means, the exercise complexity. These adjustments challenge coordination and flood the neuromuscular system with a new puzzle to solve.

Complexity may be achieved by simply selecting a more difficult exercise. But within each exercise, the player can narrow the base of support, shift to one leg, lengthen the lever, integrate load, close the eyes to take away that particular feedback, flood other sensors and receptors, or add combatives.

Combatives create unpredictable anomalies to normal movement that players regularly experience during competition. Such sensory overload teaches players to maintain sequential firing for fluidity of power production in the face of physical disturbances. Athletes at once must counteract the disturbance while continuing to produce the primary movement. This strategy will help athletes transfer full-body power gains into real sport application (not just a textbook study of a perfect skill-oriented movement), whether absorbing an open-ice hit, warding off a backchecker, containing an opponent against the boards, or fighting through a hook to release a shot on net.

As a conditioning rule, performing an exercise at a higher speed adds to the demand. But some balance exercises are more difficult to do at slower tempos. A very slow tempo heightens the muscular demand, drives up the heart rate, and brings an instant sweat response. Try the BOSU PSU superslow lat raise (page 94) at a tempo of 3:2:3 to grasp this concept.

The body functions as a unit, drawing on muscles in all parts of the body to produce the desired movement. Some muscles must contract to help produce movement, some contract to balance the body, and others contract to stabilize the spine and hold it in a safe, neutral position. Still other muscles kick in each time the body recognizes a shift in position or detects that it needs to correct an error, such as a loss of balance. Core stabilizers and spinal erectors are statically contracted to stabilize posture and fight forces of instability, protecting the spine and preventing falls. I prescribe unstable core exercises in a standing position to help develop postural muscles in a functional, reactive manner.

Balance drills are a part of prepractice and pregame dynamic warm-ups, referred to as nervous system activation. Off-season, for players working out early in the morning, I prefer to begin workouts with balance challenges to wake up the body and mind, ensuring attention for execution throughout the workout. Integrating balance with strength works well for in-season workouts when the exercise volume and workout duration is lower but the player still wants to accomplish as much as possible. The goal of the workout—developing strong and smart muscles—is consistent with the in-season focus on improving playing ability. Although players should strive to maintain the ability to lift heavier loads, the reality of the in-season often precludes this. A banged-up body from a few hard-hitting games may not allow a player to load up the bar with heavy weight. Using a moderate weight with instability can achieve excellent muscle activation and still effectively overload the muscles.

UPPER BODY AND CORE

Extreme Board Push-Ups

Purpose: Develop full-body stability, upper-body strength, and shoulder stability

Begin in a prone push-up position, with hands directly under the shoulders on the balance board. The back should be flat from shoulders to hips to ankles. Set your core. For the eccentric phase, flex slightly at the elbows, load body mass into the midback, and then lower the body and find a momentary state of balance with the chest slightly above the board. For the concentric phase, reestablish a balanced position before pushing up to the starting position by extending the arms at the elbows. The head and neck should stay naturally in line with the rest of the spine.

Advanced progressions:

- Progress to single-leg push-ups.
- Decrease speed of movement.

Stability Ball Jump Push-Ups With Pause Landing

Purpose: Develop full-body stability, upper-body strength and power, and shoulder stability

Begin in a prone push-up position, with hands on the stability ball and fingers pointing down. Set your core. Your back should be flat from shoulders to hips to ankles. For the eccentric phase, find a momentary state of balance before lowering your body toward the stability ball into the low phase of the push-up position by flexing at the elbows. For the concentric phase, forcefully push your body up and away from the ball, lifting your hands off the ball. When your hands return to the ball, stick the landing, maintaining core stability and pausing for 2 seconds before lowering into another rep.

Advanced progressions:

- After starting with very small hand displacement, increase the push-off height over a series of workouts.
- Change the position of the feet. Shift from a wide stable stance to a less stable narrow stance and eventually to a single-leg stance.

Stability Ball Hockey Stick Push-Ups

Purpose: Develop full-body stability, upper-body strength and power, and shoulder stability

Begin in prone position with the arms extended directly under the shoulders with a hockey stick on the stability ball. Grasp the stick with hands just slightly wider than shoulder-width and elbows slightly flexed. Set your core. Set up the appropriate amount of instability by choosing wide (stable) or narrow (more unstable) feet position. For the eccentric phase, lower the body by flexing at the elbows until the hands are in line with the chest and fingers are compressed into the ball at the midpoint, aiding stability. Maintain a flat line with the body from the shoulders to the ankles. For the concentric phase, raise the body away from the ball by extending at the elbows until you return to the starting position.

Advanced progressions:

- Slow the tempo of movement and include a pause hold halfway down.
- Increase the strength, stability, and reactive demands with a wider hand position on the stick.

Seated Humpty Dumpty Medicine Ball Passes

Purpose: Develop coordination, core stability, and dynamic balance in a read-and-respond environment

Face a partner who is 6 feet (2 meters) away from you. Each of you sits upright on a stability ball, with feet off the ground. While attempting to balance on the stability ball without touching the ground, pass the medicine ball chest to chest, back and forth with your partner. After catching, find the point of stability before initiating the next pass.

Advanced progressions:

- Increase the weight of the ball or increase the distance between partners.
- Pass the ball outside the body so that the partner has to catch off to the side.

Kneeling Stability Ball Balance With Lateral Shift

Purpose: Develop coordination, hip and core stability, and dynamic balance

Kneel up tall on a stability ball. Your back should be in flat position from knees to shoulders. While attempting to balance on the stability ball, shift your center of gravity laterally, pause to find your point of stability in this position, and then attempt to pull back to the midline, centered over the ball. Alternate sides.

Advanced progression: Progress the lateral distance a small amount until, over a large number of workouts, you are balancing on one knee, a feat that requires tremendous hip strength. When you move sideways far enough, your outside leg will roll off the top of the ball, netting the single-knee support and positioning the free foot close to the floor for a safe exit.

BOSU Lateral Two-Foot Jumps With Slastix Tubing ⬤DVD

Purpose: Develop core stability and dynamic balance to accommodate a load outside the midline

Place two BOSU balance trainers approximately 3 feet (1 meter) apart. Stand in an athletic ready position, holding Slastix tubing under strong stretch, in one hand at shoulder level with the elbow bent at 90 degrees and hand out in front of the elbow, away from the body. The line of pull on the tubing comes from behind the body. Triple extend through the ankle, knee, and hip to jump laterally toward the other BOSU balance trainer. Land on the second BOSU, contacting the surface with both feet simultaneously. Stick and hold the landing while continuing to keep the tubing out to the side of the body. Do not let the hand come into the shoulder. Your body can break down at its weakest link. Hold the landed position for 1 second after you regain balance and reestablish the hand position. Reverse the movement, jumping back to the original BOSU. Repeat drill with other arm.

Advanced progression: Select a heavier Slastix resistance or set up with a longer Slastix prestretch to increase the core strength required to land under control.

LOWER BODY

BOSU Alternate Single-Leg Jump and Land

Purpose: Develop single-leg dynamic balance and braking stability

Stand and balance on one leg, with the foot directly over the smallest circle (top) of the BOSU, chest up, and knee flexed. For the eccentric phase, lower the body by triple flexing at the ankle, knee, and hip. Ensure that the knee is tracking over the toes. For the concentric phase, forcefully reverse the movement by triple extending and jumping into the air, landing on the opposite leg. Stick the landing. Remain on that leg until you correct and regain balance. Then preload the leg before extending to jump off and land on the original leg. Common breakdowns include lateral flexion (side bend), forward flexion (forward bend), rotation around the hip, excessive arm movement, and unsteady ankle.

Advanced progressions:

- Preload to a deeper position before jumping off.
- Stick and hold the landing position longer.

BOSU Hockey Ready Position, Eyes Closed

Purpose: Challenge stability and develop dynamic balance

Begin in a hockey start position on the dome side of the BOSU, with knees flexed to a half squat, feet slightly wider than shoulder-width, chest up, and core braced. When you reach a point of stability, close your eyes. Your goal is to maintain stability and form, making minor corrections throughout the hold duration. If you feel out of control, open your eyes immediately and be ready to exit from the BOSU with a foot plant to the floor.

Advanced progressions:

- When solid in this exercise, have a partner push you lightly on your shoulders. You will need to counteract the push to maintain balance.
- Hold a hockey stick, blade down, in both hands. Have a partner push and pull on the stick.

Tennis Ball Drops Into Ready Position on BOSU

Purpose: Build quick hands and develop core stability with eccentric leg action while challenging balance

Put the BOSU platform side up. Stand in athletic position on the BOSU, with feet slightly wider than shoulder-width, hands at your sides, and chest up. A coach or partner stands in an upright position on the ground and holds a tennis ball in each hand at shoulder height, with palms down at arm's length. When the coach or partner drops one of the balls, quickly drop into a low athletic position by triple flexing at the ankle, knee, and hip, bringing the whole body down to catch the ball. Catch with hips low and trunk upright (chest up). When you catch the ball and achieve a point of stability, return to upright position.

Advanced progressions:

- Catch the ball with an overhand grip, which requires faster and smoother eccentric leg loading.
- Next add a cross-body catch, using the right hand to catch balls on the left side of the body and the left hand for balls on the right side of the body.

BOSU Split Lunge to Single-Leg Hold

Purpose: Build whole-body balance and core stability while integrating movement

Begin in a split squat position, front foot on the platform side of the BOSU directly in the middle, over the plug. The opposite arm is forward with the lead leg. Knees track over the toes. The back foot is balanced on the toes. For the concentric phase, initiate movement by extending at the knee and hip of the leg on the BOSU. Drive the knee of the back leg up and forward until the thigh is parallel to the floor. Move the arms athletically in opposition to the legs. Finish tall and pause at the top of the movement. For the eccentric phase, lower the body by triple flexing at the ankle, knee, and hip, returning to the starting position, cycling the arms and legs, and reaching back behind with the back foot. Switch leg positions for the second set.

Advanced progression: Complete the same exercise with the BOSU dome side up. This progression adds a lunge and requires more ankle stability. In this variation, stand behind the BOSU and lunge one leg on top of the BOSU into a split squat position. Follow the same exercise sequence but finish by pushing off the BOSU back to the start position with both legs behind the BOSU.

BOSU Lateral Bounds With Pause Holds

Purpose: Build whole-body balance, core stability, and transitional balance

Set up with one foot halfway down the BOSU convex dome surface. Plant the other foot on the floor, with feet wider than shoulder-width. Practice shifting body mass back and forth over the top of each leg. Next, shift weight to load up the BOSU leg and flex at the ankle, knee, and hip to hold a partial squat for 2 seconds. Drop the opposite foot back to the floor and repeat for the desired rep count before switching legs. Note that the BOSU foot always stays in place; the other foot moves on and off the floor.

Advanced progression: Remove the BOSU foot, loading up the outside leg. Triple extend through the ankle, knee, and hip and push off the toes to bound laterally toward the BOSU. Reach out with the lead leg to land safely on the inside convex BOSU surface with the ankle flexed and toes pulled up toward the shin to protect the ankle. Land softly and flex fluidly at the ankle, knee, and hip to absorb into a deep landing position. After you achieve a momentary state of balance, initiate a bound back to the starting position on the floor.

Lateral Crossover, Stick the Landing

DVD

Purpose: Build single-leg balance and core stability while integrating hockey movement

Balance on the left leg, with knee flexed. Preload into a deeper position before initiating movement by triple extending the leg and reaching out laterally with the right lead leg. Drive the back arm across the body to assist the action. After the right leg plants on the floor, cross the left (back) leg over the right leg. The right leg is now in a cross-under position, which you use to push off to help produce more movement. Finish by pushing off the left leg and landing laterally into the right lead leg on a positive angle, with hips inside the foot position. Load to a deep position and maintain balance. Repeat back and forth in both directions.

Advanced progression: Achieve a longer distance, producing more movement on each phase of the exercise and absorbing greater lateral eccentric braking at the finish point.

Extreme Balance Squats to Knock-Offs

Purpose: Build whole-body balance, core stability, and an even hockey ready stance

Begin in athletic position on the balance board, with feet evenly spaced, chest up, and upper body relaxed and under control. For the eccentric phase, descend into the low phase of a squat, fighting to find a balanced position. In the bottom phase, maintain a balanced position for 3 seconds, with trunk upright and knees tracking over the toes. For the concentric phase, after you have achieved a momentary state of balance, initiate the up phase of the squat by extending at the knee and hip until you have returned to athletic position.

Advanced progressions:

- In the squat hold position, have a partner tap you on the shoulders. Progressively add stronger pushes.
- Add speed to the eccentric drop. From the athletic ready stance, quickly drop down into the finished squat position, attempting to load both legs evenly.
- Remove the balance board plugs to give additional movement in the sagittal plane.

BOSU T Plyometric Jumps

Purpose: Develop the legs and improve landing stability

Stand to the left of the BOSU. Jump laterally to land on top of the BOSU with both feet (*a*). Stick and hold the landing. Jump backward off the BOSU, landing on the floor behind the BOSU. Immediately jump on top of the BOSU again and stick the landing. Jump off laterally to the right side (*b*), land on the floor, and quickly jump back to the top of the BOSU. Begin by loading each floor landing into a deep squat and jump high out of each jump, building leg power through a full range of motion.

Advanced progressions:

- Increase quickness off the floor by loading into a quarter squat before popping the feet off the ground right away, back onto the BOSU. Still stick and hold on the BOSU.
- Take less time to rest or perform longer sets so that you are performing under fatigue. Have a coach or trainer assess your movement skills and body mechanics to determine when you need to stop the drill for safety.

a   b

Chapter 7

Quickness

As an undergraduate student in the mid-1980s, I once selected sport conditioning as a project theme. Much of the information accessible came from track and field. Powerlifting, high-impact plyometrics, and linear sprinting dominated the programs. But much was unknown, and key variables of performance had not yet been identified. Athletes did not train for balance. Reaction skills were referred to as reflexes. Coaches did not differentiate between speed and quickness. Even professors stumbled over definitions of agility, which seemed to be some intangible, elusive construct. Today we enjoy greater clarity on the specific differences between each component of performance.

Several variables are related to quickness. Speed refers to acceleration and top-end velocity. Agility refers to complex whole-body multidirectional patterns, and reactivity is responsiveness to external stimuli. Quickness is first-step explosiveness and lightning footwork. Clearly differentiating these concepts is important because each requires different drills and rules of training.

Traditional speed training using the track sprint model has limited utility for on-ice stop-and-starts and tight turns in which players load their legs and shift their centers of mass outside their base of support to use their sharp skate edges to produce immediate and explosive force in the opposite direction.

Coaches dream of players with "explosive speed"—but much of their vision of a dangerous hockey player is quickness. Quickness is the first-step explosion from a stationary position or to exit out of deceleration. It is evident as the first move that follows a reaction. Players also draw on quickness during repetitive fast footwork such as repeated crossovers when cycling out of the corner. Hockey is a game of one-on-one battles and races for loose pucks. The ability to initiate movement faster than opponents is critical—teams rarely lose if they are consistently the first to the puck and always right on top of the play.

During a hockey game, quickness is manifested in many ways: to execute the draw on a face-off, to drop down and position the body to block a shot or make a save, to cross over and accelerate away from an opponent, to stop quickly and control the body to maintain a defensive position, to shoot the puck, and to deliver a bodycheck. First-step quickness produces game-breaking plays.

A player has the advantage if he can initiate movement and skate at a higher speed sooner than his opponents, who may just be getting their first steps going. Although speed is all about acceleration, first-step quickness is about stopping and starting. Quickness contributes to one-on-one tactics by enabling the player to cut on a dime. Aggressive braking from high speed is a deceptive tactic that is difficult to contain. In shortening the time to move from point A to point B, the rate of the stop is as important as the rate of the start. In fact, the rate of the stop contributes to a faster start. Plyometric training harnesses the mechanisms of these phenomena.

THE POWER OF PLYOMETRICS

Over the past decade, plyometric training has become an integral part of athletics training programs for coaches in most multidirectional sports. Strength and explosive power are the foundation for success in anaerobic (sprinting energy systems) sports such as hockey, rugby, basketball, and football. Today all top hockey coaches and trainers integrate plyometrics into their hockey-specific conditioning programs. Their goal is to take weight room strength gains and better express explosive power on the ice in the form of stops and starts, aggressive exits out of turns, slap shots, bodychecks, and dynamic skating patterns.

Plyometric training refers to a distinct method of training for power or explosiveness. It is a method of training, not a specific exercise. Jump training in the 1970s targeted depth drops from high heights converted into vertical jumps and massive bounding drills. Coaches today prescribe exercises more specific to hockey, including single-leg multidirectional moves, lateral moves, and whole-body rotary power. Emphasizing the appropriate intensity on the landing and loading of the legs prevents deceleration injuries and forms the base to drive up acceleration.

I measure plyometric intensity by the impact caused by the amount of displacement. A jump from a greater height will, by nature, impose greater stress on the muscles, ligaments, and bones. For me, the risk outweighs the benefit. When jumping and bounding, the joints must absorb body weight as it lands on the ground. This impact can greatly stress the joints. The greater the height of the jump, the more force the ankle, knee, hip, and spine have to endure. Also, the more an athlete weighs, the greater the risk of injury. Players who weigh 220 pounds (100 kilograms) stress their joints far more than do players who weigh 170 pounds (77 kilograms). And the lower the relative strength, the greater the risk of injury. Players who weigh 170 pounds and lack sufficient muscle development and leg strength are also at risk.

Players in the pubertal phase of growth and maturation, who are developing longer skeletal levers but have not yet built muscles of corresponding mass and strength, experience their peak height velocity. The joints connecting longer bones are less able to handle lateral deceleration forces; epipheaseel growth plates do not like repeated high impact; and a player's new height throws off his mechanics. Traditional plyometrics must be avoided during this period of awkward growth when players are more susceptible to injury.

Many athletes have participated in traditional plyometrics and netted excellent gains without injury. But today's plyometric exercise options reduce the risk of injury. Most modern plyometric drills were created with the dual goal of producing sport-specific benefits and improving explosiveness without totally thrashing the legs, training for results but with consideration for decreasing the recovery time. This attribute is important for hockey players, who also tax their legs by doing strength training, anaerobic sprint intervals, balance drills, agility drills, speed training, on-ice practice, and power skating. Multisport athletes face these daily demands all year long.

Thrashing is a nonscientific term, but it accurately describes the level of stress that high-impact plyometrics impose on the legs. Regeneration time is required to repair and prepare for more physical challenges during the next workout, practice, or game.

A quick, easy generalization to help differentiate between plyometric exercises for first-step quickness and plyometric exercises for speed focuses on the depth of landing, the effort required to initiate power, and the focus on powering through triple extension. In training stride power for speed, players land or stop lower (deep) and power back the opposite way through a full stride. For pure quickness, they strive to pop the feet off the ground immediately, coupling the eccentric and concentric phases. In quickness plyometrics, the hips drop only slightly and the knees flex just a couple of inches (5 centimeters). First-step quickness and foot rapidity are trained through two key methods: short-range plyometric coupling and lightning foot repeat drills.

PLYOMETRIC SCIENCE

Plyometrics involve a rapid eccentric contraction immediately followed by a concentric contraction, which allows for a more powerful concentric contraction. When a player puts on the brakes to stop, she rapidly loads the muscle with an eccentric (muscle lengthening), or negative, contraction, with an effort to follow immediately with a concentric (muscle shortening), or positive, contraction. This technique results in more explosive power initiation. You see this kind of movement during the quick backswing before an explosive slap shot or a quick stop with rapid knee flexion and an immediate explosion into action in the opposite direction.

Sensors in the muscle spindles keep track of the length of the muscle and its rate of lengthening. If the muscle is lengthened quickly, as when the legs bend to absorb a quick two-foot stop, the sensors detect this and inform the brain, which tells the muscle to contract immediately to protect itself. This contraction helps the player transition abruptly out of a stop. This kind of countermovement is common to many hockey actions and the key component of plyometric training.

The countermovement also produces potential kinetic energy. Muscle is a pliable tissue that stores elastic energy when quickly lengthened, as a stretched elastic band does. An immediate transition to move in the oppo-site direction harnesses this elastic energy for more powerful movement. Loading slowly or pausing at the bottom of the countermovement does not contribute to a quicker first step, because the extra potential energy is lost as heat. Likewise, the muscle sensors no longer signal for explosive muscle action.

A balanced and even landing, fast lowering on the braking phase, and quick coupling between the braking and starting all contribute to an explosive first step. An effective countermovement is evident when defense-men prepare for open-ice bodychecks. Just before hitting an approaching opponent, a defenseman will quickly drop the hips and bend at the knees, and then immediately explode in the opposite direction to deliver the bodycheck. Plyometrics are a key link from strength and lean muscle mass to quickness and explosive power.

PLYOMETRIC TOOLS

New training equipment makes plyometric exercise safer while producing more specific results. This new equipment has helped me modify and create drills that will transfer onto the ice and reduce the strain on the knees and shins. The traditional use of high jump heights to shock the muscles and load up the eccentric phase produced heavy loading on the muscles and high impact on the bones and joints at a high velocity, increasing the risk of ACL injury and repetitive strain stress fractures. Microhurdles and ladders keep the feet close to the ground, emphasizing rapid footwork and minimizing impact. Ladders provide structure for lightning footwork drills, forcing players to keep their feet moving. Microhurdles can be arranged to work hockey-specific patterns: stops and starts, backward-to-forward motions, and lateral movement.

BOSU balance trainers are used for plyometric jump drills. The player is quick off the floor and then sticks and holds the landing on the BOSU. The cue is "quick-stick." The aim is fast movement off the floor as opposed to jump height. Athletes should aim for explosiveness at the point of foot contact on the ground but stick and hold each landing on the BOSU. To improve the focus on each rep, they should pause after each landing atop the BOSU before continuing through the pattern. These drills improve the foot–ground relationship, increasing the rate of the stop-and-start, while adding benefit from the unstable stick-and-hold on the BOSU. The drills add to the ability to stop in balance, decrease the risk of injury from deceleration and direction change, and provide a high-quality eccentric loading that will best funnel into acceleration.

A Power Plyo box system can be set up in different configurations for resisted vertical jumps and angled lateral jumps. Flat-topped plyometric boxes of three heights will accommodate players of different heights and permit the fine-tuning necessary for training explosiveness. The angled-side configuration permits independent leg action and provides a safe surface to absorb lateral moves, protecting the ankles and mimicking the joint angles required on the ice for aggressive stops and starts and cornering. The resisted vertical jumps emphasize leg explosiveness.

HOCKEY BENEFITS

Plyometric training is the best method to ready the player for on-ice quickness. As Jeremy Roenick notes, "For overall explosiveness, if you want to be a faster and quicker player, then plyometrics is going to be of tremendous benefit to you."

• **Shifting gears**. A forward in full flight down the wing can tax defensemen beyond their abilities by shifting gears. Instantaneous speed adjustments, rapidly alternating between decelerating and accelerating, challenge defensemen to read and react to maintain coverage. When the forward sees the defenseman shift his weight in reaction to the forward's quick change in speed (deceleration), the forward can then explode back up a gear, cutting laterally inside to the net or moving around the defenseman. The ability to quickly change speed while already skating is extremely effective in throwing off a defender. Being able to shift from fourth gear down to second and back up to fifth in the blink of an eye is a valuable offensive tool that makes the attacker more deceptive.

• **Checking**. Quickness, combined with strength, is also useful during open-ice bodychecks. When perfectly executed, bodychecks are one of the most beautiful hockey movements. Strength is an obvious component of the movement, but to execute open-ice hits correctly, a player has to be able to read the play and react quickly to move into position for the hit. Then he must quickly lower his body into a power position and thrust explosively upward, first with the legs and then quickly following through with the arms. The weight transfer from low to high must be explosive to overpower an opponent who is skating in the opposite direction. This technique can also be used to check players against the boards, ward off defensemen when driving to the net, and by defensemen retrieving dumped-in pucks, and overpowering a forechecking opponent.

• **Skating quickly**. Hockey players can gain an edge on their competition by improving their foot speed. Fast-feet drills lead to better first-step quickness, more explosive changes in direction, and enhanced agility. When a player sees a breakdown in the play, good reads and quick reaction skills are only one piece of the equation. She must be able to capitalize on the opportunity with fast feet. One style of drills for quickness uses plyometric coupling to improve first-step quickness. Other drills are used to keep the feet moving.

In a game with tight one-to-one checking as well as team systems to back that up, players who can fire their feet quickly, keep their feet moving, and always be in action will be successful. Coaches must forever remind players to keep their feet moving! By quickly turning over the feet, a player creates separation between herself and a defender. This technique allows the player to get to the net quickly and get in position to score before being checked. The player becomes a threat even when in the corner. When opponents learn that a player has fast feet and is difficult to contain tightly, they will make the mistake of backing off and giving the player space.

Pure fast-feet drills are not specific to the skating movement pattern or leg movements needed to change direction. The purpose at this stage is to increase the mind's ability to command the muscles to fire quickly.

QUICKNESS TRAINING GUIDELINES

At all ages and all levels, at any time in the training schedule, players should learn new drills by beginning with slow movement. They should not increase foot speed until their technique is perfect. New drills should be introduced at warm-up pace so that players can safely learn proper technique and acclimate to new demands.

A training program that incorporates a variety of drills to develop overall athleticism and coordination is critical during the neural maturation period from age 0 to about age 12, the prepubertal phase of growth and maturation. At young ages, agility is more important than quickness to ongoing development. Coaches should devote a greater volume of drills to agility and less to quickness.

Repetition is key. Players need enough practice time to learn, correct, rehearse, and benefit from each drill. For example, if a ladder is set up to drill quickness, select four footwork patterns and repeat four times rather than do eight patterns twice each.

Preparticipation screening is necessary to be sure that players are ready for plyometric training. Readiness for plyometrics used to be tested by the player's ability to squat 1.5 to 2.0 times his body weight. My current method is to see whether a player can skip and play hopscotch—I am sure you get what I mean! Most young hockey players can do low-intensity plyometric exercises, but they should first complete a 6- to 8-week strength program before participating in quickness drills. After improving their strength base and muscle readiness, players can begin with a small volume of drills (six to eight sets).

Trainers need to keep initial drills simple. Before increasing tempo, they should make sure that players can land and stop in balance. Players should hold each direction change transition point for 2 seconds. Players must pass through this pause-and-hold version of each quickness drill, demonstrating that they can coordinate the deceleration mechanics, before going full out. Then when players can execute the entire exercise at top speed, the trainer can later add similar exercises to the volume or replace an exercise with a more demanding one, netting the same volume.

To enter each exercise, the player establishes a ready position with knees flexed and hips low. If a player has to move into the ready position before he is set to accelerate, he will suffer a critical delay in initiating the required movement. The player needs to keep his center of gravity within the base of support. The less lateral weight transfer that the player has to absorb, the more rapid is the foot movement that he can achieve. An aggressive angle, with hips outside the base of support, can increase power, but for pure fast-feet drills, players should keep the feet close to the midline and minimize vertical displacement. They should keep the feet close to the ground, eliminate impact forces, and focus on turning over foot position rapidly. The sound of the movement offers a useful cue. Players should eliminate any loud pounding on the floor by modifying their technique to ensure a soft landing.

Quickness training is quality, not quantity, training that requires full-out effort for a few strides followed by active recovery. Improvement is not just a physical adaptation that requires overload; it is a neuromuscular adaptation that requires explosive and correct movement patterns with perfect technique. This adaptation increases the ability of the brain to turn on the machine more quickly. Players should perform at full effort until neuromuscular fatigue occurs. Trainers should not seek to induce physical fatigue. When fatigued, explosiveness slows and technique falters. Instead, athletes should rapidly complete precise movements so that the neuromuscular system learns to organize high-velocity movements. Limit drill duration to 10 seconds, ensuring the ATP-PC energy system dominates.

Rest intervals must be long enough that the player does not begin any repetition in a fatigued state. This is not a test of endurance. Between-set recovery time should allow the player to attack each drill in a perfect condition to generate the fastest movement possible. A 1:5 work-to-rest ratio provides time to resynthesize enough ATP to fuel another high-quality drill. For 24 athletes, four groups of 6 is the ideal setup; while 4 players complete the drill, 20 rest. Line of 4 players waiting their turns establishes the 1:5 ratio without requiring microattention to a stopwatch to time rest periods. Focus on the execution of active players and let the lines roll through.

Incorporate visual or auditory stimulus in varied movement patterns. For example, drop a ball in front of players so that they have to explode into action to catch it before it hits the ground again. Work in a tight, confined area with several repeats in 10 seconds.

Plyometric drills can be modified to be easier on the joints. Athletes can make the following modifications to obtain quickness benefits but ease stress on the joints:

- Increase foot quickness by popping the feet off the ground. As in a game of hot potatoes, as soon as the foot starts to touch the ground, pop it back off again. Pop off the balls of the feet. Try to increase the number of foot contacts made in a set amount of time.
- Practice quickly reversing movement and exploding in the opposite direction.
- In an effort to turn the feet over faster, a tendency is to pound harder on the ground. Listen to the foot strike and aim to produce no sound. Silence comes from soft landings.

- Eliminate the pause that occurs at the exact point at which the direction of movement is going to reverse. This point is the coupling time between the eccentric and concentric contractions. A pause between lowering and pushing off will lose the potential elastic energy and turn off the muscle sensors, detracting from the potential power for the push-off. Focus on coupling the stop and start as opposed to lowering into a deep loading.
- Keep the feet close to the ground, where they return sooner for additional foot contacts. In sport, movement occurs only when the foot is in contact with the ground, applying force.
- First, complete two-legged drills to share the load and maximize quickness. Next, add simple drills with a single leg, starting slowly with low volume but progressively training until each leg can coordinate well with equal independent quickness.

QUICKNESS

Forward Line Drill

Purpose: Develop quick feet

For method A, face toward a line on the floor. Stand ready with knees slightly flexed and your weight on the toes. Move through the complete pattern (illustration), with two quick touches behind the line followed by one foot touch in front of the line. Next, complete the same pattern, but when planting L3 and R6, turn your foot in (inwardly rotate leg from hip).

For method B, face away from the line and complete the reverse pattern (two quick touches in front of the line and one step behind the line).

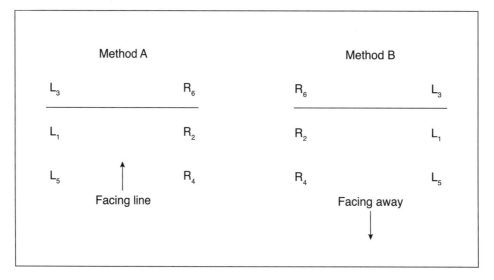

Lateral Crossover Line Drill

Purpose: Develop quick feet in the crossover pattern, dryland and on the ice

Stand to the right of a line on the floor, sideways to the line. Jumping up, touch your right foot and then your left foot to the ground. Cross your outside (right) foot over the inside foot and plant it across the line (R3). Next, unload your right foot and load up the left foot. Then touch the right foot to the ground and cross the left over the right, landing the left across the line (L6). These are repetitive crossovers back and forth across the line. For method A (illustration), keep your foot touches close to the line. For method B, move side to side as wide as possible, so that you perform more lateral movement.

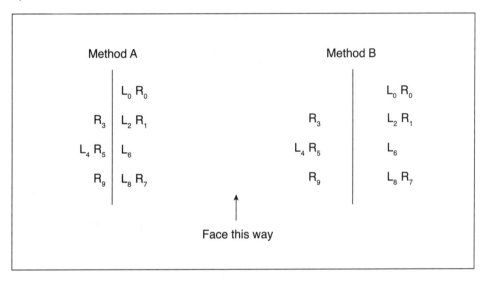

Octagon Drill

Purpose: Build quick feet, directional change, and agility

Set up an octagon pattern with agility slats. Begin in the middle of the pattern with feet close together, weight on the toes, and knees slightly flexed. Hop up to the first position and immediately return to the middle. Complete the entire pattern without pausing at any position. When landing at each position, overcome the countermovement and spring out to the next spot. Complete the pattern once clockwise and once counterclockwise.

Variations:

- Adjust the agility slats to make the octagon smaller to accommodate lower strength or to increase the countermovement pace.
- Advanced athletes can complete the pattern with a single leg.

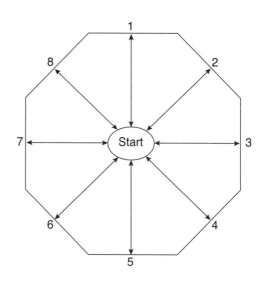

HURDLES

Two-Foot Lateral Hurdle Hops

Purpose: Develop leg quickness, lateral movement, and countermovement speed

Line up five microhurdles, spaced about 3 feet (1 meter) apart. Stand beside the first hurdle, with feet close together. Hop sideways over all the hurdles. Be sure that both feet land on the ground at exactly the same time. Immediately return over the hurdles to the starting position.

Variations:

- If you land unevenly or with excessive body or arm movement, regress to improve the quickness foundation. Land deeper and emphasize a higher jump. This approach slows the movement and emphasizes the landing phase.
- Advance the drill by incorporating a two-down, one-back hop sequence. Jump over two hurdles, return over one, jump over two hurdles, and so on. Try to maintain pace on the direction change.

Two-Foot Hurdle Zigzag Hops

Purpose: Develop leg quickness, lateral movement, and countermovement speed

Line up 10 microhurdles turned end to end. Stand with feet close together, knees flexed, and ready to start at one end. Hop down the hurdles in a zigzag pattern. Land close to the hurdle and use a low jump height for a pure quick-feet drill.

Variation: Try jumping for more lateral distance, landing as far from the hurdles as possible while minimizing the decrease in countermovement pace. Keep the hips angled toward the hurdles while the feet land farther away.

LADDERS

Ladder drills improve footwork and foot speed. Ladder rungs are foot placement markers that bring replicable structure to footwork drills. Because the rungs are a set distance apart, athletes cannot increase their stride length as their center of mass moves from stationary and accelerates. Ladder drills emphasize leg turnover and foot frequency.

Lateral Two In, Two Out

Purpose: Develop footwork quickness

At one end of the ladder, start by straddling the outside bottom end of the first rung. The shoulders are back, the core is set, and the eyes are up, looking down the ladder. Place one foot into the rung followed by the second foot (two in). Step out of the ladder with the first foot and then with the second foot so that you are now straddling the ladder again just below the second rung (two out). Continue this all the way down the ladder. Be sure to switch your starting leg so that you use both the right and left foot as the lead foot.

Variation: Try to keep the tempo so that the two in steps are not separated from the two out steps. Stay close to the ladder and work on fast footwork and soft contacts with the ground.

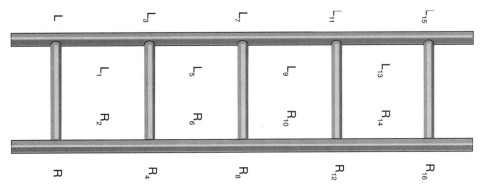

Quick-Feet Narrow Shuffle

DVD

Purpose: Develop footwork quickness while increasing the complexity of movement skills

Begin placing one foot inside the first rung. The second foot steps into the rung beside the first foot. The first foot now steps out of the ladder and the second foot moves up to the next rung. The first foot, which is now outside the ladder, joins the second foot inside the second rung. The second foot steps outside the ladder and first foot moves up to the third rung. The pattern continues down the length of the ladder.

Variation:

After establishing the movement pattern, increase lateral movements, making the pattern move more laterally outside the ladder. This variation will add more movement skills for agility, developing positive body weight transfer for direction change.

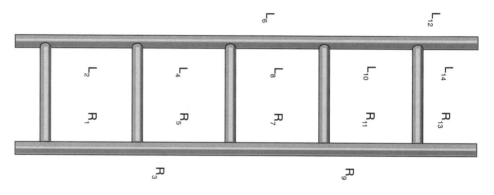

Single-Leg Zigzag

DVD

Purpose: Challenge balance while developing quickness; develop single-leg eccentric landing control of forward, lateral, and rotational stability; develop quick coupling and explosive takeoffs into the next hop

Start on one foot outside the ladder. Perform consecutive zigzag hops as quickly as possible down the ladder by hopping in and out of the rungs. Hop into the first rung, hop diagonally outside the second rung, and then hop diagonally back into the third rung. Continue this pattern all the way down the ladder so that you hop into every other rung.

After landing with triple flexion, quickly reverse direction with triple extension and hop to the next position. Hips and shoulders must remain square, and the core must be stable throughout. The foot should land outside the hip, creating a positive body angle. This skill requires increased focus on balance and linked system control; absorption of explosive angular, vertical, and rotational deceleration in an unstable landing position; and quick, explosive movement from one hop to the next.

Variation: Try hopping into every rung. This variation will decrease the load on the landing but increase the number of foot contacts. A progression to this pattern is taking the hops wider outside the ladder.

Crossovers

Purpose: Develop quick movement skills, lightning quick footwork, and lateral movement

Start to the right of the first rung. With the right foot, cross over into the ladder. With the left foot, step to the outside of the second rung. With the right foot, step out beside the left foot, getting into position on the left side of the ladder. (Cue words are "cross step in, two steps out"). Now the left foot is free to cross into the third rung. Continue the pattern quickly down the ladder, crossing into every other rung. Focus on keeping the hips and shoulders square, with your body weight centered down the midline. This technique will enable you to stay narrow to the ladder and execute fast steps.

Variation:

- Increase foot contacts by crossing into every rung.
- The drill can be progressed by increasing the lateral distance of the crossovers and changing the tempo of the steps. Increasing the lateral movement of the steps will improve directional changes and movement skills. The tempo should go as follows: quick, quick, stick. The two quick steps are the second foot contacts on the outside of the ladder followed by the crossover step into the ladder. The stick is then on the wide lateral outside step.

BOSU

T-Drill

Purpose: Challenge balance and develop multidirectional explosive movement skills

Start on top of the BOSU in an athletic ready position. Jump off the BOSU with both feet at the same time and land to the left of the BOSU. Both feet should contact the floor at the same time and land shoulder-width apart. Land softly with triple flexion. Quickly pop off the ground and immediately change direction, jumping back onto the BOSU. Repeat this sequence but jump to the back of the BOSU. To complete the T pattern, jump back onto the BOSU and then jump to the right. For every takeoff and landing, the feet should leave and contact the floor or BOSU at the same time with triple flexion.

Variation: Add reaction skills by shadowing a coach or another athlete. That way, you have to react to the change in directions (left, right, or back) as well as a change in jumping tempo.

POWER PLYOMETRICS

Backward Depth Drops Into Drop Steps

Purpose: Develop explosiveness and improve movement skills specific to turning backward to forward

Start in an athletic ready position on a plyometric box 12 to 15 inches (30 to 38 centimeters) high, with your back to a coach. Step off the back of the box, absorb the landing, and drop step to either the right or left. When executing the drop step, rotate your hip 45 degrees in the desired direction and load the other leg to explode off. Take three to four strides in the desired direction before putting the brakes on. Repeat, switching the direction of the drop step.

Variation: Drop step in the direction given by the coach. As soon as you step off the box, the coach will cue you which direction to go. You must react as soon as you land.

Two-Foot Drops to Reactive Cut

Purpose: Develop explosive reaction skills for starting forward at an angle

Start on top of a box 12 to 15 inches (30 to 38 centimeters) high in an athletic ready position. Step off the box, absorb the landing through triple flexion, and react to a coach's cue to cut left or right. Externally rotate your hip to open it in the direction that you will run. Sprint for three to four strides before putting the brakes on. Repeat, switching the direction that you go.

Single-Leg Drop Into Lateral Jump

Purpose: Develop single-leg multidirectional explosiveness

Stand on a Power Plyo box 12 to 15 inches (30 to 38 centimeters) high in athletic ready position. Step off the box with the appropriate leg in the direction to which you are laterally jumping; if going left, step off leading with the right leg and vice versa. After landing, prepare for the change of direction by engaging the core and triple flexing the ankle, knee, and hip. Pop and explode laterally off one foot in the desired direction, using the arms to lead the leg movement.

Hurdle Maze Drill

DVD

Purpose: Develop fast feet and explosive movement skills in multiple directions

Set up several microhurdles randomly facing forward and sideways. Stand in athletic position beside the first hurdle. Preload the legs and have the arms ready to lead the movement. Triple extend through the ankles, knees, and hips, jumping with both feet over each hurdle in the maze, facing the same direction the whole time so that jumps are going forward as well as laterally. Do every landing and takeoff so that the feet leave and contact the ground at the same time and stay hip-width apart.

Variation: Learn the drill with deep range-of-motion jumps. Then progress to popping the feet quickly off the ground. The drill can also be advanced to single-leg hops.

ON-ICE DRILLS

React and Sprint Tennis Ball Drops

DVD

Purpose: Build first-step explosiveness

A coach stands with arms extended at the sides, holding a tennis ball in each hand about 6 inches (15 centimeters) higher than the shoulders. Stand a set distance from and square to the coach, with slight knee flexion and weight forward on toes, ready to explode into action. The coach drops one ball. As the ball leaves the coach's hand, react and sprint after the ball, trying to catch it after only one bounce. Perform this drill with no stick and use strong edging for a stationary start. Use the cue "drop and go" to remind yourself to load your legs in place for a quicker start.

Variations:

- Follow the same procedure but use a sideways start. Alternate starting by facing left or right, so that you have to react, open, and explode toward the dropped ball.

- Follow the same procedure but face away from the coach (with your back to the coach). Begin in the same ready position. The coach calls, "Drop" and drops one ball. React, turn with a quick rotation of the hips, sprint out, and cut toward the dropped ball.

Quick-Pivot Drill

Purpose: Build quickness, agility, and first-step acceleration

Always complete this drill while carrying a puck. Start on one side of the ice, carrying a puck. Build up speed to approach the first cone at high speed. Keep the hips low and the feet moving fast. Use tight pivots around the cones and pick up your feet as soon as you come around the cone. Force yourself to pick up your feet sooner than you would if you wanted to feel comfortable. Finish with a shot from the slot and return to the line.

Variations:

- For advanced skaters, increase the width between cones or decrease the length between cones.

- Players can go through on a single leg (without a puck), transferring their weight to work off both the inside and outside edges.

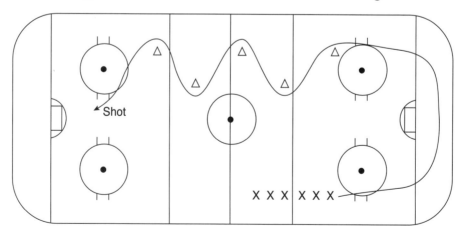

Quick Pivot, Low Drive to Net

Purpose: Develop quick feet, agility, and puckhandling

Start close to the blue line. A coach shoots the puck around the boards. Move to the boards to trap the puck and keep it inside the blue line. Immediately sprint through the cones with quick feet and tight pivots. Force the feet to pick up and cross over coming off the cone. When skating around the cone in the corner, explode and attack the net, moving up and around the slot cone. Shoot as soon as you step around the last cone in the slot.

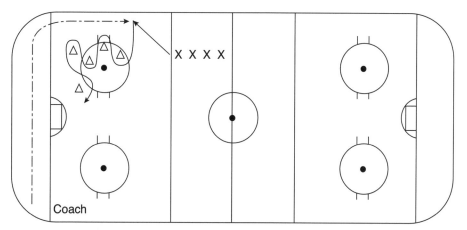

Red-to-Blue Stop-and-Start Race

DVD

Purpose: Build quickness, agility, and first-step acceleration

Start on the blue line in line with the face-off dot. The other player starts in the same position but on the other side of the ice. On the whistle, both of you sprint to the red line, complete a two-foot stop, accelerate back to where you started, and complete another two-foot stop. Then accelerate back to the red line and complete a third two-foot stop. The coach lays a puck in the middle of the ice. Race for the puck and play the puck as a one-on-one to the net. Execute all stops facing the middle of the ice and in a straight line.

Variations:

- Change the starts from crossover starts to open-hip side starts.
- Start forward. When you get to the blue line, pivot backward and skate backward back to the blue line. Then pivot forward and finish the drill.

Chapter 8

Agility and Reactivity

In a hockey game, agility and reactivity can make the difference in a number of offensive and defensive situations. Quick reactions and agile movements can make or break plays, win or lose games, and be the difference between avoiding and sustaining an injury.

High-speed agility and reactivity are undoubtedly the strongest discriminators between star major pro players and stalled minor pro players. An analysis of game-breaking plays will show that most result from an explosive tactic—the quickest players will always dominate team sports that involve one-on-one confrontations. Nowhere is this more evident than in ice hockey, in which strategies follow a pattern of read, react, and explode.

Agility is the ability to change direction quickly, effectively, and efficiently while under control and visually aware. An agile hockey player is able to move dynamically but remain ready to respond by adjusting movements in any direction. Players often display agility as a series of continuous changes in direction. In fact, agility can be thought of as multidirectional quickness.

Reflexes occur naturally in the body and at a pre-determined rate inherent in the body. Sport skills however require conscious thought; the decision to move and implementation of movement determines reaction time, a highly trainable attribute. Reactivity refers to muscle responsiveness, the ability of a nimble mind to make quick decisions and whole-body adjustments to environmental challenges. For example, a player being cross-checked while skating or stopping may jump into a lane that opens up. The speed of muscle responsiveness is moderated by the mind for responses that are not reflexive but actually reactive. These cognitive decisions can happen faster when more automatic after training. Reaction time is moderated by agility, which provides the fluid movement skills, and reactivity, which contributes fast responsiveness of both the mind and the muscles to seed direction change.

Explosive agility and muscle responsiveness allow small athletes to prosper in a big man's game and give large-mass players another dimension to their game. Both require the skills to perform complex maneuvers rapidly. Small players use agility and reactivity as the point of difference that provides a competitive advantage in lieu of size and absolute strength. Large power forwards add these attributes to redefine their position, and big defensemen build agility and reactivity to move their large mass well enough to counter fluid, explosive forwards.

For defensive coverage and positioning, "I work on quickness off ice, to get an explosive burst of speed from my first three strides, along with agility so I can quickly shift my position to always face the play," stresses Bret Hedican. "As a defenseman, I always need to keep an eye on where the puck is in the defensive zone. This means skating backward and quickly turning or using tight pivots to go with the puck. Defensemen need to be able to shift their bodies to pivot or turn forward and backward so they're always facing the play and the puck, or to stay with and cover their opponent." On the puck or off the puck, agility is a critical component.

Fans and coaches often incorrectly describe some big defensemen as slow. Given adequate space, the top speed of these players is comparable to that of other players. Although they may lack quickness, they succeed because they move efficiently. They have great mobility and lateral movement—great agility. They may not appear quick or explosive, but their agility allows them to win one-on-ones. Veteran defensemen sometimes attribute their success to experience, to knowing where to move, not even realizing that their ability to move into that position relies on agility. Agility is stored motor patterns of complex movements. Each time a player repeats a certain movement or situation, it is reinforced and becomes easier to do the next time.

But the game is getting faster. Those big defenseman with smooth agility may need to be more reactive. Extend your arms straight out to your sides and note the distance from the left hand to the right hand; reactive moves within this fingertip-to-fingertip distance can win or lose a game situation. Successful shooting, passing, hitting, skating, turning, cutting, cycling, save making, shot blocking, and other skills feed into one-on-one tactics and rely on agility and reactivity. Remember that each moment in a hockey game is completely unpredictable. Events on the ice change suddenly, so players must be able to shift body position quickly, whether carrying the puck, trying to get open for a pass, or defending the net from attackers.

From a biomechanical perspective, the 100-meter linear sprint provides an incomplete model for teaching hockey acceleration. The rules of specificity training have always been simple. To improve agility, you must train agility. Traditional linear speed training builds linear top-end sprinting speed. Training for linear speed does not translate to multidirectional speed. Practicing sprinting in a straight line is important on the forecheck and backcheck, and may improve conditioning, but does not develop the whole package for hockey games that require stops and starts, lateral movement, drop-step pivots, crossovers, turns, and cycles. Forward speed is vital in today's game, but the mechanical demands of hockey tactics are still overwhelmingly multidirectional!

Nowhere is this more evident than within one-on-one tactics. Defenders face the demand of controlling high speed to stop on a dime and explode laterally to contain an opponent. Likewise, the offensive player will cut, turn, and zigzag to evade a defender. Moreover, the ability to shift gears and quickly change speed while already moving fast is a deceptive tactic that proves effective for throwing off a defender.

This chapter contains partner drills in which forwards and D-men can assume their natural offensive and defensive positions, with forwards more often initiating agility and defenseman more often reacting. D-men will incur more forward and backward movement so that they train to face the play. Forwards tend to express their game agility more with forward skating, making tight turns, cutting, and using turn backs to create space between defenders. Goaltenders will do well to practice position-specific reactions and agility patterns in the crease. Otherwise, a wide variety of drills serve goaltenders well, because they should be the most athletic players on the team and should always be looking to enhance their overall athleticism and body control.

By harnessing attributes from quickness, balance, movement skills, deceleration, and multiplanar strength, agility and reactivity are learned skills that contribute to sport technique and individual tactics. By helping players win puck battles and gain advantageous positioning on the ice, agility and reactivity also contribute to system play. Each of these components influences the other, and all are key ingredients in the recipe for superior on-ice movement. This book has distinct chapters devoted to training quickness, balance, and strength, but it is important to clarify the movement skills and deceleration components that are the fabric of agility.

MOVEMENT SKILLS

Before developing multidirectional quickness, an athlete must first develop efficient movement skills. The battery of drills in this chapter represents a compilation of many of the common movement pattern segments used during on-ice situations. The brain and nervous system recognize movement patterns, not muscle groups. Specific movement skills include forward, stride patterns, backward, lateral movement, lateral braking, crossovers, loaded dryland training starts, on-ice v-starts, open steps, and drop steps.

Coaches spend hours creating, studying, and devising practice plans, training schedules, exercises, and drills to maximize athlete performance. Great coaches understand the needs of the sport and their athletes. They don't simply regurgitate drills and exercises until their athletes drop from fatigue; they understand the what and the why of putting these plans into action. Coaches today are likely to implement a footwork drill, but how many know how to correct mechanics? Often they just bark, "Move your feet, move your feet."

Effective training of agility requires assessment, error detection, and corrective cues to teach precise body control. During rapid movement, what are the feet, legs, hips, torso, and arms doing? At what angle are the ankle, knee, and hip joints? They all must work in an integrated, coordinated pattern.

Movement skill patterning gives definition to general athleticism, enhancing movement precision. In this skill acquisition phase, athletes methodically perform nonreactive drills, similar to the way in which they might walk through a new team system on the ice. New movements progress from slow, deliberate actions that require conscious thought and deliberation to more automatic movements that occur at high speeds.

DECELERATION TRAINING

Many hockey training programs are marketed around speed, because parents respond to the allure of acceleration training and sign up their kids. Certainly, starting fast and going fast are important. But research clearly documents that forward linear speed-based training does not transfer to complex agility tasks, which require deceleration and direction change mechanics.

In hockey, getting from point A to point B and then over to point C and on to point D requires braking skills to stop and change direction before accelerating to the next critical ice position. Deceleration exposes more weaknesses than acceleration does. Races for loose pucks are won and lost in this phase. I like to say that deceleration skill is the illusion of quickness. Indeed, the race in sport is rarely like a 100-meter track sprint, with an in-place stationary start to a linear run. Most sports demand aggressive braking and the ability to translate movement into quickness in an opposite direction.

Lack of deceleration control, strength, or balance at its worst results in injury. At its best, it results in critical delay. Many athletes lose energy when decelerating. Properly trained deceleration can be harnessed for an explosive concentric phase. A well-trained athlete will gain quickness on direction changes, creating distance from opponents and gaining time to make tactical decisions. On the defensive side, the goal is to close the gap and take away space. After the defender is tight to the opponent, reactive agility, eccentric control, first-step quickness, and good stick positioning will keep the opponent in check.

Deceleration training improves eccentric loading so that even when skaters maintain a high speed they are capable of loading the legs and adjusting mechanics to change direction into varied skating pattern.

AGILITY TRAINING

Well-executed movement skills strung together in sequence are the mark of a controlled, fluid athlete. Body control can open or widen vision. Body control with visual awareness will help slow the game and facilitate smart decisions. A player like Wayne Gretzky could read the situation correctly, predict what is going to happen, and prepare accordingly. Gretzky combined vision, hockey sense, and anticipation, allowing him to read the play, know what he needed to do, and do it better than any player ever has. Although Gretzky was known as a hard worker and a diligent practice player, refining his craft and setting the tone for those around him, much of his hockey sense was innate. Regardless of starting point, everyone can train to improve.

The ability to read a play comes with experience and that sixth sense that Gretzky was blessed with. The ability to react is a neurophysical skill that can be trained. Developing and enhancing reaction skills is the focus of reactivity, allowing athletes to maximize deceptiveness for offensive moves, react quickly in defensive situations, and shift gears quickly and efficiently.

The difference between successful completion of these movement-based drills and actual game performance is the ability to react and adapt to dynamic game situations and to perform these movements efficiently in the confined space of most game situations. Decision-making and reaction skills can be integrated into drill situations through a variety of coaching methods.

Players key on the coach for visual cues (pointing in the direction that the athlete should go), verbal cues (yelling, "Left, backward, forward, right"), or audible cues (blowing a whistle). The athlete must process these cues and react appropriately to the given situation. Shadowing or mirroring drills also develop situational decision-making skills because the athlete must shadow the coach or workout partner and react quickly to mimic changes in direction, speed, and movement. Athletes alternate between being on offense and defense during these drills so that they develop strategies and movement skills for both offensive and defensive tactics.

Race drills are not the only drills with value. In agility race drills, competing from the starting line to the finish line, players may cheat to make up for inadequate agility. Agility is about thinking quickly and moving quickly and skillfully. It is best improved with a fresh body, unencumbered by fatigue. Initial agility practice should draw on only the ATP-PC system for quality mechanics, with ample rest time. Athletes perform 10-second bouts with a 1:5 work-to-rest ratio. The coach needs to be active during drills, cueing positive angles of force, good edging, preloaded legs for explosive muscle movement, controlled arms, and solid stances. When it is time to turn up the pace, athletes should use short-range plyometric coupling and elastic energy from the skeletal muscles (see chapter 6) to initiate each movement explosively.

After developing better movement efficiency, players rehearse offensive creativity and defensive reactivity before practicing at top speed. Fast is good, but benefits also come from changing gears, changing speeds, and changing directions. Initial movements and drills should be done slowly to encourage excellent movement skill patterning, progressively building to a pace that mimics sport situations and challenges the athlete to train at game speed. The ultimate expression of reactive agility are the confined-space scrimmages used in chapter 4 to train the anaerobic system in critical gamelike conditions.

Agility and reactivity drills let the athlete determine the most effective tactics to use to outwit a partner or opponent, forcing a defensive reaction to counter and respond to the athlete's moves. These head-to-head drills add competition, fun, and intensity to the training environment. At this stage, competing under fatigue helps players prepare to draw on agility late in a shift and late in a game, when it matter most.

Early drill learning is a cognitive stage; players must think about what is happening and how best to adjust their bodies. It is slow and awkward. Players must focus, process information, and execute mechanics to stimulate the neuromuscular system, laying down motor pattern engrams until the movements become automatic. A cognitive stage reaction might take 160 milliseconds, whereas an autonomic or automatic stage reaction takes only 85 milliseconds, about half as long. Come game time, players who must think through each situation will fall behind. The body can be trained to react and move more autonomically.

AGILITY AND REACTIVITY TRAINING GUIDELINES

1. To begin, practice, correct, and rehearse fundamental movement patterns at a controlled pace.
2. Begin to string these together in sequence.
3. Lay the foundation in a dryland environment and concurrently rehearse on ice.
4. Increase the tempo of movement, with a critical eye for mechanical flaws.
5. Challenge both proficiency and tempo by adding partner mirror and shadow drills.
6. Integrate more reaction skills with coach command drills and partner challenges.
7. After improvement occurs, practice the same drill while handling a puck and practice under fatigue.

AGILITY AND REACTIVITY DRILLS

The movement skill ready position includes setting the core and midback (chapter 5, page 81). Core bracing is the key to creating leverage and stability. With training, core activation will eventually become an automatic preparatory response before any movement occurs. Establish an athletic stance, with a neutral spine, knees flexed, and weight equally distributed between toes and heels. Muscles and joints are ready to move quickly in any direction.

AGILITY AND REACTIVITY

Two In, One Out Drill (High Knees)

DVD

Purpose: Develop quick, light feet between hurdles and balanced, lateral loading outside hurdles

Place two hurdles 4 feet (120 centimeters) apart. Stand outside one hurdle on the right leg. Move laterally through the hurdles with high knees. Touch each foot once inside the hurdles and then load the left leg outside the hurdles. Repeat back and forth, left and right, with a "quick, quick, stick" foot pace.

Two BOSU Crossover and Stick

Purpose: Improve hip mobility and crossover stride power, multidirectional movement skills, and landing stability

Start beside the first BOSU. Leading with the outside leg, cross over the front of the inside leg and land on the top of the first BOSU (*a*). Bring your trail leg through and plant your foot on the floor between the two BOSU. With your outside leg, cross in front of the inside leg and land on top of the second BOSU (*b*). Bring your trail leg through, landing on the floor outside the second BOSU, stabilizing and maintaining single-leg balance. Plant your inside leg. Cross over in the opposite direction across the two BOSU. Hips should stay square and face forward throughout the drill. Keep your chest and head up. Link your arms to the movement.

a

b

Variations:

- Move BOSU closer together to work on fast footwork and quickness.
- Move BOSU farther apart. This variation requires greater power initiation.

Around, Through, and Over Drill

Purpose: Develop lateral power, first-step quickness, and agility with lateral movement forwards, backwards, and crossover movement skills

Place 5 hurdles in line, each 3 feet apart. For the around part of the drill, shuffle to the end of the hurdles. Step forward with your outside foot past the last hurdle. Without wasting a step, bring the inside leg up and around. Shuffle to the end of the row of hurdles. Plant your outside leg and immediately push off in the opposite direction. Shuffle to the end of the row. Step back with your outside foot past the last hurdle. Without wasting a step, bring the inside leg back and around. Shuffle back to the starting point.

For the through part of the drill, come around outside the last hurdle and step forward with your outside leg. Shoot your lead leg back and couple your feet. Shoot your lead leg forward and couple your feet. Continue down the line of hurdles, coming around the outside and back down to the starting point.

For the over part of the drill, push off your trail leg and cross your lead leg in front of and over the hurdle. Bring your lead leg over to meet your trail leg; each foot will contact once between the hurdles. Continue the length of the hurdles. Cross over the last hurdle and plant your outside leg. Return down the line, continuing to cross over each hurdle.

Hips should stay square. Face forward throughout the drill. Keep your chest and head up. Do not waste any steps.

D-Man Drill

Purpose: Develop first-step quickness and change of direction

Start on the outside of the back cone. Accelerate forward around the front cone and backpedal to the middle cone. Move behind the middle cone with open steps and accelerate forward to the other front cone. Come around the cone and backpedal to the back cone. Come around the cone with open steps and accelerate forward to the center cone. Come around the center cone and backpedal to the starting cone. Keep hips forward throughout the drill.

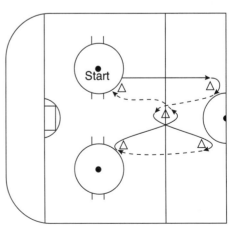

Partner Figure-Eight Shadow

DVD

Purpose: Develop first-step quickness, effective direction change, and reaction skills

Partner A begins on offense. Partner B begins on defense. Both players start in low athletic position, facing each other between and behind the cones. Partner A tries to gain a step on partner B, while partner B tries to stay with partner A. Use an open step and shoot through with the lead leg landing in front and slightly past the cone. Match with your trail leg. Shoot straight back with your outside leg and match with your other leg. Use an open step and shoot through toward the other cone with your lead leg landing in front and slightly past the cone. Shoot straight back with your outside leg and match with your other leg. Repeat the pattern. Partner A may reverse directions at any time while executing the pattern. Keep hips square and head and chest up. Stay low as you shoot through with the lead leg.

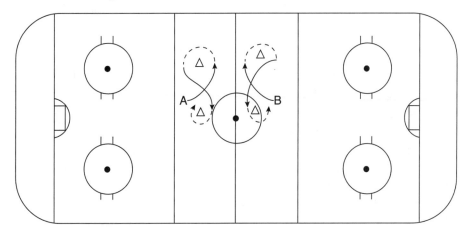

12-Hurdle Reaction Drill

DVD

Purpose: Develop agility, quick feet, and reaction skills

Step up in athletic ready position on the starting line. On the start cue, sprint up to the first row of hurdles. React to the coach's direction cue. Cross over the first and second hurdles, matching feet between the hurdles. Establish a momentary state of balance on the outside of the last hurdle. Switch directions, crossing over all four hurdles to the other end of the row. Establish a momentary state of balance on the outside of the last hurdle. Switch directions and cross over the two hurdles to return to the middle. Move up to the next row. React to the coach's direction cue and repeat the movement pattern. On the coach's final cue, perform an open step and accelerate into open space, crossing the finish line. Keep hips square and head and chest up. Stay low.

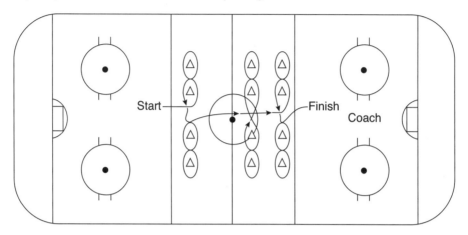

Lateral Shadow With Lateral Stepper

DVD

Purpose: Develop lateral leg power and reaction skills

Place 2 cones 15 to 20 feet apart. Partner A begins on offense, and partner B begins on defense. Both players begin in a low athletic position, facing each other between the cones. Partner A tries to gain a step (create space) on partner B, while partner B tries to stay with partner A. Both partners attach lateral steppers around their ankles. The coach indicates when to initiate the drill. Partner A moves side to side, deceptively trying to create space. Partner B attempts to mirror partner A. The drill ends when mechanical breakdown is evident or the prescribed time expires. Hips stay square, and head and chest stay up. Players stay low throughout the drill. They should dorsiflex during changes of direction. Partners must maintain the distance between their feet, keeping tension on the lateral steppers throughout the movement. They must be sure to shuffle laterally and not hop.

Reaction Diamond

Purpose: Develop quick change of direction and reaction skills

Start at the back of the diamond and come forward at the coach's cue. The coach gives a directional cue (backward, right, or left); players move as directed by the coach. The coach continues to give multidirectional cues based on the prescribed duration of the drill or until a breakdown in mechanics is observed. During the drill, stay low and maintain the distance between your feet to facilitate changes of direction. Keep hips square as you react to the coach's cues. At the end of the drill, move forward and leave the diamond, performing an open step and accelerating into open space.

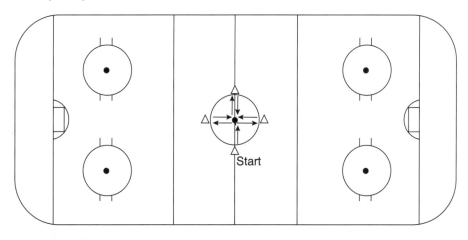

Shadow Box

DVD

Purpose: Develop quick change of direction, tight turns and forward-backward transitions, and reaction skills

Mark off two squares, end to end. Make the square for partner A slightly larger. Partner A begins on offense; he always skates forward. Partner B begins on defense; he always faces partner A's box. Both players start in a low athletic position, facing each other. Partner A starts at the back of his square. Partner B starts at the front of his square. Partner A leads the movement around the square, varying movement patterns and angles of movement to visit all the cones around the square. Partner B shadows the partner A's movement. Pace and intensity can increase as movement skills become more efficient. Players should stay low and maintain the distance between their feet to facilitate changes of direction. Hips should stay square.

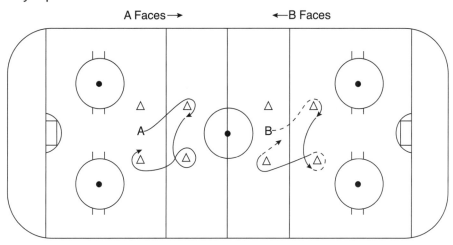

Reaction Belt Follow the Leader

Purpose: Develop agility and improve reaction time

Partner A begins on offense. Partner B begins on defense. Both players start in a low athletic position, one behind the other. Partner A tries to gain a step (create space) on partner B, while partner B tries to stay with partner A. The coach indicates when to initiate the drill. Partner A tries deceptively to create space on partner B while staying within the designated boundary. Partner B attempts to mirror partner A, following the exact same line of travel. The drill ends when mechanical breakdown is evident, when the prescribed time expires, or when the Velcro closure is pulled apart. During the drill, hips stay square, head and chest stay up, and players stay low. Dryland players should dorsiflex during lateral changes of direction.

Variations:

- Play follow the leader in a wider, more open space for anaerobic conditioning.
- In a confined space, incorporate multidirectional movements with hips staying square to the partner.

Towel Tag

Purpose: Develop agility, quick feet, reaction abilities; encourage creative maneuvers through fun challenges

Divide the team in half. Leave hockey sticks on the bench. Half of the team participates while the other half rests. Two players start as the forecheckers. All other players hang a small towel from the back of their pants. The forechecker must grab the towels from the other players. The two of them can team up to forecheck the other players. All players with a towel try to evade the forecheckers. As players lose their towels, they also become forecheckers. The drill continues until the last player has lost her towel.

Players should not have an overabundance of open ice. Mark off a boundary so that players must face many close one-on-one and one-on-two confrontations. The smaller the ice area, the more acute the direction change will be. The larger the ice area, the more flow there will be to the skating patterns.

When smaller groups of players perform the drill, adjust the game perimeter so that forecheckers can constantly challenge toweled players.

Quick-Feet Coach Directionals

Purpose: Build agility, quick feet, and direction change

Start on the face-off dot. The coach signals left, right, forward, or backward movement. Move left or right with crossovers. The coach changes signals in rapid succession. React, stop, and explode in the next direction. For team practices, set up 4 players on face off dots, the coach at center ice, and the next 4 players ready to go. Cycle through groups of 4 players.

Circle Multidirectional Quickness Drill

DVD

Purpose: Build quickness, agility, and first-step acceleration

Start at the bottom of the circle. Begin with a quick start. Skate to the top of the circle. Stop at the top and then skate backward to the middle dot. Open pivot to the left and skate forward to the left side of the circle. Complete a tight turn and then skate forward to the right side. Complete another tight turn, skate forward back to the face-off dot, and then pivot backward to the bottom of the circle. After you hit the bottom of the circle, accelerate forward all the way through the circle. Make sure that you turn tightly facing up ice so that you get both sides of the tight turn in.

Variations:

- Add a puck to the drill.
- Instead of tight turns on the side of the circle, try two-foot stops.

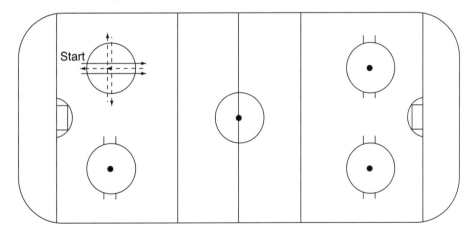

Coach's Cue Circle Agility

Purpose: Build quickness, agility, reactivity, and first-step acceleration

The coach sets up in the middle of the ice just inside the blue line. One player starts from each side on the line. On the whistle, begin with a quick start into the circle. React to the coach's directional stick cues. Players can move laterally, forward, and backward. The coach has the players change direction for 10 to 15 seconds and then blows the whistle. On the whistle, players accelerate to the blue line. The first player to make it becomes the offensive player. He picks up the puck and circles back into the zone on a one-on-one.

Variations:

- Add a puck to the multidirectional movements.
- Add another player from both sides so that the play becomes a two-on-two.

Two-Step Forward and Backward Circles

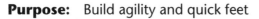

Purpose: Build agility and quick feet

Skate around one circle, turning from forward to backward and backward to forward every two steps. Always turn facing the inside of the circle. Use lighter, quicker feet than usual, increasing stride frequency. Initiate the direction turn sooner than you would if you wanted to feel comfortable. Plant your foot and initiate the next stride sooner than you would if you wanted to feel comfortable. Keep pressing to increase foot quickness while not going too far off the circle. Stay on the circle and force the body to adapt.

Forward and Backward Double Transition

Purpose: Build agility, direction change, and quick feet

Stand in the middle of two cones placed to the left and right, as close together as you can handle. Move forward and backward in and around the cones, facing square to the end zone throughout the pattern. Emphasize quick feet, quick transition from forward to backward to forward, and quick shifting of weight. Use a pattern of skating backward around the outside of the cones and forward up the middle.

Variations:

- Add coach's passes, received skating backwards on the outside of the body, and returned when skating forwards up the middle of the cones.
- Repeat the drill, skating forward up around the outside of the cones and backward down the middle.
- Reposition the cones so that both are in front in a direct line, changing the skating pattern. Skate forward through two cones, around the top cone, backward through two cones, and around the bottom cone. Jump back up to repeat.

Chapter 9

Speed

To this point, I have recommended specific training styles and drills to increase quickness, agility, and reactivity. The effect of first-step quickness, multidirectional movement skills, ability to decelerate, and reaction skills on performance on the ice have been well covered. This chapter covers the topic that I am most asked about: Who is the fastest pro player?

Full-out speed carries a certain allure and remains a valuable asset. The ability to wheel behind the net and sprint up the ice with untouchable speed on an end-to-end rush has at one time been the dream of every hockey player. Players can improve their speed, and certainly there are fast players and slow players. Although few players possess the pure straightaway speed that makes them an end-to-end threat, each league definitely has a cutoff level. If a player cannot skate at a certain pace, no matter what other attributes he can offer, he is gone. The higher the caliber of the league, the faster the game. If players cannot skate at a certain speed, they will be left behind on the ice, and out of the game.

Full-out speed is evident during aggressive forechecking and breakaways. Defensively, backchecking from the other end of the ice back to the net requires speed. If quickness is the first gear and perhaps the second, speed covers the third, fourth, and fifth gears. After the first two or three strides, a player wants to continue accelerating rapidly, attain top speed as soon as possible, reach as fast a top speed as possible, and then maintain that top speed for as long as possible.

Speed can be harnessed to get in quick on the forecheck, make contact, and cause puck turnovers. Linear acceleration and top-end speed are equally important on the backcheck, getting back into position to defend and covering opponents right to the net, as well as for making up for positional mistakes to get back into the play. This chapter targets pure speed, like that displayed by a player who races down the ice to prevent an icing call.

Most players can develop good skating technique at slow and moderate speeds. But to progress to the upper limits of speed, to full-out speed, and to handle sharp turns at high speeds, players cannot execute efficient technique unless the first develop many other physical parameters. The components listed in table 9.1 build a base for optimal speed performance.

Table 9.1 Components of High-Speed Skating

Component	Importance to speed
Proper skating technique	Makes skating most efficient. Facilitates powerful strides. Best use of edges for more production. Better placed return skate to begin next stride. Better use of momentum.
Physical strength	Allows the player to fight through hooks and checks and continue striding.
	Strong legs are able to support the body in a deep knee position so that the player can execute a longer stride and apply force over a greater distance with each stride.
	Strong legs allow the player to stay deep with bent knees during high-speed cornering. Without this strength, the player would fall, have to slow down, or have to take a wider turn.
Power	Allows the player to push off each stride and power through a long stride. The player is able to fight through opponents. Selective hypertrophy of fast-twist muscle fibers has several effects. Fast-twitch fibers have rapid contraction velocity and high peak force, which suits on-ice explosiveness, and high stores of creatine and glycogen for a high capacity of anaerobic energy production to fuel speed training.
Quickness	Improves stride frequency and foot speed.
Agility	Allows the player to change direction suddenly to evade an opponent and continue skating.
Deceleration	Allows the skater to load the legs aggressively to corner at high speeds and harness the elastic properties of muscles to accelerate in forward skating
Flexibility	Improves stride length and permits fluid technique.
	The player is able to skate fluidly and through a full range of motion.
Anaerobic energy	Fuels short bursts of high-intensity muscle action and delays fatigue, which can impede good technique.
Aerobic energy	Helps the player recover more quickly between sprinting situations and prepare for more high-speed activity.
Body composition	Low body fat facilitates relative strength and efficient movement.
Neuromuscular conditioning	Increases the player's ability to activate muscles as a high rate.

We can all remember players who were gifted with natural speed. We remember them well because they were exciting to watch. They were blessed with high capacity for speed, and although they may have worked hard in practices, most did not train specifically for speed or even condition the basic components. Imagine the speed that these players could have attained if they had developed all the components and trained for speed improvements! How fast could they have been? How much longer could they have played? Fortunately, players today have a better handle on the answers to these questions.

Some athletes are naturally faster than others, just as some are naturally better skaters. But speed development is possible for all hockey players. A skater can become faster by improving stride power, stride length, stride frequency, contractile speed, biomechanics, and anaerobic conditioning (see chapter 4).

SPEED CONDITIONING

Resistance sprinting encourages players to lengthen each stride as they strive to apply enough force to keep up the pace in a resisted condition. Resisted speed drills net slower movement by nature of the resistance imposed on the athlete, but they encourage a longer, more powerful stride that, in a free condition, will apply more force over a greater distance and produce greater speed. Randy Smythe, a speed specialist who influenced the field, quantifies the incredible potential of speed development: "Increase running stride the length of a penny, and 40-yard dash time for football will decrease 2/10ths of a second. A 100-meter dash time in track would be down 1/2 second. Add on an increase in stride frequency, and the athlete will run faster still." On the ice, player A takes 12 skating strides for one length of the ice. Player B takes 16 strides and a longer time. Player A is able to apply force over a greater distance on every stride, getting more distance from each stride.

A more powerful stride contributes to speed, providing a stronger push-off and getting greater drive from each stride to cover more distance in the same amount of time. Two players take 10 strides that are similar in length and frequency. But one player covers more ice. More aggressive edging and more powerful strides will produce greater top-end speed and help maintain speed. Stride power helps players get to pucks in front of the net. With the puck, they can drive to the net or fly down the wing, taking the puck wide before cutting to the net.

Stride frequency increases the rate of acceleration. At top speed, stride frequency determines the turnover rate and the time before the recovery leg is back in position to generate force. After a left leg stride, the player should quickly pull the leg back in and plant the skate as rapidly as possible in position to push off with the right leg. Stride frequency draws from elements of quickness, movement skills, balance, strength, and anaerobic supply. Laying down the neural pathways for skilled, high-velocity movement will help execution of the recovery stride, coordinate the gliding leg, and preferentially dial up fast-twitch fibers.

The goal of speed training is to produce as much force as possible in as short a time as possible; contractile speed contributes to this. In high-velocity conditioning, players do speed development drills full out. Even if the challenges imposed during a drill—resisted sprint conditions or absorbing body mass on a lateral jump—affect the rate of concentric contraction, just thinking about being explosive and striving to move fast will positively influence the nervous system.

Overspeed training forces athletes to increase contractile speed by making them skate much faster than they are accustomed to. The brain must signal the muscles to fire more quickly, to move the foot forward and plant it in time for the next stride. When this occurs, the neuromuscular system learns to fire the muscles more quickly and adapts to higher speed capacity.

Players need to do overspeed and free skating as fast as possible. Players cannot improve speed while working in an aerobic zone. The ATP-PC system should fuel the efforts, although anaerobic glycolysis will maintain speed potential late in a shift. Speed training needs pure ATP-PC sprint conditions to achieve the best mechanics and top speeds, as well as anaerobic capacity workouts to drive up sprint endurance and ensure that players are trained to generate high-speed efforts late in a shift.

Improving speed means improving skating technique. Major mechanical adjustments and fine-tuning include body position, maximizing the use of the skate edges, staying low with a deep knee bend, tuck position, purposeful arms, triple-stride extension, stable stride recovery, stride power, stride length, and stride frequency. Improved skating technique relies on specific strength to handle physical requirements.

Which muscles do players need to strengthen to handle the demand imposed on the body to achieve the mechanics necessary for faster skating? Developing the quadriceps (thigh), calf muscles, and hip extensors provides a powerful forward stride. Working the hamstrings (back of the upper leg) and hip flexors provides strength to pull the leg back in and position it for another push-off. Training the low-back muscles, hips, and abdominal muscles aids all parts of the stride and benefits turning and lateral movement. Strengthening the adductor and abductor muscles improves lateral movement and plays a key role in both forward and backward skating. Developing the arm and shoulder muscles is also necessary, because the arms lead the legs during acceleration. Exercise that benefits skating speed uses a full range of motion into deep squat and lunge positions, strengthening quads and glutes. Other efforts produce power across the ankle, knee, and hip into triple extension.

How much strength is needed? A common misconception that I've heard from hundreds of coaches, players, and fans is that strength and muscle mass detract from speed—that a big, strong player is muscle bound and slow. This notion could not be further from the truth. Size, muscle mass, and strength do not make a player slow. With specific training, these factors contribute to speed. When I last coached Todd Bertuzzi, he played

Mike Modano of the Dallas Stars is one of the NHL's fastest players. Although many elite players are gifted with natural speed, any player can improve his speed on the ice.

at around 246 pounds (112 kilograms) yet demonstrated very good speed and skating power. He used his muscle mass and strength for a powerful push-off on each stride.

In the new NHL, speed is at a premium. This element should trickle down to younger levels and influence how the game is played. To be clear, muscle mass and strength benefit speed. Just check out a world-class 100-meter sprinter. Then observe 200-, 400-, 800- and 1,500-meter specialists and notice the differences in body appearance. Hockey players are sprinters, but they need to repeat many sprints throughout a game and sustain pace too. In the new, faster NHL, players are examining exactly how much mass is best, tweaking their playing weight. Too light and they are not strong and powerful enough; too much mass and they cannot sustain repeated sprints all shift and all game.

To help players get faster, speed training needs structured, purposeful drills. Many coaches simply hope that their players will eventually improve through generic practice drills, using repetitive sprints up and down the ice. As fatigue sets in, the players learn only how to skate slowly with flawed technique. Drills must be designed and structured appropriately for the muscles to learn to fire more quickly and to allow the brain to learn and rehearse specific movement patterns at high speeds.

SPEED TRAINING GUIDELINES

Players should build a strength base, increase lean muscle mass, and develop the energy systems for supply and recovery. They risk injury if they take on high-intensity speed training without these base parameters. In general, players should be able to squat their body weight into a deep stance for reps and have a base of anaerobic conditioning. High-intensity speed requires an excellent strength base in the legs and core, dynamic flexibility, and a well-tuned body free from compensational restrictions that could lead to injury at high speed.

Speed development should begin with a low volume of drills, initially run at submaximal intensity. Low intensity includes using moderate speeds, limited resistance, and no overspeed. Tempo sprints allow the muscles to acclimate, gradually building the capacity to handle longer sprints and higher speed efforts.

Players should have good form and proper technique. They should improve run and skate sprint mechanics before progressing to high-speed movement. Players must not practice incorrect movements faster. Assess balance, foot placement, ready positions, edges, absorption, and use of arms during acceleration.

Training should emphasize quality over quantity. Don't confuse the most physically exhausting workout with the best workout. Some physiological parameters are best developed by physically overloading the body, but speed is best improved with bursts of high-intensity movement, interspersed with active rest and recovery. The body is learning to move fast, not slow and fatigued. Players need to rest enough between repetitions so that progressive fatigue doesn't impede technique.

After players improve their technique and anaerobic conditioning, add resisted sprint challenges. The resistance adds intensity and requires greater effort, but it targets stride power, not velocity and leg turnover rate. Excessive speed can be of greater risk.

After they improve on-ice speed, players can start carrying a puck through the drills. But they must not sacrifice speed for puck control; players likely already know how to carry the puck going at slow to moderate speed. They must maintain top speed and learn to handle the puck at those speeds.

After a number of speed training sessions, add a small volume of overspeed drills. Begin with Slastix overspeed tubing in a partial prestretch; do not go overboard. Allow time for players' bodies to adjust to higher speeds one step at a time before intensifying the overspeed environment, graduating to more aggressive pre-stretching of the tubing.

Keep speed development drills between 5 and 15 seconds in duration, long enough to allow players to draw on their anaerobic energy systems for full-out efforts but not so long that fatigue affects speed. Some hockey books list anaerobic glycolysis drills such as stop-and-start line drills for developing speed. But if you compare a player's skating technique for the first and last 10 seconds of these drills, you'll see that technique becomes terribly flawed as players become tired. Such exercises just rehearse skating slowly with poor technique. They do build leg endurance, but they don't improve upper-end speed. Additionally, 15 seconds is also a practical limit because players can skate one full lap of the ice in that time. They would never skate longer in a game without having to decelerate, stop, or change direction.

Allow approximately a minute of relief between drills. As practice progresses, players need to note how they feel—are they still fatigued or are they ready to go? Insufficient rest intervals leave players fatigued at the start of the next drill. This results in a less powerful push-off, shorter strides, less knee bend, and a slower stride rate. To improve speed capabilities, players need to produce a more powerful push-off through a longer stride, deep knee flexion, and a greater leg turnover.

SPEED TRAINING

Power Plyo Angled Lateral Jumps

a

b

Purpose: Develop lateral leg speed and power, and specific on-ice angles achieved at ankle, knee, and hip similar to those used for aggressive stopping

Begin in athletic body position. Balance on one leg on one side of the Power Plyo. Set your core. Initiate lateral movement by preloading the balancing leg. Drive your arms across your body as you forcefully jump laterally, landing (*a*) on the other leg on the opposing angled face. Absorb the landing by flexing at the ankle, knee, and hip before (*b*) initiating power to jump laterally to the original side. The arms lead the direction of the intended movement. Dorsiflex the ankle before landing to provide a firm base on which to absorb the landing.

Variation: Change the speed of movement (coupling time).

Power Plyo Resisted Vertical Jumps

Purpose: Develop vertical leg speed and power

Begin in athletic body position, with weight even distributed on both legs and on the balls of the feet. Set your core. Initiate movement by preloading the legs. Drive the arms up as you forcefully jumps against the resistance (*a*), landing into a low athletic position by flexing at the ankle, knee, and hips before initiating power to jump again (*b*). Keep the core set throughout the movement. Absorb the landing by triple flexing at the ankle, knee, and hip.

Variation: Change the speed of movement to fast repeats through quicker coupling time.

a   b

Power Skater Strides

Purpose: Develop leg speed and power through a range of motion that simulates the 45-degree skating stride; improve skating mechanics

Begin in a low athletic body position, with weight evenly distributed on both legs and feet in starting position on a Power Skater. Set the core. Staying in a low position, initiate movement

by extending one of the stride legs through a full range of motion. Drive the arms athletically and keep the hips centered as the leg travels through full extension. The stride leg flexes at the ankle, knee, and hip to return under control to the starting position before you initiate power with the other leg. Continue alternating legs for the desired repetitions or duration. Keep the core set throughout the movement. Striving for a deep stance and longer strides will transfer results to an improved on-ice technique.

Variation: For varied muscular development, slow the return phase to 4 seconds.

Power Skater Stride Repeats

Purpose: Focus on velocity and rate of contraction in the hockey stride pattern

Begin in low athletic body position on the Power Skater. Flex the support leg to support most of your body weight. Set your core. Staying in a low position, initiate movement by extending the stride leg while driving the arms athletically. Return the stride leg quickly but under control before initiating the next stride. Continue for the desired repetitions or duration. Keep the core set throughout the movement. Flex at the ankle, knee, and hip. Drive the arms athletically.

Variation: Decrease the coupling time with 1/2 strides that focus on eccentric-concentric coupling speed to build power.

Tandem Tow Resisted Sprints

Purpose: Develop stride power and stride length

This drill can be done on ice or dry land. Set up with a partner by attaching a tandem tow. Begin in low athletic body position, with chest up and core set. Your resistance partner begins in low athletic body position, with hips dropped, body prepared to provide resistance, and core set.

Initiate forward movement by driving your body forward with athletic arms. The resisting partner provides appropriate force to overload you without causing a breakdown in form, making sure that you continue to make forward progress. Continue the drill for the desired distance. Keep the core set throughout the movement and drive the movement with the arms.

Variations:

- Increase or decrease the distance.
- Increase or decrease the duration.
- Change the resistance. On the ice, the resisting partner will initially glide to allow the pulling player to overcome the resistance of his partner's weight. The resisting partner can further overload the pulling player by dragging one skate or, more aggressively, use a v-stop.

Parachute Sprints

Purpose: Develop stride power and stride length

Attach the parachute at the waist. Begin in a low athletic body position, with chest up and core set. As you initiate the forward movement, a partner opens and holds the chute up so it catches air on the first stride. Drive your body forward with athletic arms as you travel the prescribed distance or duration. Keep the core set throughout the movement. Drive the movement with the arms.

Variations:

- Increase or decrease the distance.
- Increase or decrease the duration.
- Change the resistance. Increase the size of the parachute or the number of parachutes used.

Parachute Lateral Crossovers

Purpose: Develop lateral stride power and stride length

This drill can be done on ice or dry land. Attach the parachute. The point of resistance will come off your side hip. Begin in a low athletic body position, with chest up and core set. Initiate movement with a strong crossover step. Move laterally by crossing over and pushing off. A partner holds the chute up beside you. Move the arms athletically and drive them across your body as you travel the prescribed distance or duration. Repeat, crossing over on the other side. Keep the core set throughout the movement. Drive the movement by bringing the arms across the body. Be sure to generate a strong push-off from both outside and inside crossover feet.

Variations:

- Increase or decrease the distance.
- Increase or decrease the duration.
- Change the resistance. Increase the size of the parachute or the number of parachutes used.

Stair Big-Stride Sprints

Purpose: Develop stride length and power across the ankle that will apply to strong, long on-ice strides

Power up the stairs using large strides. Drive the arms forward athletically (opposite arm to opposite drive leg) to help propel the body. Continue for the desired duration or distance. Recovery periods between working sets should be active in nature (for example, slow jog or walk). Keep the core set throughout the movement. Drive the movement with the arms.

Variations:

- Increase the total length of the working set.
- Change the resistance by choosing stairs with different steepness.

Let-Goes

Purpose: Stride through resistance and build jump in the stride, shifting gears while moving

Run or skate with resistance that is significant but does not alter mechanics. After five or six strides, your partner yells, "Go" and releases the resistance, producing a jump in the next couple of free-condition strides by tricking the nervous system, which is still dialing up enough muscle to stride through the resistance.

Overspeed Tubing Sideways Start

Purpose: Develop explosive acceleration and build agility

Stand sideways to the direction of travel. A coach holds prestretched Slastix overspeed tubing. On the coach's whistle, cross over, turn, and explode toward the coach.

Overspeed Tubing Forward

Purpose: Increase stride frequency, acceleration, and contractile speed

With Slastix overspeed tubing attached, stand ready to accelerate with knees flexed and hips low. A coach pulls the tubing to a stretched position. On the coach's whistle, accelerate straight forward. The coach should move in the same direction to help keep a stretch on the tubing and lengthen the time that you remain in an overspeed environment.

Resisted Speed and Overspeed Skating W Pattern

Purpose: Develop acceleration, stride power, agility, and direction change

Begin facing a coach who is holding the end of the Slastix overspeed tubing. The coach starts moving across the ice, so you skate on a diagonal angle. Skate backward to position 1 through a resisted skate. On the coach's whistle, skate forward in overspeed to position 2. When you get near the coach and the tubing relaxes, skate backward through a resisted skate to position 3. Repeat these movements across the ice.

Part of the goal of the W pattern is to establish an angled open-step start. The design of the drill uses a pattern that keeps the tubing out of the path of travel. To help achieve this, maintain enough separation between yourself and the coach and begin with a short enough portion of the tubing.

You can reverse the flow, skating forward away from the coach and backward in overspeed after you have refined the length of tubing and the pattern to ensure that the ice is clear.

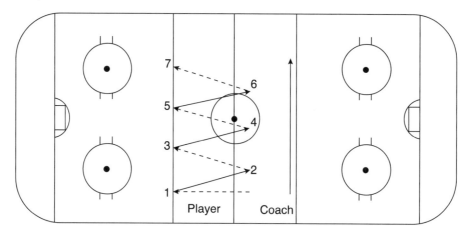

Resisted Power Pivots

Purpose: Build stride power, stride frequency, and hip power

Set up cones so that you will skate down the ice from side to side, around each cone, in a zigzag pattern. A partner wears the end of the tandem tow harness and glides down the middle of the cones while you power around each cone.

Zigzag Lateral Bounds

Purpose: Build stride length and stride power

Push off one foot at a 45-degree angle, with toes pointed slightly outward, jumping as high and traveling as far as possible (*a*). Land on one leg (*b*), absorb the landing, and push off to travel in the opposite direction. Jump from left to right to left, down the floor at 45-degree angles.

a   b

Full-Speed Sprint With Skating Start

Purpose: Increase stride frequency, stride power, stride length, and contractile speed

Skate straight down one side of the ice at 80 percent speed. Build up to 90 percent speed around the end with quick crossovers. Come out of the corner wide and accelerate to 100 percent speed at the face-off hash marks. Sprint full out straight down to the far face-off hash marks. Recover in the middle of the ice.

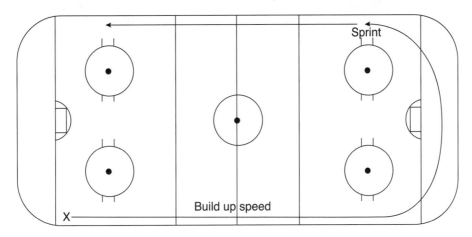

Partner Flow Puck Race

Purpose: Develop high-speed skating and acceleration

Two players start at diagonally opposite face-off circles, stationary on the face-off dot. On the whistle, they sprint out to face-off dot 1, around 2, over to 3, back down to the starting position (4), and off to the center, racing for the puck sitting on the center face-off dot. At the center, players must cross their right-hand side of the puck to avoid collisions. The player who reaches the puck first continues for a shot at the net. The player who loses the race turns backward or angles toward the skater to defend the net one-on-one but avoids head-on checking.

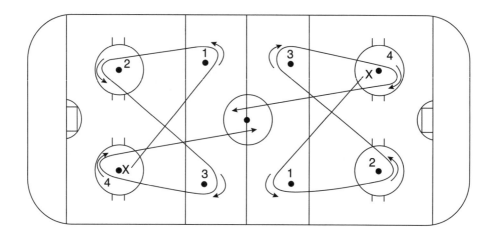

Speed Change-Up Drill

Purpose: Develop acceleration ability and stride frequency

Skate at 80 percent speed around the ice. On the coach's whistle, quickly accelerate to full speed and maintain it. On the next whistle, decelerate back to 80 percent speed. The coach should vary the time between whistles, blowing the whistle every 1 to 5 seconds, so that players practice reacting and quickly shifting gears. The action continues for up to 20 seconds before players skate easy for a rest interval.

Chapter 10

Constructing Optimal Workouts

Conditioning builds up the body. Hockey tears it down. More conditioning helps repair the body and build it back up again. Then comes the next hockey game. It is a constant cycle. In the off-season, however, players can train full time without game wounds and the fatigue of travel taking steam away from training. Players can make the best gains in conditioning and ability in the off-season.

Even with less frequent, smaller volume in-season training and well-structured on-ice practices, most players lose strength and conditioning over the course of a season. Hockey is intense, and it breaks the body down. That is in part a natural by-product of the physical on-ice battles that make the sport exciting to play and watch. The gradual breakdown of the body also results in part from the real-life *Groundhog Day* movie that many players find themselves in. They practice and play every day with very few unloading days, very little variety. Imagine weight lifting for your legs every single day. Eventually the body would break down, perhaps not because of an acute injury, but you would certainly experience a loss of strength. Many teams skate every day. Hmmmm.

Hockey conditioning aims to improve fitness, athleticism, and hockey-specific physical attributes to improve skills, individual tactics, and game performance. Those are lofty and achievable goals. Still, the underlying rule of training is "do no harm." The process of tearing down the body should occur only during hockey itself, an inevitable result in a sport that involves high-speed collisions, fatigue from a heavy schedule of games and travel, and injury set up by overuse when teams practice and compete on the ice every day.

The on- and off-ice conditioning players do should never be the cause of injury. When developing a conditioning program, always think safety first. The following guidelines will help you construct and oversee injury-free workout participation. These guidelines are especially important given the dynamic nature of the training style that I am recommending. Anytime the human body is subjected to complex motion, injury is possible. When we push the upper limits of ability, training athletes to build more speed, quickness, and power, injury may occur.

Studies of injury epidemiology from hockey and other multidirectional sports show that many sport injuries occur during deceleration, aggressive braking to cut and change direction, and high-velocity movements. It is worth noting the injury trends in other multidirectional sports such as basketball and soccer because they suggest what the body can and cannot handle in a hockey dryland environment. Ironically, rapid deceleration, aggressive direction change, and high-velocity movement produce the most dangerous hockey player. The mechanisms of injury are also the attributes of successful hockey players. A training methodology is needed that will both prevent these injuries and safely integrate these qualities to produce a skater who can call on these attributes on the ice.

How can an athlete train for dynamic action, aggressively push the limits, and stay injury free? The key elements to a safe, effective workout are preparation and maintenance of the training environment, classroom management and group dynamics skills, and teaching methodologies.

A NUTRITIONAL NOTE

Nutrition is a key link between preparation and performance. Optimal nutrition supplies energy for conditioning, allows for intense training, delays fatigue, and keeps the athlete healthy and well. Proper nutrition also aids faster, more complete recovery after workouts, so players have a full energy supply for the next practice. Eating the right things at the right times helps produce superior physiological results from workouts.

To review a list of hockey nutrition tips, refer to HockeyNutrition.com for advice on mass-gaining diets, pregame meals, carb loading, fluid replenishment, postgame refueling, nutrition during the game, eating well on the road, all-day tournaments, and back-to-back games.

PREPARATION AND MAINTENANCE OF THE TRAINING ENVIRONMENT

Ensure that the weight room is clean and organized and that equipment is stored properly. The room should have sufficient open space for movement drills and lifting sequences. Regularly check equipment to make sure that it is in good working order.

Define the flow of the room. Set up the necessary training accessories in a configuration that will help define and control subgroups. Divide the weight room into different areas. Athletes should help put away equipment before the next phase of the workout begins.

For off-ice conditioning, athletes must wear footwear that provides lateral support and good shock absorption. Players can wear cross-trainers or hiking approach shoes when performing plyometrics and agility drills.

Keep water available. Athletes need to drink plenty of water before, during, and after workouts, especially in hot weather and during intense workouts.

Wipe down sweat and spilled water from the equipment and floor. Have sweat towels available to wipe down surfaces that may be slippery from sweat, such as stability balls, BOSU balance trainers, or the floor itself.

Weightlifting belts artificially support the back and abdominal muscles and can leave the skater exposed on the ice when he must move a big opponent. Players should not compensate for inadequate torso strength with a weight belt. A tight belt during exertion actually causes the athlete to push outward, when for protection he needs to draw inward. Ironically, belts cause the opposite of what they intend to achieve.

Use Slastix tubing to apply resistance (strength and movement training) or assistance (overspeed). Slastix is thick enough to apply sufficient resistance and long enough to accommodate full-body maneuvers. Most important, Slastix is covered by a nylon safety sleeve, adding durability and offering protection in the event that the tubing breaks under stretch. The tube recoils within the safety sleeve as opposed to snapping back to hit an athlete.

CLASSROOM MANAGEMENT AND GROUP DYNAMICS SKILLS

A coach-to-athlete ratio of not more than 1:6 allows the coach to observe and coach all athletes effectively. The specific grouping of the athletes—for example, grouping those of similar abilities and size, and those who are compatible with one another—can also greatly affect observational dynamics. The coach must create a training situation that maximizes his ability to observe, interact, and actively coach throughout the practice.

The coach must organize the length of the drills, the number of participants, and the logistics of moving through the repetitions of each drill so that the desired work-to-rest ratios are maintained and the practice can move seamlessly and safely.

Although the chronological age of the participants is not a primary concern, the physical, cognitive, social, and emotional maturity of each athlete are important considerations. Do the athletes take the practice seriously? Do they focus on the tasks assigned? Are they able to understand the objectives and purpose of the practice plan? Do they have the physical readiness to participate with the group? To ensure the safety and proper development of the athletes, the coach must match the exercises chosen to the maturational readiness of players.

The style of hockey-specific conditioning and training methodologies requires an interactive element between coach and athlete. It is not enough that the players are working hard. It is not enough for the coach to demonstrate a series of exercises that the players will run through. The coach must observe, evaluate, correct, cue, engage, and motivate players for every single set. This process should affect current workout modifications and subsequent practice planning.

The coach must coach 360 degrees. He needs to be visually aware 100 percent of the time. When communicating with a specific athlete, the coach must maintain awareness of the room and what the rest of the group is doing. The active coach will constantly assess and correct with instant feedback and keep a full frame of reference of the room dynamics to coach quality training as well as head off potentially unsafe situations.

The coach needs to be a confident communicator who gives clear, concise instructions and stays positive when giving feedback. He needs to teach purposefully rather than just run players through drills.

The coach sets the tone, spirit, and level of professionalism. Athletes often take their cues in attitude, personality, and behavior from their coaches. The coach needs to enter each training session in the state of mind that he expects his athletes to be in. The coach must never let the athletes exceed his energy level. For a coach, energy is the most important tool for motivating athletes. If a coach is bored or uninterested, you can bet that the athletes will be too.

An effective active coach is not a fitness taskmaster or boot camp sergeant. The coach's ability to instruct, observe, and correct will contribute far more to an athlete's development than simply yelling for more effort.

The coach must insist that athletes contribute to the success of the workout. They must show up on time, listen to instruction, assist with setting up and putting away equipment to keep the workout flowing and the room safe, bring a positive attitude and good energy, have a solid work ethic to help themselves and other players raise the bar to a higher intensity level, and foster the camaraderie that will help everyone enjoy the process. If a player cannot commit to these simple requirements, the coach should mentor him for a short time. If he cannot develop a positive approach to training, everyone is better off if the coach removes him from the environment. The chance to learn and improve is an opportunity. A player who is too immature or simply not into it should be removed to preserve the integrity of the environment and protect the experience for those who are committed. This action will also help the coach enjoy the coaching experience. The athlete can ask to come back when he has developed enough as a person to contribute to the environment. A coach must avoid spending a disproportionate amount of time with a high-maintenance player while ignoring hard-working, enthusiastic, and motivated players.

The coach must plan for each session but should be ready to change it on the fly depending on how he reads the athletes. If the plan is for an intense session but the athletes are not physically or mentally up for it that day, the coach should adjust accordingly. Similarly, if players are keyed up and ready to push hard, the coach can increase the level of the workout to match their energy and intensity. Drills should be adaptable to players' proficiency to ensure that players are being challenged, but within safe, effective limits. Coaches often need to define a subgroup of players for whom they reduce drill demands to achieve level-appropriate training complexity.

Finally, the coach should insist that athletes use spotters when appropriate. For all heavy weight training, a spotter should assess technique, help move the weight into starting position, and, if necessary, assist with the last couple of reps and a safe exit from the exercise.

A spotter is necessary to ensure safety during weight training.

TEACHING METHODOLOGIES

The coach needs to assess player technique constantly. Elements such as body position, trunk posture, balance, foot placement, angle of leg from hip to floor, amount of knee bend, and landing position need to be checked. Technique corrections help prevent injury and optimize fitness and performance.

Even experienced players need an acclimation phase to learn new exercises. Use a break-in period when starting a new conditioning program, when introducing new components (such as plyometrics) to an existing program, and even when beginning advanced progressions of familiar exercises.

Muscles require time to adapt to new loads imposed on the body. When starting or restarting any conditioning program, begin with a progressive, gradual break-in period. During this period (about 2 weeks), initiate the program with light weights, low intensities, and low speeds. When a player starts a new conditioning program, detrained muscles are susceptible to injury during contraction. A break-in period allows safe, sensible progression to the goal training level.

Using muscles unaccustomed to weight training and conditioning will produce delayed onset muscle soreness (DOMS). If athletes do too much too soon, they will be stiff and sore 24 to 48 hours after a new workout. Overworking deconditioned muscles will slow progression because stiffness and soreness will cause athletes to miss workouts. Moreover, working through next-day workouts while dealing with DOMS places players at risk.

During a break-in period that uses a lower volume of sets, coaches need to be observant, with a focus on correcting technique. They should apply beginner-level programming that includes moderate loads, speed, and intensity until players can demonstrate strong technique, stabilization, and movement mechanics. Even a veteran athlete needs to be able to execute the basic exercise before assuming the additional challenge of a more complex variation.

After players are into their full routine, they need to rest each body part after a vigorous workout, allowing 24 to 48 hours of rest and recovery. The stimulus to a training effect is the training session itself, but the actual physical improvement or physical adaptation occurs after the training session ends. Microscopic muscle tears occur naturally during an intense workout. The muscles need time to adapt to training loads as they repair and grow to a new level. During this period of rest, the muscle responds to the training stimulus and physical development occurs.

The rest and recovery period is as important to conditioning gains as the workout. If players do not take an adequate rest period, overtraining will cause injury, delaying physical development. Players stand to benefit from physical, physiological, neural, mental, and emotional unloading. Maybe that's why Olympic athletes peak only a couple of times a year and compete in the Olympics every 4 years! We ask a lot of hockey players. From a physiological standpoint, rest is a critical ingredient in the recipe for improvement. This is an important consideration for coaches of teams in a losing funk—often they will not rest. Stepping away from their environment for mental and physical rejuvenation is usually more constructive than showing up and doing more of the same. In the off-season, for many players, "more is better"—they are reluctant to take full rest days. But achieving a peak of strength and conditioning while still feeling fresh is a meticulous challenge. The rest principle is key to best results.

Players should warm up before every workout. A dynamic warm-up prepares the body for the demands of an intense workout or on-ice session, creates a cohesive mind–muscle link, and ensures that the muscles will be warm, pliable, and compliant to meet the demands of explosive, complex movements.

Successive workouts should follow a continuum of exercise difficulty:

- Players should move from simple to more complex skills. Poor mechanics will produce bad habits and inefficient movement. Lack of control and coordination will expose players to injury. Beginners should start with low demands on the nervous system and low motor complexity.

- Players should move from unloaded to loaded exercises. As the ability to execute movement skills improves, the resistance can increase.

- Players should move from stable to unstable positions. As the athlete's ability to execute a movement skill increases, the instability challenge can increase. The athlete can alter his base of support from a stable position to a more unstable position, going from standing on both feet to standing on one foot, for example. Or the athlete can alter the training surface to an unstable one such as a balance board, stability ball, or BOSU balance trainer to encourage greater proprioceptive challenge, muscle activation, and metabolic response.

- Players should move from slow speeds to faster speeds. As the athlete's ability to execute a lift or movement skill improves, the intensity of the effort progresses from slow movements to faster, more explosive movements. For example, an athlete might progress from slow, controlled squats to explosive squat jumps.

- Players should move from static to dynamic movements. As they perfect their mechanics, movements can progress from stationary, static exercises to exercises with increased displacement of movement (lateral, vertical, and rotational). With greater displacement comes increased need for solid landings, deceleration, and transitional balance.

- Players should move from single plane to multiplane movements. As they perfect movement skills in one plane, exercises can begin to include movement in various planes. This progression will develop the ability to control deceleration and rotary forces, developing the strength and stability required for power initiation.

Knowing several guidelines to simplify or advance an exercise will allow you to modify each exercise many times over to define the level of challenge that your athletes need. If you are uncertain, choose regressions to ensure that players can complete the exercise safely, within their current abilities. But when players gain experience with an exercise and begin to find it easy, have them adopt progressions that challenge them. If an exercise is not challenging, it will not stimulate improvement. With this in mind, consider the following points in regressing or progressing exercises and successive workouts.

Training Regressions

To keep athletes safely moving forward, knowing when to regress and back off training demands can aid progression. Training regression can also be appropriate for defining the best overload, allowing solid technique with demands appropriate to linking biomechanics and physiological response. Players who must struggle beyond their ability to fight through a load too heavy or a movement too fast and complex may face injury and certainly will not improve the biomechanics of athletic performance. Training prescriptions need to define the right amount of challenge to elicit intense, best efforts and stimulate improvement. To produce optimal results, they must be neither too hard nor too easy.

Coaches evaluate players through testing, workouts, and practices to determine what challenges players can safely handle. But this is an ongoing process. The coach must have a keen, observant eye and be ready to tweak an exercise for any participant. If the athlete is lifting a weight in an unstable environment and cannot successfully lift the weight with reasonable body control, the coach could remove the instability, decrease the weight, or both. Further, the coach could retain the weight and instability but regress to a simpler exercise that requires a shorter range of motion, a more mechanically advantageous body position, or less coordination to execute. All these choices modify the exercise demand to a level more suitable for the athlete.

Progressive Overload

The exercise must be stressful enough to stimulate a physical change in the body. Often this involves working muscles and energy systems against a sufficiently heavy resistance to induce momentary fatigue (overloading). Training sets up the muscles and body parts so that they will adapt and recover to become stronger, more fit, and more skillful. As the athlete makes improvements, the conditioning program must progress to keep challenging the muscles, energy systems, and nervous system.

There are many ways to elevate the challenge imposed on the physiological and neuromuscular systems. Further physical adaptations depend on progressive overload to ensure that the training stimulus is stressful enough to keep challenging the mind and body. To increase the challenge, an athlete can increase the number of sprint repetitions (volume), decrease rest intervals for sprints (density), skate harder with a higher heart rate (intensity), progress from three to four strength-training workouts per week (frequency), run for a longer time (duration), add unpredictability (reactivity), make a lift sequence more difficult to coordinate (complexity), or emphasize more power initiation for longer sets (explosive capacity).

Changing any of the following variables can temporarily produce further improvement. Some have less utility than others. Some variables, identified first, are best applied early in a training cycle, whereas others can be drawn on forever and manipulated to challenge upper-end abilities by stimulating further adaptations.

Volume

Volume refers to the total number of sets and reps in a program. Volume is often quantified as (sets × reps × load) for a given workout. A higher training volume often produces better training results, but volume is manipulated at different times of the season to achieve specific conditioning results. A large training volume builds a base of conditioning, specifically improving strength and lean mass, decreasing fat, and sometimes improving aerobic fitness. Lower volumes are characteristic of high-intensity training that builds anaerobic power and capacity, speed, quickness, and agility. Lower volumes are also common during the in-season period to accommodate games, on-ice practices, and travel.

Frequency

Frequency—the number of times that the player trains—also affects conditioning. To achieve substantial physical changes, players must perform training three or more times a week. Maintaining a given fitness level requires at least two training sessions per week, depending on the level. Theoretically, training more frequently improves conditioning, and breaking workouts into shorter training sessions done more frequently can magnify results. For example, a player who trains 5 days per week for 2 hours may modify her program to 5 days per week, twice a day, for 1 hour each session. This scheme can produce superior results by improving the quality of each session and allowing rest and refueling before continuing efforts. But schedule logistics make this approach difficult. In addition, players often find that once they are mentally into a workout, aggressively pushing themselves, they do better staying in that mode rather than returning physically refreshed to attack a second workout that day.

Duration

For a given intensity, the greater the duration of training, the greater the training effect. The duration can be manipulated to satisfy the progressive overload principle. Common examples include lengthening the time of a run or cycling workout. But the length of time that an athlete should work out each session depends on the type of training. Remember that quality training is much more efficient and beneficial than sheer quantity training. The trend is to exert more effort during slightly shorter workouts to achieve the best results. But duration may be applied to hockey players' programs to increase the body's capacity and hence the players' readiness to tackle more intense variables such as load or speed of movement. For a player who is beginning to train anaerobically, adding more workout time (additional sprint intervals) to the workout helps build a foundation before adding more resistance or speed, shortening rest intervals, or lengthening sprint intervals.

Loading

Increasing load—the amount of weight that must be lifted—is the primary and favorite method to elicit additional strength gain. Selecting a heavier load recruits more muscle fibers and generates more muscle tension to stimulate muscle growth. Given good technique and inclusion of exercises in a standing position, the number one method of overload that my athletes use is moving more weight. They increase load by selecting a heavier dumbbell, loading an Olympic bar with more plates, or using heavy resistance Slastix tubing. Another way to challenge the body to handle a load is to place the body at a biomechanical disadvantage (for example, pushing a load in a standing position after initially training to push a load when lying supported on a bench); change the base of support (moving to a single-leg position); use the same load in an unstable environment (adding a challenging balance board); change from a dumbbell to heavy Slastix tubing (which offers more resistance toward the end of the range of motion, requiring more stabilization and eccentric control); or increase the exercise complexity for a given load. Manipulating any of these variables can make the brain recruit more muscle fibers and additional muscle groups.

Tempo and Phase Emphasis

The lowering or negative phase is known as an eccentric contraction (muscle lengthening), and the positive phase is called a concentric contraction (muscle shortening). Between lowering and raising a weight or stopping and starting a movement is the transition phase. Adjusting the tempo for each phase of movement helps define the results that the athlete will achieve. Every hockey player wants to skate faster, get his shot away quicker, and bodycheck more explosively. But training needs to follow purposeful progression. Skipping initial phases will limit the ultimate speed, quickness, and power that a player can draw on in game action.

Slow eccentric (negative phase) lifts achieve greater strength and hypertrophy gains, whereas fast concentric lifts are better for power production. Slow eccentric loadings are safest initially during movement drills, whereas fast eccentric–concentric coupling combinations will later produce the best quickness results. Following a step-by-step tempo progression will help the athlete successfully acclimate to new exercises and progress safely to advanced training methods to enjoy the best performance gains.

Step 1. Control tempo—2 seconds eccentric, 1 second transitional pause, 2 seconds concentric.

Step 2. Increase the depth of eccentric loading. An athlete who is lifting in a hypertrophy phase may opt to lengthen the eccentric phase to 4 seconds.

Step 3. Control down, pause, and power up.

Step 4. Execute a fast eccentric lift, pause, and power up.

Step 5. Add coupling. Execute a fast eccentric lift and immediately power up.

Step 6. Increase velocity throughout the lift.

Step 7. Adjust eccentric range of motion so that the athlete is initiating power at varying ranges of motion.

Density

Workout density involves the amount of rest between sets. There are different ways to apply density to a workout, depending on what results are desired. Low density is key when quality of primary results is desired, such as increasing strength or increasing quickness. Density can be quantified as work-to-rest time, such as a 1:4 work-to-rest ratio. High-density programming helps take improvements and build capacity within that system. Working on legs, a player could perform a heavy set of squats followed immediately by jump squats and then move right into unstable deep tuck holds. This program uses density to build both strength and strength endurance.

Less intense, more general workouts such as circuit training can use density (little or no rest between exercises) to maintain heart rate through a variety of exercises. This program accomplishes a well-rounded workout during a light training phase. A high-density workout usually features lower duration and volume and is therefore more time efficient. High-density workouts are sometimes used in-season to fit in a dryland strength and muscular endurance workout, often postgame. Circuit training has high energy cost but produces below-optimal results for all other components, such as strength, quickness, and speed.

But you can integrate high density into traditional work–rest lifting programs to add metabolic benefits without compromising strength improvements. The density variable can be effectively applied with three exercises that use different body parts so that the athlete can apply maximal strength and power throughout. The 3 set lift sequence is long enough to drive up heart rates but short enough to be fueled anaerobically (as compared with circuits). A player might approach a lift with a push–pull–core three-set sequence, with no rest until he completes the third exercise in the complex. The exercises draw on different musculature so strength gain is not jeopardized, and the multiple-set approach improves the anaerobic energy system.

Intensity

Intensity, a measure of physical exertion, is the most important factor in physical adaptation. The more intense the training, the greater the physical change in the body. When a player is strength training, using heavy resistance and lifting to momentary fatigue each set, will produce greater changes in the body. For aerobic activity, raising the athlete's heart rate to within a certain training zone will result in the desired cardiovascular changes. For the progressive overload principle, if something is changed to increase intensity, the player is advancing the level of overload applied to challenge the body.

Intensity can be changed by varying lifting loads or speed of movement, maintaining effort for a longer duration, or attempting to apply more force. Applying a best effort requires greater physical exertion. Every rep should be a best effort. Applying maximal efforts always magnifies the physiological response.

Neural Complexity

Strength-training programs should prepare participants for real-life movement and complex sport skills. The brain thinks in terms of movement, not muscle. This is a simple statement, but the mechanisms that control whole-body movement are complex. Neural complexity is another overload variable, challenging participants to solve the puzzle of how to coordinate mechanics to succeed at an exercise. In this process, players learn to activate the muscles that allow them to stabilize loading points before they power through concentric contractions.

In the health club setting, an effort is made to make exercise execution safe and simple, either targeting a cardiovascular response or isolating specific muscles with an aim for hypertrophy. But to optimize training and transferability of strength and conditioning to hockey performance, a more complex kind of workout that requires greater neural input is preferred.

In a traditional isolation strength setting, as strength improves, the activation level needed to recruit and command muscles to contract actually decreases. Because the individual muscle fibers are now stronger, fewer need to be recruited to lift a fixed load. But if we increase the amount of activation, more force is automatically generated and strength improvements progress more rapidly. The trick is to increase muscle size and strength and then manipulate training variables to force the nervous system to dial up the maximal number of fibers to perform the work.

We have already discussed some of the variables. Now, how can we manipulate them to attain results that carry over from the training room to the ice? Participants may be coached to move the load farther outside the midline, preload their legs more aggressively, preferentially recruit more fast-twitch fibers, place their bodies at a biomechanical disadvantage, couple eccentric–concentric actions for high-velocity power, achieve more time under tension, or integrate instability. All these changes rely on greater neural input. In the end, the goal is stronger and smarter muscles. Attaining this goal requires a specific curriculum to remap the brain and unify firing patterns, thus enhancing stabilization and kinetic chain motion.

The specificity principle implies that greater hockey gains occur when training is similar to performance patterns because of the way in which the neural system programs the option. A big, strong muscle is only as useful as the software that innervates it. A player who strength trains using an exercise like BOSU step-up to shoulder press (see page 91) will experience improvement in the strength of the shoulders, abdominals, back extensors, and quadriceps. This links the opposite leg and arm in with the hips and postural muscles so they can function well together, on the ice. If the player took his new quadriceps and shoulder strength and tried a new exercise such as leg extensions or lateral raises, the bigger and better muscles would not be able to demonstrate their full level of strength when performing the new exercises. A big, strong muscle is only as useful as the software that innervates it. The specificity principle implies that greater gains occur when training is similar to performance patterns because of the way in which the neural system programs the action.

Certain training methods can ensure that the player is laying down patterns required for all foundational hockey moves. Considerations include movement patterns, range of motion, joint angle, speed of contraction, angle of power initiation, and coupling position. The more universal the training, the greater the transference to other strength moves and to athletic maneuvers. In contrast exercises, very athletic exercises with a neural coordination challenge create better linkage to refined on-ice skills and maneuvers.

Reactivity

The body is blessed with sensors, receptors, and minibrains that assess the relative position of each limb, joint, and muscle; deviations from the center of mass; body sway; speed of muscle lengthening and joint movement; and a host of other moderators of posture and mechanics. A training program can overload and train these sensors, receptors, and minibrains to improve responsiveness.

Whole-body responsiveness and individual joint reactivity will be tested during the unexpected—play breakdowns, races for loose pucks, lanes opening, incidental contact, purposeful collision, or teams altering their attack. The ability to read, react, and respond relies on effective reactivity in each area of the body. Reactive neuromuscular training has the goal of improving immediate fine-motor adjustments that lead to a precise, high-speed, whole-body response. That is hockey!

Reactivity depends on neural connectivity trained with integrated instability, deceleration training, unpredictable agility, and coach reaction drills. The goal is to increase receptor sensitivity so that the receptor notices a biomechanical deviation sooner; to speed up the neural loop so that the player's software can detect, decide what to do, and send the message to the muscles quicker to initiate a response; and to enhance motor coordination to respond with an accurate, precise motor action. After an athlete can control his body in this way, he will have mind–muscle compliancy. That is the goal of reactive neuromuscular training. A smart hockey player does not just see the ice well and make good positional decisions. He also has a smart body that reacts quickly and accurately.

Integrated Overload Strategies

At the far end of the progressive overload spectrum is a highly conditioned player of excellent athletic ability. How does a coach continue to overload and challenge a world-class athlete? One key point to temper the enthusiasm to start players on the most difficult drills: Even the NHL's finest player needs to enter conditioning safely with testing, break-in periods, and new exercise acclimation. Only then can the coach challenge the player with high-difficulty drills. Top players do not skip steps. When they are well into their training program, mixing three key variables will continue to challenge them and produce aggressive gains:

- **Option 1: Load + slow tempo + instability.** A common progression is to move from simple to complex, from slow movement to fast movement. But combining a load at slow, controlled tempos on a BOSU Balance Trainer or a challenging balance board heightens the degree of difficulty from a strength perspective, for both prime movers and stabilizers. Surprisingly, moving a thick strength tube (Slastix tubing) through a purposefully slow, full range of motion recruits additional muscles and drives up the heart rate response to fuel the effort. I was fortunate to be part of Dr. Greg Anderson's research team who compared regular push-ups with dual-instability push-ups as measured by EMG activity. The dual-instability push-ups increased muscle activation over 1,000 percent!

- **Option 2: Load + fast tempo + neural complexity.** Moving a load at explosive speed through complex movement patterns aims to build skillful explosive power. Neural complexity advances by placing the body at a biomechanical disadvantage (such as finishing on one leg), integrating movement into a lift, or adding instability to the finish point (after generating explosive power, breaking momentum, and then holding the peak finish on an unstable surface). The load can also be body weight that preloads the legs during movement drills at higher tempos through more complex patterns. On stable surfaces, lifting against heavy resistance while coordinating more complex biomechanical requirements and trying to express power not only helps the transferability to hockey but also helps overload the body's muscles and software.

- **Option 3: Load + movement sequencing + reactivity.** Catching, absorbing, stabilizing, and throwing a medicine ball can be blended with a movement skill drill, with the movement initiated on the coach's command. For example, the athlete can load the left leg (shift weight over and down on the outside leg into a partial squat, in the one-leg ready position) before reacting to the coach's throw release by exploding laterally, landing on the right leg while catching the ball, striving to land in a controlled, strong, balanced position. The athlete holds the position until the coach cues him to throw the ball back, concurrently striding off his right leg back to the starting position (see page 87). When working with a dynamic load, the drill movement pattern is often known but the timing is unpredictable. Still, given a dynamic load, each catch requirement will be slightly different. Whether using a medicine ball catch and throw or dynamic action with Slastix tubing, dumbbells, or Olympic bars, part of the equation is setting the body to produce force in the right sequence through the kinetic chain from toe to fingertip and in hockey-relative patterns.

Specificity

Two other principles of training will influence on-ice results. Some players dedicate a lot of time and effort to general workouts, hoping that they can later benefit from this nonspecific training during hockey-specific actions. But benefits from general workouts will not transfer to the ice. At best, nonspecific training improves fitness but yields little improvement in on-ice performance. Sometimes general workouts improve fitness, which can allow players to display their existing skill level longer in a game before fatigue diminishes output. Often, however, nonspecific training is counterproductive.

Training mainly with exercises that are nonspecific in movement pattern, speed of movement, range of motion, joint angle, contraction type, and contraction force can hinder on-ice skill execution, which requires very different movement patterns, speed of movement, range of motion, joint angle, contraction type, and contraction force. The specificity principle also considers muscle groups used, work times, distances, and rest periods. The more specific the conditioning program is to game demands, the more the training effects will transfer onto the ice to benefit skills and improve hockey performance. Power Skater strides (see page 158) and Power Plyo angled lateral jumps (see page 157) are good examples of sport-specific resistance training exercises that prepare athletes for on-ice activity because they use the skating muscles and incorporate a similar movement pattern.

MUSCLE SEQUENCING

Muscle sequencing is another product of the specificity principle. Human anatomy in movement is a kinetic chain that follows a certain order. On the ice, a player's brain does not think in terms of muscle groups but rather in terms of whole-body movement. Skating and releasing a wrist shot starts in the skate and finishes with the hands. Force development crosses the ankle, knee, hips, core, and onward to the upper extremities. A hockey player who uses a toe-to-fingertip force production system, firing the muscles in the correct order, will

- produce the most total force,
- produce the most fluid action,
- minimize the risk of injury,
- achieve the same in the training environment, and
- transfer dryland strength gains to on-ice action.

Fatigue can interfere with muscle sequencing and lead to injury, so power capacity and anaerobic endurance will help maintain skillful multijoint movement. To help position players mechanically to develop toe-to-fingertip force, the coach or trainer should cue them to preload their legs and lower their mass onto their legs before producing force, putting them into an athletic ready or power position. This position will help them during open-ice hits, with containment in the corner, or when moving an opponent out of the slot. A player can preload lateral starts or ward-offs by shifting his center of mass laterally over the back leg, which he drives from. Preloading sets up the player for triple extension across the ankle, knee, and hip joints to power upper-body skills. The player who wants to produce the most power on the ice must get low and drive from the legs. This position also sets up the player to fire the muscles in the correct order.

RECORDING WORKOUT STRUCTURE AND RESULTS

Recording the results of conditioning sessions ensures proper monitoring and refinement of a player's program and shows the progression made toward goals. Documenting daily workout results also helps keep players new to training on track, improving their program adherence.

Consider keeping a hockey conditioning logbook in which you list the results of on-ice and off-ice conditioning sessions. Record the date, type of exercise (for example, strength), muscle group being worked, name of exercise, weight lifted, number of sets and reps, rest time between sets, and total workout duration. For energy system training, record peak and average heart rates, distance or time, speed or resistance, work-to-rest ratios, and the number of interval repeats.

Recording the quantifiable structure, which in essence is the workout design and exercise prescription, allows coaches and players to progress subsequent workouts logically. On-ice conditioning may target several components within one practice, so you should also record drills and drill diagrams, indicate what the drills are intended to work on, and note which players participated.

To help design future workouts, coaches and players should add subjective feedback such as "My legs were really tight and tired after that drill," "My hamstrings were tight from yesterday," "My forearms were too fatigued to max out my back exercises," or "I could have handled more." With the recording of quantifiable and subjective details, the coach can more accurately modify workouts to an optimal structure and challenge. A consistent workout log allows players to monitor and adjust training, as necessary, to help ensure that they are not overtraining or undertraining. The log will also help regulate continual upward adjustment to assure steady progress.

Chapter 11

Year-Round Conditioning

The schedule and design of year-round conditioning is called periodization, which simply means conditioning in phases in which specific physical components are developed at different volumes, densities, intensities, frequencies, durations, loads, and speeds of movement. These variables are manipulated to control the training effect, based on scientific principles and methodologies that present the best time and the best method for conditioning each physical component. From a general view, the hockey year is divided into four phases—the off-season, preseason, in-season, and postseason. What is conditioned and how it is conditioned will vary depending on the phase. The rules or guidelines within each phase will optimize results, prevent overtraining, and structure the routine so that the hockey player peaks at key times.

Coaching books in all sports break down periodization into different categories and may refer to these phases as cycles of training. The macrocycle is the entire year of conditioning. In some sports it can be longer. For Olympic athletes, the macrocycle may be 4 years long. The macrocycle is broken down into several distinct phases called mesocycles. To organize training, hockey may be divided into seven mesocycles, defined by the first half of the off-season, the second half of the off-season, the team's preseason training camp and exhibition phase, the first and second half of the in-season game schedule, the active postseason (playoffs), and the postseason recovery phase, defined by the end of playoffs to the start of off-season training. Conditioning is structured and organized during these different periods to build up selected physical attributes in a way that considers all the physical demands on the player so that sufficient rest and recovery occurs. Within each mesocycle are microcycles, typically 1 week long. Microcycles are the weekly plan that helps to meet the goals of the mesocycle.

To head in the right direction, coaches and players need to recognize that what is conditioned and how it is conditioned varies in the different cycles of a year-round hockey conditioning program. Changing the recipe of training within each main mesocycle is a great place to start. After gaining experience in manipulating the formula for training prescriptions, they can become more meticulous until they are examining each individual week, adjusting the recipe to present the most suitable demands on the athlete. Within each cycle, for each physical component within a cycle, and for each individual athlete, there are specific how-to rules and rates of progression. As the athlete progresses from one training cycle to another, the variables are structured to achieve the goals of that specific cycle.

Rules of periodization underlie both weight-room-based practices and sport practices to prepare players for competition. Oddly though, unlike the head coaches of track and field, swimming, rowing, speedskating, bicycle racing, and triathlons, who meticulously structure sport practices based on the physiology deemed suitable for the periodized plan, hockey coaches tend to think of a few good Xs-and-Os drills before practice. In the NHL, attending to the intricacies of each cycle and keeping an eye open to identify skaters' mechanical failure could help prevent many acute trauma injuries that are caused by overuse, repetitive strain, overtraining, undertraining, and imposing unsuitable demands on players in a given cycle.

Periodizing an athlete's development is both art and science. You need to understand the science behind hockey performance, how the body works, and how it adapts to different stressors. There is an art to applying sport science information: what you condition during each phase and how you condition it is a big part of the art of exercise prescription. Even with adherence to guidelines that optimize the design of year-round workouts and practices, hockey is a challenging sport to train. Players need an array of physical attributes as versatile as those required of a decathlete. Those attributes must be trained specifically for the sport demands and must integrate a unique skill set—skating on ice and using a stick to handle a puck. Hockey players are sprinters with phenomenal endurance, yet are powerful for combatives. An intricate balance is needed to secure all the attributes required of players within a short off-season and throughout an in-season packed with games and travel.

To help achieve this goal, the training style itself is designed so that the methodology used to train one component also helps to improve another component. For example, many of the upper-body multijoint lifts also strengthen the core and legs, integrate movement sequencing and balance, and drive up the anaerobic energy system. The yearly training schedule emphasizes some physical components before it does others. The physical components targeted in a hockey player's annual conditioning program are shown in figure 11.1. The base of the triangle is the building block. Various components are then progressively conditioned, leading to peak hockey performance.

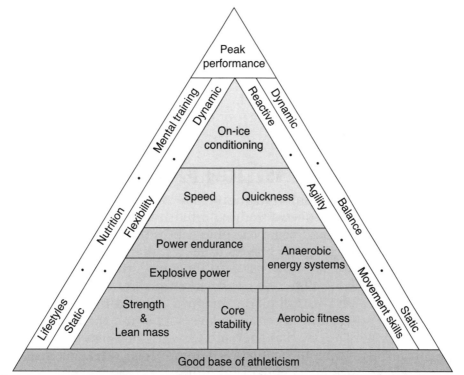

Figure 11.1   Progression from a base of fitness to hockey-specific conditioning, building to peak hockey performance.

"Players now see the opportunity in the summer to make themselves better hockey players by training for hockey. Everything is geared toward getting better as a hockey player. Not so much as getting in shape, but getting better as a hockey player," explained Tim Hunter, an experienced voice after a 16-year NHL career that included a Stanley Cup with the Calgary Flames in 1989 and a seven-game Stanley Cup final series with the Vancouver Canucks against the New York Rangers in 1994. Hunter won the Canucks' Top-Conditioned Player award at age 34 and again at age 35. Currently an assistant coach with the San Jose Sharks, he adds, "You can become a better hockey player from one season to the next, in the summer, by working on things in the off-season geared toward your hockey skills. Stickhandling, specific strength training, quick-hand drills, quick-feet drills . . . everyone's looking for an edge."

To help the annual training formula produce better results but still keep the process palatable, this chapter divides the hockey player's year-round conditioning into four phases or mesocycles. This includes a phase I off-season that may be 4 to 6 weeks long; a phase II off-season of 4 to 6 weeks; an in-season that encompasses all team time including preseason training camps, exhibition games, regular-season games, and playoffs; and a 4-week postseason that acts as a transition from the end of the season to when off-season conditioning begins.

The exact length and timing of each mesocycle varies with the level of hockey and each team's success. Players on NHL teams who do not make the playoffs finish their season in April and have almost 5 months until their next training camp. When we went to the seventh game of the Stanley Cup Championship, we had only 2 1/2 months between the playoffs and training camp, and that included the postseason recovery period! Teams and players will have to adjust the four phases of conditioning to suit the characteristics of their seasons.

POSTSEASON TRANSITION PHASE

The theme of the postseason transition phase is rest, recovery, and preparation of the body for renewed training intensities.

I expected that I would order the phases beginning with the first day of off-season training, but my players usually contact me toward the end of their season or while in the playoffs. Of course, they are focused 100 percent on their team's objective but smart enough to check in briefly to ensure that their after-season plan is mapped out and that resources are in place. For a successful off-season, players must use their after-season period effectively. The day that they end their season is the day that they begin preparing for their next season. Therefore, it is positioned here, first in line in the year-round calendar of training.

After a season ends, ideally deep in the playoffs but for some after the regular season, a formal transition phase occurs between the end of the team's season schedule and the beginning of the individual player's off-season training. In hockey, transitions rarely receive the resources that they require. How many times has a junior hockey player represented his country in a world championship, played the best hockey of his life, and then returned to his junior team and a lower level of competition, only to struggle for weeks?

A transition phase should receive as much thought and planning as an off-season program or a team playoff plan, because left to chance, the results are often disastrous. Whether the after-season phase is used effectively or not has a significant influence on off-season training results and the player's health.

The postseason phase has three key purposes. One is to rest and repair physically and recover mentally from the rigors and stress of the season. The second goal is to use the time to tune up the body so that it is operating well as the player enters the off-season training phase. The third is to maintain a base of fitness so that the player does not end up starting off-season training completely from scratch.

Physical Repair and Mental Recovery

Some coaches recommend complete rest almost immediately after the last playoff game. Generally, this is not a good idea. In that last game, the physical challenge, mental stress, emotional demands, and hormonal involvement are all at their peak. Following such intensity, the body needs to gear down gradually, not suddenly. Both mind and body are accustomed to functioning at an all-out level—abruptly shutting everything down is unhealthy.

Players do need to rest and recover, but they achieve this while remaining active in casual sport activities or light, varied workouts to taper toward active rest, recovery, and relaxation. Some of the activities that my players take up include downhill skiing, mountain hiking, swimming, road cycling. Each finds his respective activity enjoyable and the environment and circle of people positive. A positive, fun environment facilitates repair and regeneration, and has obvious mental benefits. Being bummed out after a disappointing season is OK, as is celebrating after a successful one. But the mind soon needs to unload. The best way to accomplish this is with variety—in activity, environment, and people—in a constructive situation.

Tune-Up

Some players will have injuries to rehabilitate, and most will have banged-up bodies that can benefit not only from rest but also from an effort to realign. Players need to be active participants in the process. This is the time to consult with forward-thinking chiropractors, physiotherapists, and massage therapists who can assess, apply corrective adjustments and exercises, and recommend what players need to do to tune up the body to its best alignment and function. If players take care of this now, they can attack off-season training more aggressively. If they don't, their training will be limited because they carry side issues that they must deal with later in the summer or that will surface as injuries weeks or months later.

Coaches and trainers who work with players in the off-season must recognize their core competencies and refer athletes to other professionals for expert work that may be outside their scope of practice. Postseason, a team approach should be taken to ensure that players are given a variety of checkups to assess the season's damage and receive the corrective techniques needed to enter off-season training with a finely tuned body.

Base Maintenance

Without question, players must take a break, experience a variety of activities, rest, have fun. Some players are too eager to jump right back into training. On the other end of the continuum, other players are completely sedentary and stretch that out too long, placing themselves at a disadvantage. Middle ground is the place to aim for.

Because active unloading is healthier than suddenly becoming completely sedentary, maintaining a base is natural. But how much and how hard? The general rule is to take it easy, but this phase is somewhat intuitive. Players need to listen to their bodies, especially their minds. If they are enthusiastic or find activities that they love, and their bodies respond well, they could pick up the frequency and intensity a step. The goal is to recover, rest, and have fun but also maintain some fitness and even take fitness up a step, so that the body is used to moving going into the first day of the formal off-season program. More specifically, players should participate in an aerobic activity three times a week and complete some core stability exercises three times per week to secure a minimum base of fitness and readiness for the off-season program.

OFF-SEASON PREPARATION PHASE I

The theme for off-season preparation phase I is to grab the lead in strength and conditioning.

Just as the style of training, the game itself, and the athletes have changed, so too has the schedule. Players at all levels face a heavier game schedule. Counting exhibition games, regular-season games, and possible playoff games, the NHL schedule includes over 100 games a year. The off-season is almost a month shorter than basketball's, 1 1/2 months shorter than baseball's, and less than half that of football's. Many minor hockey players endure a high volume of games and then add a separate spring league to secure more high-caliber games. Overall, down time away from hockey is shrinking. The margin for error is smaller. When training begins, taking the right steps is critical.

The off-season begins by building a base of aerobic fitness and strength. Upcoming high-intensity anaerobic conditioning, speed development, muscular endurance and power, and on-ice activity will rely on a solid aerobic and strength base. Strength and aerobic fitness are trained concurrently with the style outlined in chapters 4 and 5, which feeds strength and drives upper-end fitness levels.

But if the season ends by March, as it will for many college teams, or in April, as it will for many other levels, players can enjoy a full-recovery postseason, a full 6-week phase II off-season, and still be left with a phase I off-season that is more than 6 weeks long. Players who need to add mass and can net out a longer phase I off-season would begin with a full schedule of strength training but limit aerobic conditioning to twice per week. "When you combine both for extended periods, strength can suffer while the aerobic base will continue to build," says Coach Lorne Goldenberg, who trained the Quebec Nordiques, Ottawa Senators, St. Louis Blues, Chicago Blackhawks, and Florida Panthers. "I usually try to allow for 3 to 4 weeks of strength training without any aerobic work," says Goldenberg. The player who has the luxury of a long off-season can work first on building his strength base and gaining lean muscle mass. Then he can build strength and aerobic base together over the last 6 weeks of the off-season. Initially, expending all effort on strength training will maximize strength and mass gains. Then, limiting the heavy aerobic period to 6 weeks of higher speed intermittent aerobic workouts will build the important aerobic base while keeping physical changes more specific to the demands of hockey.

During the off-season, players should stretch daily to complement full-range-of-motion strength training and improve their flexibility for on-ice speed, quickness, and agility. Players should continue to tune up the body, making sure that it is aligned properly before graduating to more explosive work in phase II.

Players should learn and rehearse techniques and movement patterns for quickness, agility, and speed development, at a slow, easy pace as part of warm-ups and cool-downs. This is the time to identify potential strength imbalances and technique flaws that can be worked on to enhance future high-intensity drill technique and skill execution.

In the sample phase I off-season workout (table 11.1), the exercise curriculum uses a chest–back, push–pull lift with complementing core stabilization. Movement skill acquisition is targeted at this stage of the off-season, which also provides a well-rounded warm-up.

Table 11.1 Off-Season Conditioning Phase I

Focus: movement skill foundation, push–pull strength lift, core stabilization (90-minute workout)

Coach's notes: Early summer warm-ups teach and rehearse specific movement skills that will later feed into agility. A short volume quickness workout targets fast feet without significant displacement of the center of mass, while the player is warmed up but fresh. The quickness exertion and good sweat put the player in a good mental state to push hard in the lift. A lift prep warms up the chest and back while preparing the core and shoulders to support the exercises. A push–pull lift overloads the chest and back and integrates core stabilization. Additional core exercises complete the workout.

Drills and exercises	Sets × reps	Tempo	Details
Dynamic warm-up: movement skills (15 minutes)			Zigzag cone formation
Cool walk with knee drive	1 × floor	Control	Extend up tall on toes, pause on toes
Butt kickers	3 × floor	Control	Light feet, heels to butt, use arms
High knees	3 × floor	Control	Light feet, knees up, use arms
Backpedal	3 × floor	Control	Stay low, reach back, use arms
Hockey lunge walk	1 × floor	3-second hold	45-degree lunge, hockey arm swing
Zigzag lateral bound and hold	1 × floor	Control	Land soft and hold for 3 seconds
Plant-and-go sprint (open or drop steps)	3 × floor	Quick	Low plant, positive angle
Lateral side shuffle	3 × floor	Quick	Stay low, back straight
Sumo squat reverse pivot	1 × floor	3-second hold	Wide stance, drop down low
Lateral bound and hold	1 × floor	Hold	Land low, light landing, knee over toe
Carioca shuffle	3 × floor	Quick	Swivel hips, light feet

(continued)

Table 11.1 (continued)

Crossover and cross-under pushes	3 × floor	Quick	Push off with cross-under leg, fully extend
Forward line drill	4 × 10	Quick	Inward rotate front planting last 2 sets
Lateral crossover-line drill	4 × 10	Quick	Use method B, wide
Ladder narrow shuffle	4 × 10	Quick	Light feet, rapid, soft on ground
Linked system strength prep (10 minutes)			
Extreme board push-ups	2 × 10	3:1:3	Flat back, core set, shoulders over wrists
Stability ball jump push-ups with pause landing	2 × 10	1:3:1	Flat back, arms bent on landing, core set
Medicine ball shoulder-to-shoulder pass	2 × 10	1:1:2	Shoulders level to ground, use hips, finish in extension
Strength lift complex I (25 minutes)			
Olympic rock singers with lat step	3 × 12 per side	1:3	Athletic position, core set, arm slightly bent
Supine pull-ups with towel grip	3 × 12	3:1:3	Flat body, neutral grip, scapula retracted
Stability ball hockey stick push-ups	3 × 12	3:1:3	Feet hip width apart, grip outside the ball
Squat to row	3 × 12 per arm	1:1:3	Elbows in, shoulder blades retracted
Strength lift complex II (25 minutes)			
BOSU drop step to Slastix tubing push	3 × 12 per arm	1:3	Athletic position, initiate with legs
Single-leg, opposite-arm row	3 × 12 per arm	1:2:3	Core set, shoulders set, bend at the hip
TRX push-ups	3 × fatigue	3:2:3	Prone, lean on toes, arms out from body
TRX row	3 × fatigue	1:2:3	Supine, palms facing out, core set
Core stabilization (15 minutes)			
Partner knock-offs	2 × 30 seconds	Hold	Low athletic position, core engaged
Partner ball hold on BOSU holding stability ball	2 × 12	Hold	Arms slightly bent and out from body
Up, up, down, down	2 × max	Control	Plank position, elbow, elbow, hand, hand
Two-ball instability rollouts	3 × 12	Hold	Hips level, arm and leg extended out

The ratio in the tempo column defines in seconds the time for the positive phase, midhold, and negative phase. For example, if the tempo is 1:2:2, the player would lift the weight in 1 second, hold strong at midpeak for 2 seconds, and take 2 seconds to lower the weight under control.

Flexibility

- Stretch daily *after* each workout and perform myofascial release.

Aerobic

- Complete the aerobic workout twice per week before the last 6 weeks of the phase I off-season (before the last 6 weeks of the first half of the summer).
- Complete the aerobic workout three to five times per week over the last 6 weeks.
- Begin with continuous aerobic workouts.
- Progress by increasing the duration of each workout. Next, increase the intensity, completing it at a faster pace.
- Progress to intermittent aerobic workouts with a high-speed emphasis.

Anaerobic

- During the last 4 weeks of this phase, perform full anaerobic sprint intervals once per week.

Strength and power

- Complete the strength workout four times per week, with a focus on strength and mass.
- Continue a core emphasis as stand-alone sets but also integrated into most upper- and lower-body lifts. Build from the inside out.
- Use moderate weights and high reps (12 to 15) for a 1-week break-in period.
- Graduate into a full program with low reps (6 to 12), progressively heavier weights, and controlled lift tempos, using a slow 3- to 4-second eccentric loading in some of the exercises and a constant pace on others, 2 seconds up and 2 seconds down, plus some pause holds at mid positions.
- As you adapt to the program, increase the volume (number of exercises and number of sets) in the workouts.
- Continue to increase the amount of weight that you use for each exercise.
- In the last week of the off-season, decrease the rest intervals between sets.

Balance

- Use instability three to four times per week, within the dynamic warm-up and integrated into core and strength exercises.

Quickness

- You can get started with a small volume of quickness drills twice per week.

- Select simple fast-feet drills that have little body (center of mass) displacement and low heights (low impact), such as ladder drills.
- Focus on light, soft feet and rapid foot turnover.

Agility and reactivity

- Target agility several times per week by placing drills within other workout sections.
- Incorporate controlled, paced agility movement skills into warm-ups and cool-downs to give time to assess techniques and improve mechanics. This training will make future preseason high-intensity work more efficient.
- You can separate specific movement skills or blend them together to create agility patterns, but save reaction skills for phase II. Make sure that players know the movement skill or movement pattern ahead of time and focus on precise repetition. Rehearse the known so that you can harness skilled movement for reactive and competitive games in phase II.
- Practice deceleration in multidirectional movement patterns at controlled velocities.
- Occasionally mix in some varied movement skills and controlled tempo stop-and-starts into aerobic conditioning—forward, backward, or multidirectional—which provides time to ramp up deceleration while also helping to sustain a heart rate in the training zone and unload from repetitive forward running mechanics.

Speed

- A speed break-in is achieved during higher paced intermittent aerobic exercise, which is less than a full-out best rep sprint but much faster than traditional aerobic exercise. Ultimately, it is the highest pace that you can sustain for 2 to 2 1/2 minutes.
- In the last four weeks of phase I, you can mesh initial speed training twice per week on leg strength or anaerobic days by adding reps of resisted speed drills, such as tandem tows. Given the resisted condition, the expressed velocity is low, which is inherently safer, but the overloaded stride power will be harnessed toward free sprint conditions in phase II.

On-ice

- I recommend less ice time throughout the off-season, unless skating skills are poor. If this is the case, power skating three times per week and treadmill skating once per week would be beneficial. But even poor skaters need to make sure that they are not using up too much of their available training time and expending too much energy on the ice. Practicing skating technique will yield few results unless the player first develops the physical attributes needed to support skill execution. Players should use the off-season time to build the physical tools that they can use to enhance skating technique in the preseason. If a poor skater opts for early work on the ice and skate treadmill, emphasize either quality mechanics in low-volume practices to retain the energy for conditioning or a sustained effort sufficient to elicit a training effect. On average, my players skate from zero to two times per week in phase I. Instead, adding more drill sets on the power skater would also help skating mechanics as you train leg strength.

Structured conditioning is needed to prepare specifically for hockey, but in early off-season players can sometimes replace or complement workouts with other sport activities and still gain benefits, as well as variety in the program. For example, an intense, well-played 70-minute tennis or squash match may replace an aerobic workout and a quickness and agility workout, or complement those workouts by following the tennis or squash match with a 20-minute aerobic workout and a small volume of specific quickness and agility drills. Other sports that involve constant movement along with directional changes and lateral movement (such as small-space soccer or basketball) may be used, as long as the pace is high enough. Having said that, remember that nonspecific activities occasionally have their place. Mountain biking or swimming might not impose the right load on the body for optimal hockey improvements, may be of insufficient intensity, and may not be specific, but if a player finds the activity fun, it *is* healthy, keeps him moving, and changes the demands placed on the body and mind, giving him a change from the structured routine. Think about what will help produce the best results over a *long* periodized process, not just that one day.

OFF-SEASON PREPARATION PHASE II

The theme of off-season preparation phase II is that training with intensity and specificity wins.

The second main off-season training mesocycle packages the second half of the summer and leads right into training camp. This phase is characterized by high-intensity anaerobic work, explosive power, speed, sprint endurance, quickness, and agility. A shift occurs toward higher intensity work, explosive movements, high speeds, intervals, and sport specificity. Figure 11.2 shows the relative change in volume, intensity, specificity, and skill work as a player progresses from the first half of the off-season through the full summer and into the regular season.

As they move into the second half of their off-season, players work less frequently on aerobic fitness to allow more time for sprint work. During the off-season, I stay away from too much bike training or track running. There is a shift away from these repetitive mechanics that trace a straight-ahead path. Off-season anaerobic work is characterized by multidirectional

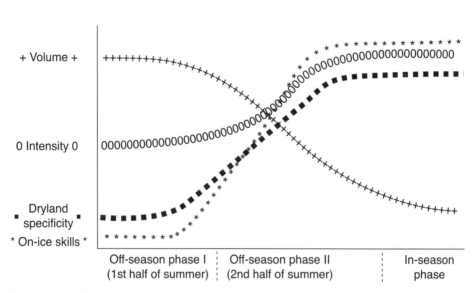

Figure 11.2 The relationship between volume, intensity, skills, and specificity at different times of the season.

intervals, competitive and unpredictable shadowing drills, and resistance tools such as parachutes and resistance harnesses that force harder efforts to skate and run to build stride power and allow crossovers, cornering and turns, and backward and lateral movement.

Strength is trained differently, to develop explosive power and muscular endurance, building off the base of strength and lean muscle mass. Lifts focus on power initiation, higher velocity movements, and the capacity to be powerful under fatigue. Balance training becomes more complex and movement oriented, and speed, quickness, and agility are trained with competition and unpredictability.

The sample phase II off-season workout (table 11.2) focuses on legs–shoulders–core rotation. From the perspective of movement sequence and reciprocal contribution, these fit well together within one workout. This workout, targeting the legs during most exercises, warms up with balance to ready the leg muscles and mind to perform at their best, and then ends with anaerobic capacity training to push the limits of what the legs can do.

Flexibility

- Continue stretching daily after each workout and perform myofascial release.
- Gain range of motion preexercise with a dynamic movement-oriented warm-up and joint mobility exercises.

Aerobic

- Complete one intermittent aerobic workout and one high-intensity continuous workout each week. Use a shorter duration but higher intensity (speed, heart rate).

Table 11.2 Off-Season Conditioning Phase II

Focus: balance, leg and shoulder power, rotary power, anaerobic energy development

Coach's notes: Instability and movement force the mind to think immediately for a focused warm-up that activates the core and warms the muscles. The slow-tempo lift prep routine gets the muscles firing in the legs–core–shoulder sequence, readies the posterior chain, and elevates heart rate and muscle temperature. Strength complexes mix legs and shoulders. Leg exercises for power are followed by power capacity. Some shoulder strength exercises *use* the legs; others *overload* the legs. When a shoulder exercise overloads the legs, it occurs earlier in the sequence. Rotary power finishes the lift, with legs and shoulders contributing to movement execution. Anaerobic conditioning ends the workout, scheduled with the leg lift to net out lower demand days for the legs, yet it is done after the rotary exercises, providing time for the legs to recover a bit from the lift. At this time of the off-season, anaerobic drills are often multidirectional, using relays and partner competition drills to push efforts higher.

Drills and exercises	Sets × reps	Tempo	Details
Dynamic warm-up: balance and core prep (12 minutes)			
BOSU hockey ready position, eyes closed	2 × 30 sec	Hold	Ready position, core set, scapula retracted, legs loaded
BOSU alternate single-leg jump, land, and hold	2 × 10	1:3:1	Land low, chest up, shoulders back and hold
Tennis ball drops into ready position on BOSU	2 × 10	Quick hold	Drop quick and under control, pause at bottom
BOSU split lunge to single-leg hold	2 × 10 per leg	3:2:3	Core set, start long stride, finish up tall
Linked system strength prep (8 minutes)			
Lateral squat to lateral raise with Slastix tubing	2 × 8 each arm	2:2:3	Strong posture, engage core and mid back
Multijoint squat to rotator cuff pulls	2 × 8 each arm	1:2:1	Drive elbow back, rotate up and around
BOSU PSU squat to shoulder press	2 × 10	3:1:3	Use light weight, finish tall, link legs and core
Strength lift complex I (30 minutes)			
Back squat to toes	3 × 4	Power up	Quick coupling, link up to toes, heavy load, focus powering out of hole
BOSU PSU squat to shoulder press	3 × 6	1:2	Finish tall, link legs and core
Lateral bound to lateral raise	3 × 6 each arm	1:1	Load low, link legs to core to shoulder
Leapfrog lateral jumps	3 × 10 per leg	Speed	Load low, link in arms
Speed squats	3 × 25	Speed	Light weight, speed, endurance, link up to toes

(continued)

Table 11.2 *(continued)*

Strength lift complex II (30 minutes)			
Crossover lunge (Olympic bar) to side of Power Plyo	3 × 6 each leg	1:1	Keep shoulders and bar square to wall, drop low
BOSU step-up to shoulder press	3 × 6 each side	1:1	Opposite arm and leg, drive off bench leg
Power Skater strides	3 × 12 each side	Speed	One leg at a time, quick coupling, fast and full stride
Front-raise repeats	3 × 6	1:1	Power up, link legs and hips
BOSU T-drill	3 × 6	Quick:2: Quick	Two-foot jumps quick off ground, hold on BOSU
Rotary power (15 minutes)			
Hockey stick rotations	2 × 10 per side	1:1	Rotate at trunk, link in hips, shoulders level
Woodchops with hold	3 × 10 per side	1:3:1	Rotate hips, finish in extension, pause at midline
Prone plank hold with cross-body knee drives	2 × 10 per leg	1:2:1	Flat back, core set, drive knee to opposite elbow
Push–pull to rotation	2 × 10	1:2:1	Split stance, athletic position, link legs
Anaerobic energy (15 minutes)			
Around, through, and over relay	6 × 30 seconds at 1:2	Speed	Lateral moves, pivots, crossovers
D-man drill	6 × 30 seconds at 1:2	Speed	Stay low, use arms, smart steps

The ratio in the tempo column defines in seconds the time for the positive phase, midhold, and negative phase. For example, if the tempo is 1:2:2, the player would lift the weight in 1 second, hold strong at midpeak for 2 seconds, and take 2 seconds to lower the weight under control.

Anaerobic

- Increase anaerobic workout frequency to three times per week.
- Progressively increase the number of sprint repetitions and the length of the sprint interval time, and decrease the between-sprint recovery time.
- As your season approaches, complete one or more of the weekly anaerobic sprint workouts on the ice.
- Your program might instead use pwer-based sets of 4-6 reps, and at other times in the workout complete sets of 15 reps for power endurance; thinking powerfully and attempting to initiate power through all reps.

Strength and power

- Lift four times per week, with a focus on harnessing strength and mass for pure explosive power as well as the capacity to maintain power output.
- Use sets of 4 to 8 reps for power and 12 or more reps for power capacity. You can challenge power capacity by performing exercises for the same muscle group with no rest between sets. For example, do a set of 6 heavy weight speed squats followed by a set of 6 lighter weight jump squats for a total of 12 reps. In this example, you would do quality power reps with heavy load at the beginning and attempt to be powerful under fatigue at the end throughout the second exercise.
- Your program might instead use power-based sets of 4 to 6 reps and, at other times in the workout, complete sets of 15 reps for power endurance, thinking powerfully and attempting to initiate power through all reps.
- Select exercises that are more sport specific, especially in the whole-body movement patterns.
- Increase the speed of movement. Aim for greater power initiation on each rep.

Balance

- Many exercises and drills in this phase are performed with maximum weight and maximum speed on flat ground or ice, but some of the sets incorporate instability.
- Use instability four times per week, within the dynamic warm-up and integrated into core, push, pull, shoulder, and leg-strength exercises.
- Use instability in some of the drills for lateral movement and deceleration, learning how to load into balanced power positions.
- Unstable surfaces also come into play for single-leg reactivity and combatives.

Quickness, agility and reactivity, and speed

- In the second half of the off-season (table 11.3), increase the intensity and volume of drills and group them together in a stand-alone workout.
- Workouts can be done both off and on the ice for a total of three per week. On a given week you could do two full sessions off the ice and one on the ice; on another week you might do three off-ice workouts but with only half the volume because you will include some drills on the ice three times per week as well. If you split dryland and on-ice training, try to pair these on the same day so that you have some days without this type of training.
- You can implement distinct on-ice drills (from chapters 7, 8, and 9) and structure some of the on-ice sprints (chapter 4) into one-on-one drills that require best efforts. Be careful you are actually developing top speed and not just skate conditioning.

Table 11.3 Off-Season Conditioning Phase II, Speed, Agility, and Quickness Session

Focus: fast feet, agility, speed, quickness, anaerobic conditioning

Coach's notes: In the second half of the summer, workouts are programmed separately to accommodate the focus on high-velocity movement drills. If players and coaches front load fast-feet and quickness drills and spend time on speed quality, the ATP-PC system and anaerobic power have received training. After finishing, they can progress into high-volume speed and agility drills to complete their anaerobic capacity conditioning as well. Getting closer to the players' training camps, quickness and agility drills follow a 1:2 work-to-rest ratio. Pure speed drills are held to a 1:4 ratio, but when speed–power drills are used for anaerobic intervals, go back to a 1:2 ratio.

Drills and exercises	Sets × reps	Tempo	Details
Dynamic warm-up: movement skills (10 minutes)			Use agility ladder
Ladder cool walk	1 × length	Control	Extend up tall on toes, pause on toes
Ladder high knees	2 × length	Control	Light feet, link in arms, drive knees up
Ladder butt kicks	2 × length	Control	Heels to butt, straight body, use arms
Ladder lateral high knees	2 × per side	Control	Light feet, link in arms, drive knees up
Ladder lateral side shuffle	2 × per side	Control	Light feet, stay low, shoulders back
Ladder lateral two in, two out	2 × per side	Control	Upper body is still, light feet
Ladder single-leg zigzag	2 × length	Control	Absorb landing, knee over toe, body control
Hockey lunge walk across ladder	1 × length	Control	45-degree lunge, skating stride arm swing
Ladder sumo squat	1 × length	Control	Wide stance, skip two rungs per pivot
Quickness (fast feet) (20 minutes)			1:4 work-to-rest ratio
Ladder lateral two in, two out	4 × length	Quick	Pop feet quickly off ground
Ladder crossovers	2 × per side	Quick	Stay low, stay narrow to ladder
Two-foot hurdle zigzag hops	4 × length	Quick	Link in arms, light landing, quick coupling
Hurdle maze drill	3 × per leg	Quick	Alternate legs each rep

Agility (15 minutes)			1:2 work-to-rest ratio
Two in, one out drill (high knees)	4 × 10	Quick	Plant on full foot with small pause
Two BOSU crossover and stick	4 × 10	Quick	Land low, absorb landing
12hurdle reaction drill	4 × 1	Quick	Athletic position, head up, plant on full foot
Partner figure-eight shadow	2 × 15 seconds (defense) 2 × 15 seconds (offense)	Quick	Efficient steps, look at chest of offensive player, stay low
Reaction belt follow the leader	2 × 20 seconds (defense) 2 × 20 seconds (offense)	Quick	Efficient steps, athletic posture, smart cutting
Speed (25 minutes)			1:4 work-to-rest ratio
Overspeed tubing sideways start	5 × each	Speed	Athletic position, drive knees up, open up hips
Overspeed tubing forward	5 × each	Speed	Athletic position, balls of feet, drive knees up
Resisted speed and overspeed skating W pattern	3 × each side	Speed	Efficient steps, stay low on backpedal, use positive angles
			1:2 work-to-rest ratio
Let-goes	6 ×	Speed	Drive knees up, create positive angle
Tandem tow resisted sprints	4 × 10 meters 4 × 20 meters 4 × 30 meters	Speed	Drive knees up, create positive angle

- Quickness and agility drills now use unpredictability and shadowing for reactivity.
- Continue the resisted speed work and complete some sprints in a free condition. Add a small volume of overspeed work.

On-ice

- Skate three to four times per week.
- Practice on-ice skill work—puckhandling, passing, shooting, skating, angling, and so on—and integrate these into high-speed skating and one-on-one tactics.
- Use small-space scrimmages to challenge skating skills, read-and-react ability, and anaerobic conditioning.
- The progression of on-ice activity, from the first on-ice session through readiness to full-intensity scrimmages, is outlined in figure 11.3.

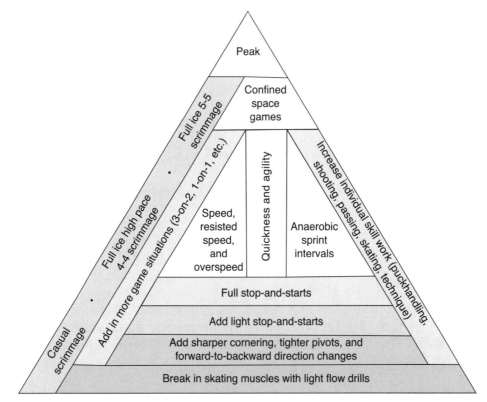

Figure 11.3   Preseason on-ice progression.

IN-SEASON PHASE

The theme of the in-season phase is to keep building.

Depending on the age, level, and league, the length and complexity (game schedule, travel, tournaments, playoffs) of each team's in-season varies. But the common theme of in-season conditioning is maintenance.

Even players who devote the entire summer to preparing for hockey will be deconditioned by the end of the season if they do not commit to in-season conditioning. If players do not schedule maintenance workouts, they will have a lower level of conditioning by playoff time, exactly when they need optimal conditioning! On-ice activity can maintain or improve some physical components. Other components need to be maintained off the ice. For example, hockey performance draws on aerobic power and muscular strength, but a hockey game does not provide the specific stimulus needed to build those components.

The high density of games and their grueling physical nature can leave players deconditioned throughout a season. Hockey demands a lot from the body for optimal performance. The constant wear and tear on the body results in fatigue that can make in-season maintenance of physical components extra challenging. Periodized training, realized in the weight room and on the ice in well-structured, well-run practices, helps maintain conditioning levels through to the playoffs; it prevents players from losing the strength and fitness that they have gained over the summer. In this way, periodization prevents undertraining and helps maintain in-season conditioning levels. Scheduled carefully, players may even make good gains during the in-season.

In the NHL and junior hockey, in-season conditioning and game readiness really tests periodization skills because the game schedule; travel; practice intensity, volume, and frequency; practice content; injuries and illnesses; and, in some cases, public relations events, media demands, demotions, call-ups, and trades are all factors that influence when and how a player should be conditioned. Coaches in charge of conditioning may have 3 hours a day with some players. At other times and with other players, they may only have 15 minutes at the end of practice to work on quickness and agility.

For those reasons, off-season programs focused only on muscles inherently fail. Players who build muscle strength with significant neuromuscular adaptation experience less strength drop-off in-season, using the complex demands of hockey along with in-season lifts that achieve overload with moderate loads and neural complexity to maintain more of their strength. Players built primarily on muscle mass will experience a significant strength drop-off in-season when performing a high volume of heavy lifts is not realistic.

University varsity players have the best training schedule, with two games per week skewed toward Friday and Saturday nights, often giving a Sunday rest day and allowing big practice and lift days on Monday, Tuesday, and Wednesday. They can typically lift a little heavier and with greater volume.

Young minor players are ideally playing other sports besides hockey that cost energy, and nonsport activities likely take up part of their schedule. Supplemental dryland training needs to be specific, purposeful, and intense to elicit desired results in the smaller amount of time that they can commit.

In-season, all players achieve anaerobic conditioning within practices (and, of course, games) through varied movement patterns and stop-and-start actions. Although skate treadmills offer benefits off-season, and my players participate in multidirectional agility sprints and running in the mountains all summer, I recommend staying away from skating treadmills when players are already on the ice many times each week (overuse injuries can result from too much skating) and also use much less agility type dryland drills. Players can unload from the multidirectional on-ice demands by selecting bike intervals. One of the reasons that triathletes traditionally experience so few injuries is their cross-training. In-season, having an exercise mode that challenges the heart, lungs, and legs but unloads the core and legs from the demands of direction change is valuable.

Knowing what concepts to challenge, how to challenge them, and which ones to unload is instrumental to injury prevention. When I was conditioning coach of the Vancouver Canucks, my players went three seasons without incurring a groin injury, a common hockey injury. Their off-season program helped determine that outcome, but an effective in-season program must complement it. Ensuring that players adhered to a specific in-season program was a significant contributor. In today's game, with all the awareness and knowledge available, players must commit themselves to working at their craft, to pursuing their goals with passion. A team needs players who are focused on improving and diligently make this a daily habit. If a hockey player is not committed to working on his physical tools, you may want to match him with a more appropriate sport to compete in, such as chess or a knit-off!

During the in-season, my goal for athletes is to maintain their overall conditioning and improve one aspect of their game. Considering coaches' evaluations of players and fitness test results, I select one weakness to key on. One player may have the goal to improve footwork and quickness; another may target improving anaerobic endurance or reducing body fat. Improving one aspect of a player's game may sound simple, but working in the required time in the face of heavy game, practice, and travel schedules, along with fatigue and minor injuries, presents a great challenge for both coach and athlete.

Improving one main area for each player will have a tremendous effect on the play of both that individual and the team as a whole. Incremental improvements by every player will make a big difference in team performance.

In-season conditioning may take various forms and play a variety of roles. It may involve conditioning within on-ice practice drills, off-ice conditioning practices, or extra on-ice and off-ice conditioning on game days for players not in the lineup. In-season conditioning plays a huge role for injured players, aggressively rehabilitating injuries and bringing the player to full game readiness. Players shouldn't have to play themselves into shape in the first few games after returning from an injury. They should return to the lineup in better shape and more game ready than anyone else on the team. Other players have been wearing down their bodies by playing games; the injured player has had time to build up and improve specific physical and skill areas.

During my 11 years with the Vancouver Canucks, immediately after most games all players completed anaerobic bike sprint intervals and full-body multijoint lifts with balance, cross-body patterns, single-leg, and core rotation characteristics built in. Scheduling our most intense off-ice training right after games allowed maximum recovery time before the next game. Although most teams do not have the facilities to accommodate this kind of workout schedule, our plan emphasizes the importance of in-season training. Teams who do not train in-season are deconditioned by the time playoffs begin. Players who do too many aerobic drills become slower and tired. Teams training for strength and anaerobic conditioning enhance their power and power capacity; that's what the game is all about!

Conditioning also emphasizes rest and recovery. Coaches need to provide adequate rest intervals between on-ice drills and during off-ice conditioning, monitor the intensity of practices, track each player's ice time during games, allow time for postgame recovery, and schedule days of complete rest. Workouts may be done after an evening game specifically to assist in recovery or to fit in a strength workout so that players can take the next day completely off for rest and recovery. Working toward optimal in-season conditioning does not always mean doing intense work. Sometimes it may require scheduling short, specialty core strength workouts, light recovery routines, or a day of complete rest, away from the weight room and away from the rink.

Table 11.4 shows a sample in-season workout. Whole-body lifts work well in-season, with the use of major complexes in which several sets are sequenced with no rest, to maintain elevated heart rates. Be sure to include core work within the complexes and quick-feet drills after the warm-up but before the lift.

Flexibility

- Continue flexibility workouts daily, doing dynamic warm-ups and joint mobility exercises before practices and games, and static stretching and myofascial release afterward.

Aerobic

- Complete off-ice continuous aerobic workouts to maintain aerobic power. These workouts are shorter (20 to 30 minutes) and less frequent (once to twice a week) but with superhigh intensity.
- Use aerobic activity of light intensity to flush the legs and speed postgame recovery. Aim for 15 minutes at 70 percent of maximum heart rate.

Table 11.4 In-Season Conditioning

Focus: balance, rapid excitation, full-body strength and power, core stabilization

Coach's notes: Integrated balance–core drills quickly warm and ready the legs, hips, core, and upper body. Small-displacement ladder drills increase the heart rate, further warm and potentiate muscles, and lead into the quickness drills. Quickness drills target footwork and deceleration without significant impact, while turning on the system to make the transition into an effective lift. The first lift complex combines legs, shoulders, and rotation, using more single-leg functional exercises that require a strong core and including a finishing move with the shoulders. The second strength complex packages chest and back together in push–pull moves. Core stabilization is inherent within the push–pull lifts selected. Standing rollouts finish up the lifts with a focus on posture and strong bracing.

Drills and exercises	Sets × reps	Tempo	Details
Dynamic warm-up: balance and core prep (10 minutes)			
Seated Humpty Dumpty medicine ball passes	2 × 10	Hold	Core engaged, shoulders back
Kneeling stability ball balance with lateral shift	2 × 60 seconds	Hold	Chest out, core engaged, hips in
BOSU lateral two-foot jumps with Slastix tubing	2 × 8	1:3:1	Athletic position, keep tubing to the outside of body
Ladder quick-feet narrow shuffle	1 × 1 2 × 1		Light feet, core set, shoulders back
Ladder lateral two in, two out	1 × 1 2 × 1		Light feet, core set, shoulders back
Ladder crossovers	1 × 1 2 × 1		Quick crossovers, pause and hold the lateral landing
Rapid excitation and quickness (10 minutes)		1:2 work-to-rest ratio	
Octagon drill	4 × 15 seconds	Quick	Two-foot jumps, quick off ground, maintain knee bend
Two-foot lateral hurdle hops (two down and one back)	4 × 1	Quick	Quick off ground, positive angles, light feet
Single-leg drops into lateral jump	10 × per leg	Quick	Quick coupling, link in arms
Strength lift complex I (20 minutes)			
Hockey lunges to lateral raise	2 × 8	1:1	45-degree lunge, chest up
Single-leg, opposite-arm lat raise	2 × 8 each side	1:1:1	Squat to extension
Lateral crossover box step-ups	2 × 8 each side	1:1	Square shoulders up, power off bench leg

Extreme board arm curl–shoulder press combo	2 × 8 each side	2:2	Legs stay balanced, dumbbells shoulder height with palms in
Single-leg rotations	2 × 8 each side	1:1:1	Hips ups, core set, one foot on the ball
Strength lift complex II (20 minutes)			
Dual-arm chest push repeats (fast feet)	2 × 8	1:2:1	Link legs, quick coupling, positive angle
Single-leg, opposite-arm row	2 × 8 per arm	1:2:2	Forward lean, knee bent
Multijoint stick push	2 × 8	Quick	Partner resistance, start low, finish in extension
Partner towel rows	2 × 8 per arm	2:2	Stay low, shoulders back, chest up
Standing rollout	2 × 15	1:2:1	On toes, shoulders higher than hips, push into the ball

The ratio in the tempo column defines in seconds the time for the positive phase, midhold, and negative phase. For example, if the tempo is 1:2:2, the player would lift the weight in 1 second, hold strong at midpeak for 2 seconds, and take 2 seconds to lower the weight under control.

Strength

- Complete short strength workouts twice per week for maintenance. At our Twist Athlete Conditioning Centers, whole teams report in twice a week for in-season lifts, beginning after their team's training camp and running straight through to the playoffs.

- During the season, grip strength and leg strength do not suffer great decrements. Many players maintain or build leg strength from on-ice activity, whereas others incur slight decreases. But all players commonly lose significant upper-body strength over a season. For maintenance purposes, consider spending at least 80 percent of workouts on upper-body strength and abdominal work and the rest on legs. (Players who are below average in leg strength or stride power may need to devote more time to working on leg strength in-season.)

- Decrease the volume of workouts while keeping the same high intensity. Because of fatigue or general soreness that results from physical contact in games, many players feel more comfortable using less weight than they do in their off-season lifts. If a player's body will accept heavy loads, definitely go there—that works great. But when necessary, to accommodate a moderate loading and still overload the muscles maximally, manipulate the between-set rest periods, repetitions per set, and speed of movement to stimulate muscle strength adaptations. You can use lighter loads and faster movements, with enough reps to lift right up to full fatigue each set. This method will maintain some strength while also building muscular endurance. Alternatively, use instability with lighter loads and slow controlled reps on both the positive and negative phases of the lift to increase muscle activation, keep the muscle under tension, and increase neural input to help overload the muscle and maintain strength. Reducing rest times between sets is another option that will produce some strength maintenance and muscular endurance benefits while using lighter weights.

- Perform neurally complex exercises to impose greater challenges on the mind–muscle system and to overload the muscles as much as possible. Match the lift style with the athletic skillfulness appropriate to on-ice demands. Use mainly whole-body and multijoint lifts that complement whole-body skillfulness and combatives on the ice and exercise many muscles at once.

- Be flexible. Depending on the game schedule, a strength workout may be a 45-minute workout on a practice day or a 10-minute routine of push-ups and partner towel rows right in the dressing room after a game. Squeeze in what you can. Do not wait for the perfect workout day during a string of nongame days. By the time the perfect day comes, you will have missed so many days that you risk delayed soreness following a good lift. Constantly chip away at the work required to maintain in-season strength. Consistent and frequent short lifts pay off over a long season. Infrequent and irregular big lifts are of little value.

Anaerobic

- Generally, you can achieve anaerobic conditioning on the ice in regular practice drills or practice conditioning drills. But don't guess and hope. Structure to optimize the training effect and know when to unload as well. Define drills with a consideration to the physiology, much like a swim coach or track coach would think.

- Players whose ice time is limited or who are not dressing for games should add anaerobic sprints on the ice after practice or on the bike. Active players who need to lengthen their shifts can also add anaerobic sprints. Doing this may help them extend their ability to go full out from 35 seconds to a longer 45-second shift, for example. Supplemental bike sprints drive up conditioning by applying resistance to overload the legs while unloading from the skating movement pattern and top-end speed output, a beneficial variation over a long season.

Quickness and agility

- On-ice practice should cover these elements. But I do have players complete supplemental quickness and agility exercises if they need improvement in this area or if they are not dressing for several games in a row. Even world-class athletes need to improve quickness. Young players are just beginning to develop, and if they have a sufficient strength base, they can improve explosiveness. Older players need to key on this area to help maintain their abilities as they age. With specific practices, my athletes over age 30 still make substantial improvement.

- Quickness and agility will not decline during the season, but two 15-minute sessions per week can easily lead to improvement during a season.

Speed

- Assess practice plans to make sure there are speed challenges accomplished in some of the drills. If not, I would be more inclined to improve the structure of practices than to add supplemental speed training on top.

- In-season I coach an athlete for speed development only if that area has been identified as a specific weakness and is the most important area for that player to develop. Usually three or four players on a team need to improve overall speed or stride power. For other players, I stress speed development during the preseason and then leave specific game speed to the practice drills (and game participation).

- Three exceptions may apply to this general guideline for in-season speed periodization. One is including extra speed work for the very slow player who lacks speed more than he lacks quickness. Second, I may incorporate top-speed drills for highly skilled players to work on skill execution at faster speeds. Third, for players who are very fast, repeated resisted speed intervals on the ice are an option to train several components at once—for example, leg power, leg strength and endurance, and the anaerobic energy system.

Index

Note: The italicized *f* and *t* following page numbers refer to figures and tables, respectively.

About the Author

Peter Twist is the former strength and conditioning coach for the Vancouver Canucks and is currently president of Twist Conditioning Incorporated (www.sportconditioning.com), an athlete conditioning company with franchised athlete conditioning centers; one-on-one and team training; a line of 350 sport conditioning products; and sport conditioning specialist certifications delivered by Twist Master Coaches throughout Canada, the United States, Australia, and the United Kingdom. A frequent guest lecturer at international fitness conferences and coaching clinics, Twist delivers workshops on sport conditioning to personal trainers, conditioning coaches, sport coaches, and medical professionals around the globe.

An NSCA-certified strength and conditioning specialist with a master's degree in coaching science from the University of British Columbia, Twist served as president of the Hockey Conditioning Coaches Association, editor of the *Journal of Hockey Conditioning*, and NSCA provincial director for British Columbia. Twist lives in North Vancouver with his wife Julie, daughters Zoe and Mackenzie, and dogs Rico and Loosy.

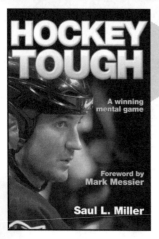
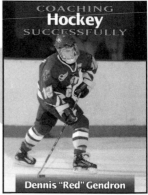
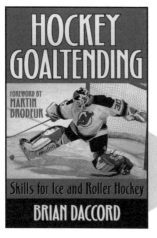